高职高专"十二五"规划教材

化工专业英语

杨春华　陈　刚　主编
侯　炜　副主编
张　龙　主审

化学工业出版社
·北京·

内容简介

全书分为十个单元，每个单元均由课文、阅读材料和科技英语翻译组成。课文和阅读材料均源于原版的英文教材和期刊，选材上与专业知识衔接，深度和广度适当，主要内容包括：化工基础知识、化工单元操作、化工设备、无机化工、有机化工、石油化工、高分子材料、精细化工、煤化工和绿色化工。

本书是为高职高专化工类专业编写的专业课教材，各院校可以根据本校的专业研究方向选学其中的内容，本书也可供同等英语程度的化工技术人员或相近领域人员使用。

图书在版编目（CIP）数据

化工专业英语/杨春华，陈刚主编. —北京：化学工业出版社，2011.7（2023.5重印）
高职高专"十二五"规划教材
ISBN 978-7-122-11605-5

Ⅰ. 化… Ⅱ. ①杨…②陈… Ⅲ. 化学工业-英文-高等职业教育-教材 Ⅳ. H31

中国版本图书馆 CIP 数据核字（2011）第 122898 号

责任编辑：窦　臻　张　亮　　　　　　　　文字编辑：颜克俭
责任校对：顾淑云　　　　　　　　　　　　装帧设计：王晓宇

出版发行：化学工业出版社（北京市东城区青年湖南街 13 号　邮政编码 100011）
印　　装：北京虎彩文化传播有限公司
787mm×1092mm　1/16　印张 10½　字数 270 千字　2023 年 5 月北京第 1 版第 6 次印刷

购书咨询：010-64518888　　　　　　　　　售后服务：010-64518899
网　　址：http://www.cip.com.cn
凡购买本书，如有缺损质量问题，本社销售中心负责调换。

定　　价：30.00 元

前　　言

化工英语是高等院校化工类专业的一门专业必选课。由于各省院校的化工类专业研究方向不同，化工英语选学的内容也应有所侧重。本教材由不同地区长期工作在高职院校并从事一线教学与研究的教师编写而成。在其编写过程中，致力于体现下述原则。

1. 专业性强。本教材课文的选材均源于原版的英文教材和期刊，选材上与专业知识衔接，深度和广度适当，从第一个单元的化学化工基础知识到最后一个单元的绿色化学，均能体现化工领域典型产品和其生产工艺。

2. 实用性强。本教材分为十个单元。囊括化学化工基础知识、化工单元操作、化工设备、无机化工、有机化工、石油化工、高分子材料、精细化工、煤化工和绿色化工等。不同地区的学校可根据化工专业开设的学时数和研究方向选学不同章节的内容。

3. 针对性强。本教材每个单元都是由课文、阅读材料和科技英语翻译知识组成。课文和阅读材料均选用化工领域代表性最强、最具时代特征的工艺。科技英语翻译部分针对科技英语的特点、翻译标准和翻译方法，结合每单元内容，主要从科技英语词和句子的翻译来展开，选编了词的翻译方法、词性转换译法和增词省词译法；句子的翻译选编了名词性从句、定语从句、状语从句和被动语态等的译法。使学生能融知识性与实用性于一体、专业培养与翻译技能于一体、英语学习与素质培养于一体，一举多得。

本教材由吉林工业职业技术学院的杨春华、陈刚任主编，内蒙古化工职业学院的侯炜任副主编、晋城职业技术学院的吉晋兰、吉林工业职业技术学院范美青参编，长春工业大学张龙任主审。具体分工如下：杨春华（第 1、6、7、8 单元，科技英语翻译一和科技英语翻译六～八）；陈刚（第 4、10 单元，科技英语翻译四和科技英语翻译十）；侯炜（第 5 单元，科技英语翻译四～五和科技英语翻译十）；吉晋兰（第 9 单元，科技英语翻译二～三和科技英语翻译九）；范美青（第 2、3 单元）；另外，全书由杨春华、陈刚和侯炜统稿；侯炜对全书单词的译注进行了校对工作。吉林工业职业技术学院的张小丽等老师对本书稿提出了许多宝贵意见，在此表示感谢。

由于编者水平有限，疏漏和不妥之处在所难免，恳请广大同行与读者提出宝贵意见和建议，以便完善。

编者

2011 年 6 月

CONTENTS

Unit One   Basic Knowledge of Chemical Engineering

Lesson One   Chemical Composition

Most materials encountered in nature and in chemical process systems are mixtures of various species. The physical properties of a mixture depend strongly on the mixture composition. In this text, we will review different ways to express mixture compositions.

1. Moles and Molecular Weight

The atomic weight of an element is the ratio of the average mass of atoms of an element to 1/12 of the mass of an atom of carbon-12 (the isotope of carbon whose nucleus contains six protons and six neutrons). The molecular weight of a compound is the sum of the atomic weights of the atoms that constitute a molecule of the compound: atomic oxygen (O), for example, has an atomic weight of approximately 16, and the therefore molecular oxygen (O_2) has a molecular weight of approximately 32.

A mole mass of a species is the amount of that species whose mass is numerically equal to its molecular weight. Carbon monoxide (CO), for example, has a molecular weight of 28, 1 mol of CO therefore contains 28g CO .

If the molecular weight of a substance is M, then there are M kg/kmol, M g/mol of this substance. The molecular weight may thus be used as a conversion factor that relates the mass and the number of moles of a quantity of the substance. For example,
34 kg of ammonia (NH_3:M=17) is equivalent to

$$\frac{34 \text{ kg } NH_3}{} \left| \frac{1 \text{ kmol } NH_3}{17 \text{ kg } NH_3} \right. = 2.0 \text{ kmol } NH_3$$

2. Mass and Mole Fractions and Average Molecular Weight

Process streams occasionally contain one substance, but more often they consist of mixtures of liquids or gases, or solutions of one or more solutes in a liquid solvent.

The following terms may be used to define the composition of a mixture of substances including a species A.

Mass fraction $x_A = \dfrac{\text{mass of A}}{\text{total mass}} (\dfrac{\text{kg A}}{\text{kg total}} \text{ or } \dfrac{\text{g A}}{\text{g total}})$

Mole fraction $y_A = \dfrac{\text{moles of A}}{\text{total moles}} (\dfrac{\text{kmol A}}{\text{kmol total}} \text{ or } \dfrac{\text{mol A}}{\text{mol total}})$

Note that the numerical value of a mass or a mole fraction does not depend on the mass units in the numerator and denominator as long as these units are the same. If the mass fraction of benzene (C_6H_6) in a mixture is 0.25, then $x_{C_6H_6}$ equals 0.25 kg/kg total, 0.25 C_6H_6 g/g total, and so on.

A set of mass fractions may be converted to an equivalent set of mole fractions by (a) assuming as a basis of calculation a mass of the mixture (e.g., 100 kg); (b) using the known mass fractions to calculate the mass of each component in the basis quantity, and converting these masses to moles; and (c) taking the ratio of the moles of each component to the total number of moles. An analogous procedure is followed to convert mole fractions to mass fractions, differing only in that a total number of moles (e.g., 100 mol) is taken as a basis of calculation.

EXAMPLE　Conversion from a Mass Composition by Mass to a Molar Composition

A mixture of gases has the following composition by mass:

O_2	16%	(x_{O_2} =0.16g O_2/g total)
CO	4.0%	
CO_2	17%	
N_2	63%	

What is the molar composition?

SOLUTION　Basis: 100 g of the mixture.

A convenient way to perform the calculations is to set them up in tabular form.

Component i	Mass Fraction x_i	Mass (g) $m_i=x_i m_{total}$	Molecular Weight M_i (g/mol)	Moles $n_i=m_i/M_i$	Mole Fraction $y_i=n_i/n_{total}$
O_2	0.16	16	32	0.500	0.150
CO	0.04	4	28	0.143	0.044
CO_2	0.17	17	44	0.386	0.120
N_2	0.63	63	28	2.250	0.690
Total	1.00	100		3.279	1.000

The mass of a species is the product of the mass fraction of that species and total mass (basis of 100g). The number of moles of a species is the mass of that species divided by the molecular weight of the species. Finally, the mole fraction of a species is the number of moles of that species divided by the total number of moles (3.279mol).

The average molecular weight (or mean molecular weight) of a mixture, $\bar{M}$, is the ratio of the mass of a sample of the mixture(m_t) to the number of moles of all species (n_t) in the sample. If y_i is the mole fraction of the ith component of the mixture and M_i is the molecular weight of this component, then

$$\bar{M} = y_1 M_1 + y_2 M_2 + \cdots = \sum_{\substack{all \\ components}} y_i M_i$$

3. Concentration

The mass concentration of a component of a mixture or solution is the mass of this component per unit volume of the mixture (g/cm^3, kg/m^3,...). The molar concentration of a component is the number of moles of the component per unit volume of the mixture (kmol/m^3, mol/cm^3,...).

Consider, for example, a 0.02mol/L solution of NaOH (i.e., a solution containing 0.02mol NaOH/L): 5 L of this solution contains:

$$5\,L\left|\frac{0.02 \text{ mol NaOH}}{L}\right. = 0.1 \text{ mol NaOH}$$

New Words and Expressions

encounter [in'kauntə] *vt.* 遭遇，邂逅；遇到

various ['vɛəriəs] *a.* 各种各样的；多方面的

mole [məul] *n.* [化]摩尔，克分子(量)[亦作 mol]

molecular [məu'lekjulə] *a.* 分子的；由分子组成的

isotope ['aisəutəup] *n.* [化]同位素

proton ['prəutɔn] *n.* [物]质子

neutron ['nju:trɔn] *n.* 中子

average ['ævəridʒ] *a.* 平均的

atomic [ə'tɔmik] *a.* 原子的，原子能的；微粒子的

constitute ['kɔnstitju:t] *vt.* 组成，构成；建立；任命

molecule ['mɔlikjul] *n.* 分子；微小颗粒，微粒

approximately [ə'prɔksimitli] *adv.* 大约，近似地；近于

numerically [nju:'merikli] *adv.* 数字上；用数字表示

substance ['sʌbstəns] *n.* (化学成分明确的) 物质；实质

monoxide [mɔ'nɔksaid, mə-] *n.* [化]一氧化物

conversion [kən'və:ʃən] *n.* 转换；变换；兑换

relate [ri'leit] *vt.* 使…有联系；叙述

quantity ['kwɔntəti] *n.* 量，数量；大量；总量

ammonia [ə'məunjə] *n.* [化]氨

fraction ['frækʃən] *n.* [数]分数；部分；小部分；稍微

occasionally [ə'keiʒənəli, əu-] *adv.* 偶尔，间或

solution [sə'lju:ʃən] *n.* 溶液；溶解；解答

solute ['sɔlju:t, sɔ'lju:t, 'səulu:t] *n.* 溶质；溶解物

solvent ['sɔlvənt, 'sɔ:l-] *a.* 有溶解力的；有偿付能力的
　　　　　　　　　　　　 n. 溶剂；解决方法

numerical [nju:'merikəl] *a.* 数值的；数字的；用数字表示的

numerator ['nju:məreitə] *n.* 分子；计算者；计算器

denominator [di'nɔmineitə] *n.* 分母；命名者

calculate ['kælkjuleit] *vi.* 计算；以为；作打算
　　　　　　　　　　　　 vt. 计算；预测；认为；打算

component [kəm'pəunənt] *a.* 组成的，构成的
　　　　　　　　　　　　 n. 成分；组件；元件

equivalent [i'kwivələnt] *a.* 等价的，相等的；同意义的
　　　　　　　　　　　　 n. 等价物，相等物

ratio ['reiʃiəu, -ʃəu] *n.* 比率，比例

analogous [ə'næləgəs] *a.* 类似的

convenient [kən'vi:niənt] *a.* 方便的

tabular ['tæbjulə] *a.* 列成表格的；扁平的

concentration [,kɔnsən'treiʃən] *n.* 浓度；集中；浓缩；专心

molecular weight   [化]分子量

atomic weight   原子量

mole mass   摩尔质量

be equal to   相等；胜任；合适

conversion factor   换算因数；转换因子；变换因数

mole fraction   摩尔分数；克分子分数

average molecular weight   平均分子量

be converted to   被转化成

the product of A and B   A 与 B 的乘积

Notes

1. The atomic weight of an element is the ratio of the average mass of atoms of an element to 1/12 of the mass of an atom of carbon-12 (the isotope of carbon whose nucleus contains six protons and six neutrons).元素的原子量是一种元素的平均原子质量与碳12（原子核包含6个质子、6个中子的碳同位素）原子质量的1/12之比。the ratio of A to B，A与B的比。

2. The molecular weight of a compound is the sum of the atomic weights of the atoms that constitute a molecule of the compound: atomic oxygen(O), for example, has an atomic weight of approximately 16, and the therefore molecular oxygen(O_2) has a molecular weight of approximately 32. 化合物的分子量是组成该化合物原子的原子量之和：例如，氧原子(O)，原子量约为16，那么氧气(O_2)的分子量约为32。that constitute a molecule of the compound为定语从句，先行词为the atoms.

3. The molecular weight may thus be used as a conversion factor that relates the mass and the number of moles of a quantity of the substance.分子量可以用做质量和物质摩尔数之间的换算因子。

4. Note that the numerical value of a mass or a mole fraction does not depend on the mass units in the numerator and denominator as long as these units are the same. 注意只要分子和分母的单位是一致的，质量分数和摩尔分数的数值大小与分子和分母的单位没有关系。

Exercises

1. Put the following into Chinese

molecular   weight   atomic weight

mole mass   average molecular weight

2. Put the following into English

摩尔   分子量

质子   中子

溶液   溶质

浓度   原子量

摩尔质量   平均分子量

质量分数   摩尔分数

3. Questions

1) Calculate the average molecular weight of air from its approximate molar composition of 79%N_2, 21%O_2.

2) Calculate the average molecular weight of air from its approximate composition by mass of 76.7% N_2, 23.3%O_2.

Lesson Two   Chemical Reaction Stoichiometry

The stoichiometric equation of the reaction imposes constraints on the relative amounts of reactants and products in the input and output streams (if A → B, for example, you cannot start with 1 mol of pure A and end with 2 mol of B). In addition, a material balance on a reactive substance does not have the simple form input =output, but must include a generation and/or consumption term.

1. Stoichiometry

Stoichiometry is the theory of the proportions in which chemical species combine with one another. The stoichiometric equation of a chemical reaction is a statement of the relative number of molecules or moles of reactants and products that participate in the reaction. For example, the stoichiometric equation

$$2SO_2 + O_2 \longrightarrow 2SO_3$$

indicates that for every two molecules of SO_2 that react, one molecule of O_2 that reacts to produce two molecules of SO_3. The numbers that precede the formulas for each species are the stoichiometric coefficients of the reaction components.

A valid stoichiometric equation must be balanced; that is, the number of atoms of each atomic species must be the same on both sides of the equation, since atoms can neither be created nor destroyed in chemical reactions. The equation

$$SO_2 + O_2 \longrightarrow SO_3$$

can not be valid, for example, since it indicates that three atoms of atomic oxygen (O) are produced for every four atoms that enter into the reaction, for a net loss of one atom, but

$$2SO_2 + O_2 \longrightarrow 2SO_3$$

are balanced.

The stoichiometric ratio of two molecular species participating in a reaction is the ratio of their stoichiometric coefficients in the balanced reaction equation. This ratio can be used as a conversion factor to calculate the amount of a particular reactant (or product) that was consumed (or produced), given a quantity of another reactant or product that participated in the reaction. For the reaction

$$2SO_2 + O_2 \longrightarrow 2SO_3$$

you can write the stoichiometric ratios

$$\frac{2 \text{ mol } SO_3 \text{ generated}}{1 \text{ mol } O_2 \text{ consumed}}$$

If you know, for example, that 1600 kg/h of SO_3 is to be produced, you can calculate the amount of oxygen required as

$$\frac{1600 \text{ kg } SO_3 \text{ generated}}{h} \left| \frac{1 \text{ kmol } SO_3}{80 \text{ kg } SO_3} \right| \frac{1 \text{ kmol } O_2 \text{ consumed}}{2 \text{ kmol } SO_3 \text{ generated}} = 10 \frac{\text{kmol } O_2}{h}$$

$$\Longrightarrow 10 \frac{\text{kmol } O_2}{h} \left| \frac{32 \text{ kg } O_2}{1 \text{ kmol } O_2} \right. = 320 \text{ kg } O_2/h$$

It is a good practice to include the terms "consumed" and "generated" when performing conversions of this sort: simply writing 1 mol O_2/2mol SO_3 could be taken to mean that 2 mol of SO_3 contains 1 mol of O_2, which is not true.

2. Chemical Equilibrium

Two of the fundamental questions of chemical reaction engineering are，given a set of reactive species and reaction conditions，(a) what will be the final (equilibrium) composition of the reaction mixture，and (b) how long will the system take to reach a specified state of equilibrium? The field of chemical equilibrium thermodynamics concerns itself with the first question，and chemical kinetics deals with the second.

Some reactions are essentially irreversible；that is，the reaction proceeds only in a single direction (from reactants to products) and the concentration of the limiting reactant eventually approaches zero (although "eventually" could mean seconds for some reactants and years for others).

Other reactions (or the same reactions at different conditions) are reversible；reactants form products and products undergo the reverse reactions to reform the reactants. For example，consider the reaction in which ethylene is hydrolyzed to ethanol：

$$C_2H_4 + H_2O \Longleftrightarrow C_2H_5OH$$

If you start with ethylene and water，the forward reaction occurs；then once ethanol is present，the reverse reaction begins to take place. As the concentrations of C_2H_4 and H_2O decrease，the rate of the forward reaction decreases，and as the C_2H_5OH concentration increases，the rate of the reverse reaction increase. Eventually a point is reached at which the rates of the forward and reverse reactions are equal. At this point no further composition change takes place and the reaction mixture is in chemical equilibrium. At this point you have enough knowledge to be able to calculate equilibrium compositions if the relations are given to you.

New Words and Expressions

stoichiometry [ˌstɔikiˈɔmitri] n. 化学计量学
stoichiometric [ˌstɔikiəˈmetrik] a. 化学计量的；化学计算的
equation [iˈkweiʒən, -ʃən] n. 方程式，等式；相等；反应式
constraint [kənˈstreint] n. 约束；局促，态度不自然；强制
reactant [riˈæktənt, riː-] n. [化]反应物；反应剂
generation [ˌdʒenəˈreiʃən] n. 产生；一代人；一代
consumption [kənˈsʌmpʃən] n. 消费；消耗
procedure [prəˈsiːdʒə] n. 程序，手续；步骤
proportion [prəˈpɔːʃən] n. 比例；部分；面积；均衡
statement [ˈsteitmənt] n. 声明；陈述，叙述；报表，清单
participate [paːˈtisipeit] vi. 参与，参加；分享
indicate [ˈindikeit] vt. 表明；指出；预示；象征
precede [priːˈsiːd, pri-] vt. 领先，在…之前；优于，高于
formula [ˈfɔːmjulə] n. 公式，准则；配方

coefficient [ˌkəui'fiʃənt] *n.* [数]系数；[物] (测定某种质量或变化过程的)率；协同因素

valid ['vælid] *a.* 有效的，有根据的；正当的

consume [kən'sjuːm] *vt.* 消耗，消费

fundamental [ˌfʌndə'mentəl] *a.* 基本的，根本的

　　　　　　　　　　　　　　n. 基本原理；基本原则

equilibrium [ˌiːkwi'libriəm] *n.* 平衡；平静；保持平衡的能力

specified ['spesifaid] *a.* 规定的；详细说明的

thermodynamic [ˌθəːməudai'næmik, -di-] *a.* 热力学的；使用热动力的

kinetic [ki'netik, kai-] *a.* 动力学的；运动的；活跃的

essentially [i'senʃəli] *adv.* 本质上；本来

irreversible [ˌiri'vəːsəbl] *a.* 不可逆的；不能取消的；不能翻转的

proceed [prəu'siːd] *vi.* 开始；继续进行；发生；行进

eventually [i'ventʃuəli] *adv.* 最后，终于

approach [ə'prəutʃ] *vt.* 接近；着手处理

　　　　　　　　　　vi. 靠近

　　　　　　　　　　n. 方法；途径；接近

reversible [ri'vəːsəbl] *a.* 可逆的；可撤销的；可反转的

undergo [ˌʌndə'gəu] *vt.* 经历，经受；忍受；进行

reform [ri'fɔːm] *vt.* 改革，革新；重新组成；重新生成

ethylene ['eθiliːn] *n.* [化]乙烯

hydrolyze ['haidrəlaiz] *vt.* 使水解

　　　　　　　　　　vi. 水解

ethanol ['eθəˌnɔl] *n.* [化]乙醇，酒精

decrease [di'kriːs, 'diː-, 'diːkriːs, di'k-] *vi.* 减少，减小

　　　　　　　　　　　　　　n. 减少，减小；减少量

knowledge ['nɔlidʒ] *n.* 知识，学问；知道，认识

impose constraints on 施加约束

carry out 执行，实行；贯彻；实现；完成

participate in 参加；分享

good practice 良好的做法；良好的习惯做法

chemical equilibrium [化]化学平衡

Notes

1. The stoichiometric equation of the reaction impose constraints on the relative amounts of reactants and products in the input and output streams.反应计量方程式对输入和输出物料中反应物与产物的量的相对关系是有约束的。impose constraints on 施加约束于…。

2. The numbers that precede the formulas for each species are the stoichiometric coefficients of the reaction components.每一物质分子式前的数字是反应组成的计量系数。that precede the formulas for each species 是定语从句，先行词是 The numbers。

3. Two of the fundamental questions of chemical reaction engineering are, given a set of

reactive species and reaction conditions, (a) what will be the final (equilibrium) composition of the reaction mixture, and (b) how long will the system take to reach a specified state short of equilibrium? The field of chemical equilibrium thermodynamics concerns itself with the first question, and chemical kinetics deals with the second.如果参加反应的物质和反应条件是已知的，那么化学反应工程的两个基本问题是(a)反应混合物的最终（平衡）组成是什么，(b)体系需要多长时间达到规定的平衡状态？第一个属于化学平衡热力学问题，第二个是化学动力学解决的问题。该句较长，也是科技英语句子的一个主要特点。主体结构是 Two of the fundamental questions are…(a)…, and (b)…。其中 given a set of reactive species and reaction conditions 是过去分词短语作条件状语；what will be the final (equilibrium) composition of the reaction mixture, 和 how long will the system take to reach a specified state short of equilibrium 是表语从句做主句的表语。

Exercises

1. Put the following into Chinese

chemical reaction stoichiometry   material balance

a generation or consumption term   reaction component   a conversion factor

2. Put the following into English

计量方程式   计量系数

换算因数   化学平衡

化学反应工程   化学平衡热力学

化学动力学   可逆反应

不可逆反应   正反应

逆反应   平衡组成

3. Questions

Consider the reaction

$$C_4H_8 + 6O_2 \longrightarrow 4CO_2 + 4H_2O$$

1) Is the stoichiometric equation balanced?

2) What is the stoichiometric coefficient of CO_2?

3) What is the stoichiometric ratio of H_2O to O_2?

Lesson Three   Balances on Reactive Processes

Certain restrictions imposed by nature must be taken into account when designing a new process or analyzing an existing one. You cannot, for example, specify an input to a reactor of 1000 g of lead and an output of 2000 g of lead or gold or anything else. Similarly, if you know that 1500 kg of sulfur is contained in the coal burned each day in a power plant boiler, you do not have to analyze the ash and stack gases to know that on the average of 1500 kg sulfur per day leaves the furnace in one form or another.

The basis for both of these observations is, which states that mass can neither be created nor destroyed. Statements based on the law of conservation of mass such as "total mass of input = total mass of output" are examples of mass balances or material balances. The design of a new process or analysis of an existing one is not complete until it is established that the inputs and outputs of the entire process and of each individual unit satisfy balance equations.

1. Process Classification

Chemical processes may be classified as batch, continuous or semibatch and as either steady state or transient. Before writing material balances for a process system, you must know into which of these categories the process falls.

Batch process. The feed is charged (fed) into a vessel at the beginning of the process and the vessel contents are removed sometime later. No mass crosses the system boundaries between the time the feeds are charged and the time the products are removed. Example: Rapidly add reactants to a tank and remove the products and unconsumed reactants sometime later when the system has come to equilibrium.

Continuous process. The inputs and outputs flow continuously throughout the duration of the process. Example: Pump a mixture of liquids into a distillation column at a constant rate and steadily withdraw product streams from the top and bottom of the column.

Semibatch process. Any process that is neither batch nor continuous. Examples: Allow the contents of a pressurized gas container to escape to the atmosphere; slowly blend several liquids in a tank from which nothing is being withdrawn.

If the values of all the variables in a process (i.e., all temperatures, pressures, volumes, flow rates) do not change with time, the process is said to be operating at steady state. If any of the process variables change with time, transient or unsteady-state operation is said to exist. By their nature, batch and semibatch processes are unsteady-state operations, whereas continuous processes may be either steady-state or transient.

Batch processing is commonly used when relatively small quantities of a product are to be produced on any single occasion, while continuous processing is better suited to large production rates. Continuous processes are usually run as close to steady state as possible.

2. Balances

(1) The General Balance Equation
Suppose methane is a component of both the input and output streams of a continuous process

unit，and that in an effort to determine whether the unit is performing as designed，the mass flow rates of methane in both streams are measured and found to be different ($m_{in} \neq m_{out}$).

$$\xrightarrow{\quad m_{in} \quad} \boxed{\text{Process Unit}} \xrightarrow{\quad m_{out} \quad}$$

There are several possible explanations for the observed difference（the measured flow rates）.

① Methane is being consumed as a reactant or generated as a product within the unit.

② Methane is accumulating in the unit—possibly adsorbing on the walls.

③ Methane is leaking from the unit.

④ Those measurements are wrong.

If the measurements are correct and there are no leaks，the other possibilities—generation or consumption in a reaction and accumulation within the process unit—are a difference between the input and output flow rates.

A balance on a conserved quantity (total mass, mass of a particular species, energy, momentum) in a system (a single process unit，a collection of units，or an entire process) may be written in the following general way:

$$\text{input + generation - output - consumption = accumulation} \tag{1-1}$$

input	+	generation	−	output	−	consumption	=	accumulation
(enters through system boundaries)		(produced within system)		(leaves through system boundaries)		(consumed within system)		(buildup within system)

(2) Balances on Continuous Steady-State Process

For continuous processes at steady-state，the accumulation term in the general balance equation (1-1) equals zero，and the equation simplifies to

$$\text{input + generation = output + consumption} \tag{1-2}$$

If the balance is on a nonreactive species，the generation and consumption terms equal zero and the equation reduces to input=output.

New Words and Expressions

restriction　[ri'strikʃən]　*n.* 限制；约束；束缚

analyze　['ænəlaiz]　*vt.* 对…进行分析，分解

specify　['spesəfai, -si-]　*vt.* 指定；详细说明；列举；把…列入说明书

similarly　['similəli]　*adv.* 同样地；类似于

stack　[stæk]　*n.* 堆；堆叠；大量，许多

observation　[,ɔbzə:'veiʃən]　*n.* 观察；监视；观察报告

conservation　[,kɔnsə'veiʃən]　*n.* 保存，保持；保护

design　[di'zain]　*vt.* 设计；计划；构思

individual　[,indi'vidjuəl, -dʒəl]　*a.* 个人的；个别的；独特的

classification　[,klæsifi'keiʃən]　*n.* 分类；类别，等级

batch　[bætʃ]　*n.* 间歇式；一批；一炉；一次所制之量

transient　['trænziənt, -si-, -ʃənt, 'tra:n-]　*a.* 短暂的；路过的

n. 瞬变现象

category　['kætigəri]　n. 种类，分类；范畴

vessel　['vesəl]　n. 反应器；容器，器皿；脉管，血管；船，舰

cross　[krɔːs]　vi. 交叉；杂交；横过

vt. 杂交；渡过；使相交

boundary　['baundəri]　n. 边界；范围；分界线

unconsumed　[ˌʌnkən'sjuːmd]　a. 未消耗尽的；未吃光的；未遭毁灭的

throughout　[θruː'aut]　prep. 贯穿，遍及

adv. 自始至终，到处；全部

duration　[djuə'reiʃən]　n. 持续；持续期间，存在期间

distillation　[ˌdisti'leiʃən]　n. 蒸馏，净化；蒸馏法；精华，蒸馏物

column　['kɔləm]　n. 圆柱，柱形物；纵队，列；专栏

constant　['kɔnstənt]　a. 不变的；恒定的；经常的

n. 常数；恒量

steadily　['stedili]　adv. 稳定地；稳固地；有规则地

withdraw　[wið'drɔː, wiθ-]　vt. 撤退；收回；撤销；拉开

vi. 撤退；离开

container　[kən'teinə]　n. 集装箱；容器

escape　[i'skeip]　vt. 逃避，避免；被忘掉

vi. 逃脱；避开；溜走

atmosphere　['ætməˌsfiə]　n. 气氛；大气；空气

blend　[blend]　vt. 混合

variable　['vɛəriəbl]　n. 参数；[数]变量；可变物，可变因素

occasion　[ə'keiʒən, əu-]　n. 时机，机会；场合；理由

methane　['miːθein]　n. [化]甲烷；沼气

measure　['meʒə]　vt. 测量；估量；权衡

explanation　[ˌeksplə'neiʃən]　n. 说明，解释；辩解

accumulate　[ə'kjuːmjuleit]　vi. 累积；积聚

vt. 积攒

leak　[liːk]　vi. 漏，渗；泄漏出去

vt. 使渗漏，泄露

measurement　['meʒəmənt]　n. 测量；度量；尺寸；量度制

conserve　[kən'səːv, 'kɔnsəːv]　vt. 保存；使守恒；（物理、化学变化或进化过程中）使（能量等）守恒

momentum　[məu'mentəm]　n. 动量；动力；冲力；势头

simplify　['simplifai]　vt. 简化；使单纯；使简易

take into account　考虑；重视；体谅

law of conservation of mass　物质守恒定律

based on　以…为基础，基于

fall into　分成

batch process　间歇过程；分批工艺，分批法；批流程

continuous process　连续过程；连续法；连续加工

semibatch process   半间歇过程
in an effort to   企图（努力想）；试图要

Notes

1. Certain restrictions imposed by nature must be taken into account when designing a new process or analyzing an existing one.当设计新的过程和分析现存的过程时，必须从本质上考虑限制这一过程的因素。该句的主语是certain restrictions imposed by nature，其中imposed by nature是过去分词短语做定语修饰certain restrictions，该句给出的参考翻译采用了意译、倒译和增译的方法。

2. Similarly，if you know that 1500 kg of sulfur is contained in the coal burned each day in a power plant boiler，you do not have to analyze the ash and stack gases to know that on the average of 1500 kg sulfur per day leaves the furnace in one form or another.类似地，如果已知电厂锅炉每天燃烧的煤中含硫1500 kg，那么就没有必要分析灰分和放出的气体，就可以知道每天以一种或其他种形式离开燃烧炉的硫的平均数量是1500 kg。本句是由一个主句，一个条件状语从句组成。从句中burned是过去分词做定语修饰the coal。

3. Statements based on the law of conservation of mass such as "total mass of input = total mass of output" are examples of mass balances or material balances.基于质量守恒定律如输入的总质量=输出的总质量的陈述，是质量平衡或物质平衡的例子。该句的主体是Statements…are examples…。句中based on the law of conservation of mass是过去分词短语做后置定语修饰Statements。过去分词短语做后置定语是科技英语的主要特点之一。

4. The design of a new process or analysis of an existing one is not complete until it is established that the inputs and outputs of the entire process and of each individual unit satisfy balance equations.直到整个过程和每种物质的输入和输出满足的平衡方程式成立，才能完成对新过程的设计和已有过程的分析。Until引导的时间状语从句中的it是形式主语，真正的主语是主语从句that the inputs and outputs…equations。

5. Allow the contents of a pressurized gas container to escape to the atmosphere.让气体压力容器中的内容物逃逸到大气中。这是一个祈使句。

Exercises

1. Put the following into Chinese

a power plant   the law of conservation of mass
batch process   continuous process
semibatch process   operation conditions

2. Put the following into English

反应过程平衡   反应器
甲烷的质量流速   连续稳定态过程

3. Questions

Classify the following processes as batch，continuous，or semibatch，and transient or steady-state.

1) A balloon is filled with air at a steady rate of 2g/min.

2) A bottle of milk is taken from the refrigerator and left on the kitchen table.

3) Water is boiled in an open flask.

Reading Materials: Catalyst

1. Introduction

Catalysis is a phenomenon by which chemical reactions are accelerated by small quantities of foreign substances, called catalysts. A suitable catalyst can enhance the rate of a thermodynamically feasible reaction but cannot change the position of the thermodynamic equilibrium. Most catalysts are solids or liquids, but they may also be gases.

The catalytic reaction is a cyclic process. According to simplified model, the reactant or reactants form a complex with the catalyst, thereby opening a pathway for their transformation into the product or products. Afterwards the catalyst is released and the next cycle can proceed.

However, catalysts do not have infinite life. Products of side reactions or changes in the catalyst structure lead to catalyst deactivation, In practice spent catalysts must be reactivated or replaced.

2. Types of Catalysis

If the catalyst and reactant or their solution forms a common physical phase, then the reaction is called homogeneously catalyzed. Metal salts of organic acids, organometallic complexes, and carbonyls of Co, Fe, and Rh are typical homogeneous catalysts. Examples of homogeneously catalyzed reactions are oxidation of toluene to benzoic acid in the presence of Co and Mn benzoates and hydroformylation of olefins to give the corresponding aldehydes. This reaction is catalyzed by carbonyls of Co or Rh.

Heterogeneous catalysis involves systems in which catalyst and reactants form separate physical phases. Typical heterogeneous catalysts are inorganic solids such as metals, oxides, sulfides, and metal salts, but they may also be organic materials such as organic hydroperoxides, ion exchangers, and enzymes.

Examples of heterogeneously catalyzed reactions are ammonia synthesis from the elements over promoted iron catalysts in the gas phase and hydrogenation of edible oils on Ni-kieselguhr catalysts in the liquid phase, which are examples of inorganic and organic catalysis, respectively.

Electrocatalysis is a special case of heterogeneous catalysis involving oxidation or reduction by transfer of electrons. Examples are the use of catalytically active electrodes in electrolysis processes such as chlor-alkali electrolysis and in fuel cells.

In photocatalysis light is absorbed by the catalyst or a reactant during the reaction. This can take place in a homogeneous or heterogeneous system. One example is the utilization of semiconductor catalysts for photochemical degradation of organic substances, e.g., on self-cleaning surfaces.

In biocatalysis enzymes or microorganisms catalyze various biochemical reactions, The catalysts can be immobilized on various carriers such as porous glass, SiO_2, and organic polymers. Prominent examples of biochemical reactions are isomerization of glucose to fructose, important in the production of soft drinks, by using enzymes such as glucoamylase immobilized on SiO_2, and the conversion of acrylonitrile to acrylamide by cells of corynebacteria entrapped in a polyacrylamide gel.

The main aim of environmental catalysis of environmental protection. Examples are the reduction of NO_x in stack gases with NH_3 on V_2O_5-TiO_2 catalysts and the removal of NO_x, CO, and hydrocarbons from automobile exhaust gases by using the so-called three-way catalyst consisting of Rh-Pt-CeO_2-Al_2O_3 deposited on ceramic honeycombs.

The term green catalytic processes has been used frequently in recent years, implying that chemical processes may be made environmentally benign by taking advantage of the possible high yields and selectivities for the target products, with little or no unwanted side products and also often high energy efficiency.

The basic chemical principles of catalysis consist in the coordination of reactant molecules to central atoms, the ligands of which may be molecular species (homogeneous and biocatalysis) or neighboring atoms at the surface of the solid matrix (heterogeneous catalysis). Although there are differences in the details of various types of catalysis (e.g., solvation effects in the liquid phase, which do not occur in solid-gas reactions), a closer and undoubtedly fruitful collaboration between the separate communities representing homogeneous, heterogeneous, and biocatalysis should be strongly supported.

科技英语翻译一　科技英语的特点

　　有关科学著作、论文、研究与实验报告和方案、各类科技情报和文学资料、科技实用手段（包括仪器、仪表、机械、工具等）的结构说明和操作说明等方面的资料均属科技文体。此类文章不同于文学类的文体，科技英语更多的是叙述普遍真理、描述特性、功能或过程及交代推理或假设等，因此它具有自己独特的语言特点和规律：清晰、准确、精练、严密、正式和客观。了解和掌握科技文体的特点及规律将有助于翻译实践。这里主要阐明科技英语在词汇和句法上的特点。

一、词汇上的特点

1. 科技词汇多源于希腊语和拉丁语

　　希腊语和拉丁语同立于世界上成熟最早、完备最佳的语林之中，其词汇不再发生词形、词义上的变化。这种词汇上的稳定性恰是科技英语所需要的，并且具有推动科技英语新词汇产生的特征，如下。

➢ pharmaceutical药品、mechanical机械的、technology技术、levogyrate左旋的、kerosene煤油、carbonhydrate碳水化合物等。

➢ Amphiphile　Amphiphile is derived from the Greek word amphi, meaning both.
这个词源于希腊的amphi，意思是两个。

2. 专业名词、术语多

　　科技英语专业性强，文体正式，使用大量的专业名词和术语。如：

➢ **Soaps** are still included in smaller amounts in many **detergent formulations** but the bulk surfactants in use today are synthetic **non-ionics** and **anionics**, with **alcohol ethoxylates**, **alkylaryl sulfonates**, **alkyl sulfates** and **alkyl ether sulfates** being the most prominent. 许多洗涤剂的配制仍使用少量的皂类，但是现在大量使用的是非离子和阴离子表面活性剂，比较典型的产品有醇聚氧乙烯醚、烷基芳磺酸盐、烷基磺酸盐和烷基醚硫酸盐。

　　这一段话中出现了soaps、detergent、surfactants、non-ionics、anionics、alcohol ethoxylates、alkylaryl sulfonates、alkyl sulfates、alkyl ether sulfates 九个专业术语。

3. 词形越长，词义越专一

　　长的词形在化工和医学英语中很常见，它们词义专一，能用来表达确切的含义，它们往往是由一些基本的科技英语词素组合而成，所以掌握一些基本科技英语词素以及它们的组合规律，对我们快速理解英文科技资料是非常有益的，如下。

➢ hexachloro-cyclohexane 六氯化苯、scizosaccharomyces 裂殖酵母　遇到长而复杂的单词，考察其构词，也能猜明其词意。

➢ manetohydrodynamics 磁流体力学　　maneto+hydro+ dynamics

➢ phonophotograph 声波照相　　phono+photo+graph

➢ telemicroscope 望远显微镜　　tele+micro+scope

➢ macromolecular 大分子的；高分子的　　macro+molecular

> thermoplastics热塑性塑料　　thermo+plastics
> electromagnetics电磁　　electro+ magnetics

4. 前后缀出现频率高

英语的构词法主要有 3 种：合成法、转化法和派生法。很多科技英语的词汇产生于派生法。派生法的核心是依靠添加前缀或后缀构成新词，这就导致了前缀和后缀使用频率高。

例如在科技英语中：

由前缀 semi-构成的词汇有 230 多个，

由前缀 auto-构成的词汇有 260 多个，

由前缀 micro-构成的词汇有 300 多个，

由前缀 thermo-构成的词汇不少于 130 个。

仅这四个前缀，就构成了近千个科技词汇。后缀构成的词汇不仅数目可观，而且还富有某一方面的概念特点。

例如：后缀-ance,-ence,-ity,-ment,-ness,-sion,-tion,-th,-ure 等构成的科技词汇，表示行为、性质、状态等抽象概念；以-able,ible,-ant,-ent,-al,-ic,-ical,-ive,-ous 等后缀构成的科技词汇，表示某种性质和特征等。

例如：烷烃的尾缀是**-ane**，那么甲烷、乙烷、丙烷等烷烃的词汇构成末尾都出现了-ane。methane 甲烷、ethane 乙烷、propane 丙烷、butane 丁烷、pentane 戊烷、hexane 己烷、heptane 庚烷、octane 辛烷、nonane 壬烷和 decane 癸烷等。

5. 广泛使用缩写词

缩写词采用，可以缩略文章篇幅空间，加快文本传输速度。且缩写词简练易记，一目了然，如下。

> **NMR**(nuclear magnetic resonance)核磁共振、**PVA**(polyvinyl alcohol)聚乙烯醇、**EDTA**(ethylene diamine tetraacetic acid) 乙二胺四醋酸、**LAS**(linear dodecylbenzene sulfonate)线型十二烷基苯磺酸盐、**FCC**(fluid catalytic cracking)流化床催化裂化、**PE**(polyethylene)聚乙烯等。

二、句法上的特点

1. 无人称句多

这是由于科技文体的主要目的在于阐述科学事实、科学发现、实验结果等。尽管这些科学活动或科学实验是人类所为，但这些文章或报告主要是为了说明科学技术活动所带来的结果、证明的理论或发现的科学现象或客观规律，而不是介绍发明者或发明者的主管感受，因此，科技文章往往不用第一、第二人称句，如下。

> A valid stoichiometric equation must be balanced; that is, the number of atoms of each atomic species must be the same on both sides of the equation, since atoms can neither be created nor destroyed in chemical reactions.

一个有效的计量方程式必须是平衡的；也就是说方程两边每种原子的个数是相同的，因为在化学反应中原子既不能被创生也不能被销毁。

> Chemical processes may be classified as batch, continuous or semibatch and as either steady state or transient.

化学过程分为间歇、连续和半间歇过程；也分为稳定态或者瞬时态。

以上两句中没有出现人称词，科技英语中这样的句子到处可见。

2. 广泛使用被动语态

据统计，科技英语中至少有 1/3 是被动语态。因为科技文体多描述的是事物、过程及现象等，侧重叙事推理、强调客观准确，所以句子的中心对象是它们，因而句子往往以被动语态出现，比主动语态更能说明需要论证的对象，使其位置鲜明、突出，如下。

➢ The feed **is charged (fed)** into a vessel at the beginning of the process and the vessel contents **are removed** sometime later.

在化学过程开始时向容器中加入原料，一段时间后把容器内容物移除。

➢ Batch processing **is** commonly **used** when relatively small quantities of a product are to **be produced** on any single occasion.

当一次生产的产品数量相对较少时，通常采用间歇操作过程。

3. 长句子多

科技文章为了表达一个复杂的概念或事实，突出逻辑性强、结构紧凑的特点，常常使用长句。长句中往往包含各种从句（尤其是定语从句）与短语结构，如下。

➢ The most commonly used type of catalytic reforming unit has three reactors, each with a fixed bed of catalyst, and all of the catalyst is regenerated in situ during routine catalyst regeneration shutdowns which occur approximately once each 6 to 24 months.

最常用的催化重整系统有3个反应器，每个反应器均有催化剂固定床，在常规的催化剂再生停车期间，所有这些催化剂原位再生，大约每6~12个月停车一次。

本句是一个复合句，由两个并列分句，一个定语从句组成。

4. 大量使用非谓语动词

科技文章要求行文简练、结构紧凑，为此常常使用非限定性动词代替各种从句或并列分句，如下。

➢ Most materials **encountered** in nature and in chemical process systems are mixtures of various species.

自然界和化学过程中遇到的大部分物质是不同物种的混合物。

句中过去分词 encountered 做定语修饰 most materials，避免使用结构复杂的定语从句 that are encountered。

➢ Before **writing** material balances for a process system，you must know into which of these categories the process falls.

在写一个过程系统的物质平衡前，必须知道该过程属于这些种类中的哪一种。

句中 Before writing material balances for a process system 是现在分词短语做时间状语，代替了时间状语从句 before you write。

5. 大量使用名词化结构

在科技英语中，常用一个名词词组"表示动作意义的名词+介词+名词+修饰语"代替一个句子的情况，也就是说，在普通英语中用动词表达的内容在科技英语中常用名词表达，这种名词词组称为名词化结构。

名词化结构到处可见，这是由于科技文献包含大量诸如定义、原则、定律以及结论等抽象概念，要阐述这些概念需要大量修饰语和限定成分，为了使行文简洁、表达客观、内容确切、信息量大、强调存在的事实，而应用了大量的名词化结构。

比较：

➢ The earth rotates on its own axis，which causes the change from day to night.

➢ **The rotation of the earth on its own axis** causes the change from day to night.

地球绕轴自转，引起昼夜的变化。

名词化结构 "the rotation of the earth on its own axis"使复合句变成了简单句，而且使表达的概念更加严密准确。

➢ Archimeds first discovered the principle of **displacement of water by solid bodies**.

阿基米德最先发展固体排水的原理。

句中 displacement of water by solid bodies 是一个介词短语结构，一方面代替了同位语从句 that water was displaced by solid bodies,另一方面强调了 displacement 这一事实。

6. 广泛使用后置定语结构

科技英语要求语言简练、内容准确，后置定语经常被使用。常见的主要有 3 种：过去分词和过去分词短语、介词短语、形容词及形容词短语作后置定语。

➢ The heat produced is equal to the electrical energy **wasted**.

产生的热量等于浪费的电能。

过去分词 produced、wasted 做后置定语分别修饰 the heat 和 the electrical energy。

➢ Pressure **in a liquid** is at right angles to the walls of a container.

液体的压力与容器壁垂直。

介词短语 in a liquid 作后置定语修饰 Pressure。

➢ In this factory the only fule **available** is coal.

该厂唯一可用的燃料是煤。

形容词 available 做后置定语修饰 fule。

Unit Two   Chemical Unit Operation

Lesson Four   Glossary of the Chemical Process Terms

Absorption A process in which a gas mixture contacts a liquid solvent and a component (or several components) of the gas dissolves in the liquid. In an absorption column or absorption tower, the solvent enters the top of a column, flows down, and emerges at the bottom, and the gas enters at the bottom, flows up (contacting the liquid), and leaves at the top.

Adsorption A process in which a gas or liquid mixture contacts a solid and a mixture component adheres to the surface of the solid.

Boiler A process unit in which tubes pass through a combustion furnace. Boiler feedwater is fed into the tubes, and heat transferred from the hot combustion products through the tube walls converts the feedwater to steam.

Boiling point (at a given pressure) For a pure species, the temperature at which the liquid and vapor can coexist in equilibrium at the given pressure. When applied to the heating of a mixture of liquids exposed to a gas at the given pressure, the temperature at which the mixture begins to boil.

Bottoms product The product that leaves the bottom of a distillation column. The bottoms product is relatively rich in the less volatile components of the feed to the column.

Bubble point The temperature at which the first vapor bubble appears when the mixture is heated.

Condensation A process in which an entering gas is cooled and/or compressed, causing one or more of the gas components to liquefy. Uncondensed gases and liquid condensate leave the condenser as separate streams.

Crystallization A process in which a liquid solution is cooled, or solvent is evaporated, to an extent that solid crystals of solute form. The crystals in the slurry (suspension of solids in a liquid) leaving the crystallizer may subsequently be separated from the liquid in a filter or centrifuge.

Dew point The temperature at which the first liquid droplet appears when the mixture is cooled at constant pressure.

Distillation A process in which a mixture of two or more species is fed to a vertical column that contains either a series of vertically spaced horizontal plates, or solid packing through which fluid can flow. Liquid mixtures of the feed components flow down the column and vapor mixtures flow up. Interphase contact, partial condensation of the vapor, and partial vaporization of the liquid all take place throughout the column. The vapor flowing up the column becomes progressively richer in the more volatile components of the feed, and the liquid flowing down becomes richer in the less volatile components. The vapor leaving the top of the column is condensed; part of the condensate is taken off as the overhead product and the rest is recycled to the reactor as reflux, becoming the liquid stream that flows down the column. The liquid leaving the bottom of the column is partially vaporized; the vapor is recycled to the reactor as boil up, becoming the vapor stream that flows up the column, and the residual liquid is taken off as the bottoms product.

Drying A process in which a wet solid is heated or contacted with a hot gas stream, causing some or all of the liquid wetting the solid to evaporate. The vapor and the gas evaporate to emerge as one outlet stream, and the solid and remaining residual liquid emerge as a second outlet stream.

Evaporation (vaporization) A process in which a pure liquid, liquid mixture, or solvent in a solution is vaporized.

Extraction (liquid extraction) A process in which a liquid mixture of two species (the solute and the feed carrier) is contacted in a mixer with a third liquid (the solvent) that is immiscible or nearly immiscible with the feed carrier. When the liquids are contacted, solute transfers from the feed carrier to the solvent. The combined mixture is then allowed to settle into two phases that are then separated by gravity in a decanter.

Filtration A process in which a slurry of solid particles suspended in a liquid passes through a porous medium. Most of the liquid passes through the medium (e.g., a filter) to form the filtrate, and the solids and some entrained liquid are retained on the filter to form the filter cake. Filtration may also be used to separate solids or liquids from gases.

Heat Energy transferred between a system and its surroundings as a consequence of a temperature difference. Heat always flows from a higher temperature to a lower one.

Heat exchanger A process unit through which two fluid streams at different temperatures flow on opposite sides of a metal barrier. Heat is transferred from the stream at the higher temperature through the barrier to the other stream.

Overhead product The product that leaves the top of a distillation column. The overhead product is relatively rich in the most volatile components of the feed to the column.

Pump A device used to propel a liquid or slurry from one location to another, usually through a pipe or tube.

New Words and Expressions

absorption   [əb'sɔːpʃən]   *n.* 吸收，吸收过程；吸收作用

contact   ['kɔntækt]   *n.* 接触，联系，联络，交往，触点，接头

emerge   [i'məːdʒ]   *vi.* 出现；显出；暴露

adsorption   [æd'sɔːpʃən]   *n.* 吸附(作用)

adhere   [əd'hiə]   *vi.* 黏附，附着

furnace   ['fəːnis]   *n.* 熔炉，火炉

species   ['spiːʃiːz]   *n.* 物种，种，种类；类型

volatile   ['vɔlətail]   *a.* 易变的，反复无常的，易激动的，(液体或油)易挥发的

bubble   ['bʌbl]   *n.* 气泡，泡沫，泡状物；透明圆形罩，圆形顶
　　　　　　　　vi. 沸腾，冒泡；发出气泡声
　　　　　　　　vt. 使冒泡；滔滔不绝地说

condensation   [ˌkɔnden'seiʃən]   *n.* 冷凝，凝聚，冷凝液

compress   [kəm'pres]   *vt.* 1.压紧，压缩 2.精简

liquefy   ['likwə,fai]   *vt. & vi.* 液化，溶解，液化

crystallization   [,kristəlai'zeiʃən]   *n.* 结晶化

evaporate   [i'væpəreit]   *vt. & vi.*   (使某物)蒸发掉

crystal   ['kristəl]   *n.* 水晶；结晶，晶体；水晶饰品

                                         a. 水晶的；透明的，清澈的

slurry   ['slə:ri, 'slʌ-]   *n.* 泥浆；悬浮液

suspension   [sə'spenʃən]   *n.* 暂停；悬浮；停职

subsequently   ['sʌbsikwəntli]   *adv.* 随后，其后；后来

filter   ['filtə]   *n.* 过滤，过滤器

                   vt. & vi. 透过，过滤

centrifuge   ['sentrifju:dʒ]   *n.* 离心机

droplet   ['drɔplit]   *n.* 小滴，微滴

distillation   [,distə'leiʃən]   *n.* 1.(各种释义的)蒸馏(过程) 2. 蒸馏物

vertical   ['və:tikəl]   *a.* 垂直的，竖的

horizontal   [,hɔri'zɔntəl]   *a.* 水平的，与地平线平行的

vapor   ['veipə]   *n.* 蒸汽；烟雾

                 vt. 使…蒸发；使…汽化

                 vi. 蒸发；吹牛；沮丧

interphase   ['intə(:)feiz]   *n.* 界面

                     a. 界间的,相间的

vaporization   [,veipərai'zeiʃən, -ri'z-]   *n.* 蒸发；喷雾器；蒸馏器

recycle   [,ri:'saikl]   *vt.* 回收利用

reflux   ['ri:flʌks]   *n.* 逆流,退潮

residual   [ri'zidʒuəl]   *a.* 存留下来的；剩余的；残余的

mixer   ['miksə]   *n.* 搅拌器,混合器

immiscible   [i'misəbl]   *a.* 不能混合的,不融和的

transfer   [træns'fə:]   *vt. & vi.* 转移；迁移

gravity   ['græviti]   *n.* 万有引力；地心引力；重力

decanter   [di'kæntə]   *n.* 玻璃水瓶

porous   ['pɔ:rəs]   *a.* 能穿透的，能渗透的，有毛孔或气孔的

medium   ['mi:djəm]   *n.* 媒介，手段，方法，工具

surroundings   [sə'raundiŋz]   *n.* 环境；(周围的)事物

consequence   ['kɔnsi,kwəns]   *n.* 结果；重要性；推论

barrier   ['bæriə]   *n.* 栅栏，关卡，障碍，隔阂

overhead   ['əuvəhed, ,əuvə'hed]   *adv.* 在头顶上；在空中；在高处

                             a. 高架的；在头上的；在头顶上的

                             n. 天花板；经常费用

propel   [prəu'pel]   *vt.* 推进；推动

location   [ləu'keiʃən]   *n.* 位置，场所

absorption column   吸收塔

flow down   向下流

flow up   向上流
combustion furnace   燃烧炉
distillation column   蒸馏塔
bubble point   泡点
boiling point   沸点
dew point   露点
boil up   上升蒸汽
porous medium   多孔介质
filter cake   滤饼
volatile component   易挥发组分；轻组分

Notes

1. In an absorption column or absorption tower, the solvent enters the top of a column, flows down, and emerges at the bottom, and the gas enters at the bottom, flows up (contacting the liquid), and leaves at the top. 在吸收塔中，溶剂从塔顶进入，向下流动，从塔底采出，气体从塔底进入，向上流动，从塔顶采出。本句是由两个并列分句组成，第一个分句中，enters the top of a column，flows down和emerges at the bottom是the solvent的并列谓语。第二个分句中，enters at the bottom，flows up和leaves at the top都做the gas的并列谓语。

2. A process in which a mixture of two or more species is fed to a vertical column that contains either a series of vertically spaced horizontal plates, or solid packing through which fluid can flow. 是指两种或是多种物质的混合物被送到包含一系列的垂直间距的塔板或者是流体可以流动的有固体填充物的塔中的过程。本句的主体结构就是A process。in which a mixture of two or more species…can flow.是定语从句，对process进行解释说明。Either…or…要么…或…。

3. The vapor leaving the top of the column is condensed; part of the condensate is taken off as the overhead product and the rest is recycled to the reactor as reflux, becoming the liquid stream that flows down the column. 离开塔顶的气相被冷凝，部分冷凝液作为塔顶产品被采出，其余的冷凝液以回流的形式返回到反应器内，并且成为液体的一部分在塔内向下运动。leaving the top of the column现在分词短语修饰主语the vapor。

4. A process in which a liquid mixture of two species (the solute and the feed carrier) is contacted in a mixer with a third liquid (the solvent) that is immiscible or nearly immiscible with the feed carrier. 是指含有两种物质（溶质和物料载体）的液体混合物在搅拌器中与第三种液体（溶剂）相接触的过程，溶剂与物料载体不互溶或是不完全互溶。本句的主体结构就是A process，定语从句in which a liquid mixture of two species…with the feed carrier. 对process进行解释说明。

Exercises

1. Put the following into Chinese

tube wall   given pressure

liquid condensate   residual liquid

interphase contact   transfer from...to…

2. Put the following into English

泡点	露点	回流
易挥发组分	多孔介质	过滤器
塔顶产品	釜残液	

3. Questions

(1) What are the definitions of bubble point and dew point?

(2) Try to find out some examples of absorption.

Lesson Five   Distillation

A plant for continuous distillation is shown in Figure 2.1. Reboiler A is fed continuously with the liquid mixture to be distilled. The liquid is converted partially into vapor by heat transferred from the heating surface B. The vapor formed in the reboiler is richer in low boiler than the unvaporized liquid, but unless the two components differ greatly in volatility, the vapor contains substantial quantities of both components, and if it were condensed, the condensate would be far from pure. To increase the concentration of low boiler in the vapor, the vapor stream from the still is brought into intimate countercurrent contact with a descending stream of boiling liquid in the column, or tower, C. This liquid must be rich enough in low boiler so that there is mass transfer of the low boiler from the liquid to the vapor at each stage of the column. Such a liquid can be obtained simply by condensing the overhead vapors and returning some of the liquid to the top of the column. This return liquid is called reflux. The use of reflux increases the purity of the overhead product, but not without some cost, since the vapor generated in the reboiler must provide both reflux and overhead product, and this energy cost is a large part of the total cost of separation by distillation.

The reflux entering the top of the column is often at the boiling point; but if it is cold, it is almost immediately heated to its boiling point by the vapor. Throughout the rest of the column, the liquid and vapor are at their boiling and condensing temperatures, respectively, and the temperatures increase on going down the column because of the increase in high boiler concentration, and in some cases, because of increase in pressure.

Enrichment of the vapor occurs at each stage because the vapor coming to a stage has a lower concentration of the low boiler than the vapor that would be in equilibrium with the liquid fed to that stage. For example, the vapor coming to the top stage is less rich than the overhead product, and the reflux, which has the same composition as the product, has an equilibrium vapor composition which is even richer than the product. Therefore, vapor passing through the top stage will be enriched in low boiler at the expense of the reflux liquid. This makes the reflux poorer in low boiler, but if the flow rates have been adjusted correctly, the liquid passing down to the second stage will still be able to enrich the lower quality vapor coming up to the second stage. Then at all stages in the column, some low boiler diffuses from the liquid into the vapor phase, and there is a corresponding diffusion of high boiler from the vapor to the liquid. The heat of vaporization of the low boiler is supplied by the heat of condensation of the high boiler, and the total flow rate of vapor up the column is nearly constant.

The enrichment of the vapor stream as it passes through the column in contact with reflux is called rectification. It is immaterial where the reflux originates, provided its concentration in low boiler is sufficiently great to give the desired product. The usual source of reflux is the condensate leaving condenser D. Part of the condensate is withdrawn as the product, and the remainder is returned to the top of the column. Reflux is sometimes provided by partial condensation of the overhead vapor; the reflux then differs in composition from the vapor leaving as overhead product. Provided an azeotrope is not formed, the vapor reaching the condenser can be brought as close to complete purity as desired by using a tall tower and a large reflux.

From the reboiler, liquid is withdrawn which contains most of the high boiling component, because little of this component escapes with the overhead product unless that product is an azeotrope. The liquid from the reboiler, which is called the bottom product or bottoms, is not nearly pure, however, because there is no provision in the equipment of Figure 2.1 for rectifying this stream.

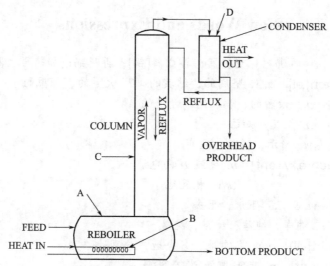

Figure 2.1   Continuous distillation

A—reboiler; B—heating surface; C—column; D—condenser

The column shown in Figure 2.1 often contains a number of perforated plates, or trays, stacked one above the other. A cascade of such trays is called a sieve-plate column. A single sieve plate is shown in Figure 2.2. It consists of a horizontal tray A carrying a downpipe, or downcomer C, the top of which acts as a weir, and a number of holes B. The holes are all of the same size, usually 0.25 to 0.5 in. in diameter. The downcomer D from the tray above reaches nearly to tray A. Liquid flows from plate to plate down the column, passing through downcomers D and C and across the plate. The weir maintains a minimum depth of liquid on the tray, nearly independent of the rate of flow of liquid. Vapor flows upward from tray to tray through the perforations. Except at very low vapor rates, well below the normal operating range, the vapor velocity through the perforations is sufficient

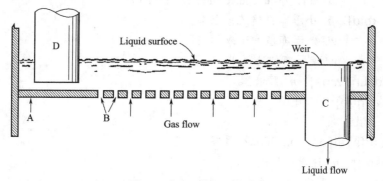

Figure 2.2   Sieve plate

A—tray or plate; B—perforations; C—downcomer to plate below; D—downcomer from plate above

to prevent leakage or "weeping"of the liquid through the holes. The vapor is subdivided by the holes into many small bubbles and passes in intimate contact through the pool of liquid on the tray. Because of the action of the vapor bubbles，the liquid is actually a boiling frothy mass. The vapor space above the froth contains a fine mist of droplets formed by collapsing bubbles. Most of the drops settle back into the liquid，but some are entrained by the vapor and carried to the plate above. Sieve-plate columns are representative of an entire class of equipment called plate columns.

New Words and Expressions

reboiler   [riːˈbɔilə]   n. 再沸器；重沸器；再煮器[锅]；再蒸锅；加热再生器

substantial   [səbˈstænʃəl]   a. 1. 坚固的；结实的   2. 大量的，可观的

intimate   [ˈintimət]   a. 亲密的；私人的；精通的

　　　　　　　　　　　　n. 至交；知己

　　　　　　　　　　　　vt. 暗示；通知；宣布

countercurrent   [ˈkauntəˌkʌrənt]   n. 逆流,反向电流

　　　　　　　　　　　　　　adv. 相反地

descend   [diˈsend]   vt. & vi.   下来，下去

purity   [ˈpjuəriti]   n. 纯净；纯洁；纯粹；纯度

respectively   [risˈpektivli]   adv. 各自地，各个地，分别地

enrichment   [inˈritʃmənt]   n. 丰富,肥沃,浓缩,富集

rate   [reit]   n. 比率，率，(运动、变化等的)速度；进度

adjust   [əˈdʒʌst]   vt. & vi. (改变…以)适应；调整；校正

diffusion   [diˈfjuːʒən]   n. [物,化]扩散；漫射

rectification   [ˌrektifiˈkeiʃən]   n. [化]精馏

immaterial   [ˌiməˈtiəriəl]   a. 不重要的，不相干的

originate   [əˈridʒəneit]   vt. 引起；创作

　　　　　　　　　　　　vi. 发源；发生；起航

remainder   [riˈmeində]   n. 剩余物；残余部分

azeotrope   [əˈziːətrəup]   n. 共沸混合物,恒沸物

perforated   [ˈpəːfəreitid]   a. 穿孔的；有排孔的

　　　　　　　　　　　　v. 穿孔 (perforate 的过去分词)

cascade   [kæsˈkeid]   n. 小瀑布；喷流；层叠

　　　　　　　　　　　vi. 像瀑布般冲下或倾泻

　　　　　　　　　　　v. 使瀑布似地落下

downcomer   [ˈdaunˌkʌmə]   n. 降液器

diameter   [daiˈæmitə]   n. 直径

weir   [wiə]   n. 溢流堰

perforation   [ˌpəːfəˈreiʃən]   n. 穿孔；贯穿

velocity   [viˈlɔsəti]   n. 速率；迅速；周转率

weeping   [ˈwiːpiŋ]   a. 哭泣的，滴水的；垂枝的

leakage   [ˈliːkidʒ]   n. 泄漏；渗漏物；漏出量

subdivided　[ˌsʌbdiˈvaid, ˈsʌbdivaid]　*vi.* 细分，再分

vt. 把…再分，把…细分

frothy　[ˈfrɔθi]　*a.* 多泡的；起泡的；空洞的，浅薄的

mist　[mist]　*n.* 薄雾；视线模糊不清；模糊不清之物

entrain　[inˈtrein]　*vt.* 导致；产生；携带；带走

continuous distillation　连续蒸馏

flow rate　流速

diffuse from…into…　从…扩散到

perforated plate　筛板

be subdivided into　被再分成

sieve-plate column　筛板塔

plate column　板式塔

Notes

1. The vapor formed in the reboiler is richer in low boiler than the unvaporized liquid, but unless the two components differ greatly in volatility, the vapor contains substantial quantities of both components, and if it were condensed, the condensate would be far from pure. 若轻重组分的相对挥发度相差很大，则在再沸器中形成的蒸气与未汽化的液体相比，含有较多的轻组分；若轻重组分的相对挥发度相差不大，则上升蒸气中两种组分的含量都较多，并且冷凝后，冷凝液的纯度很低。formed in the reboiler 过去分词短语作定语修饰主语 the vapor，richer in low boiler than the unvaporized liquid 作表语，but 引导转折句 but unless 引导条件从句，if it were condensed，the condensate would be far from pure 为虚拟语气，if 引导条件从句 it were condensed，此逗号后为主句，the condensate 主语，would be far from pure 系表结构。

2. The use of reflux increases the purity of the overhead product, but not without some cost, since the vapor generated in the reboiler must provide both reflux and overhead product, and this energy cost is a large part of the total cost of separation by distillation. 回流的液体增加了塔顶产品的纯度，但是由于再沸器产生的上升蒸气同时提供了回流液和塔顶产品，因此并不是没有能量消耗。并且消耗的这部分能量是蒸馏分离过程中消耗的整体能量的一大部分。since 引导条件从句，generated in the reboiler 过去分词短语做定语修饰从句主语 the vapor。

3. For example, the vapor coming to the top stage is less rich than the overhead product, and the reflux, which has the same composition as the product, has an equilibrium vapor composition which is even richer than the product. 例如，塔顶蒸气的浓度比塔顶产品的浓度低，与产品有相同组成的回流液的平衡气相组成的浓度比产品高。coming to the top stage 现在分词短语做定语修饰主语 the vapor。which 引导非限定性定语从句，先行词为 the reflux。

4. This makes the reflux poorer in low boiler, but if the flow rates have been adjusted correctly, the liquid passing down to the second stage will still be able to enrich the lower quality vapor coming up to the second stage. 这使得下降的回流液中的易挥发组分的含量降低，如果液体的流速调节为正常的话，下降到第二层塔板的液体与上升到第二层塔板的蒸气接触时，上升蒸气中的易挥发组分的含量会进一步富集。but if 引条件从句 the flow rates have been adjusted correctly，the liquid 主句主语　passing down to the second stage 现在分词短语做定语修饰主语，coming up to the second stage 现在分词短语做定语修饰宾语 the lower quality vapor。

5. Provided an azeotrope is not formed，the vapor reaching the condenser can be brought as close to complete purity as desired by using a tall tower and a large reflux. 如果不形成共沸物，且采用很高的塔以及大量的回流，则到达冷凝器的蒸气可以近似达到所要求的100%的纯度。Provided引导条件从句an azeotrope is not formed，reaching the condenser现在分词短语做定语修饰the vapor。

Exercises

1. Put the following into Chinese

| condensate | perforated plate | low boiler |
| overhead product | at low vapor rate | vapor bubble |

2. Put the following into English

| 再沸器 | 精馏段 | 冷凝器 |
| 共沸物 | 降液管 | 溢流堰 | 筛板塔 |

3. Questions

(1) What's the definition of distillation? And elaborate the principle of distillation briefly.

(2) How many parts does the sieve plate consist of ? What are they?

Reading Material: Fluid Flow Phenomena

Mass transfer takes place at the interface between two mutually insoluble fluids or at the interface between a fluid and a solid. Since the phenomenon is closely related to fluid flow, we have to understand the fundamental nature of flow before going into details of the phenomenon.

O. Reynolds was the first to address the fundamental aspects of the mechanism of flow. In 1883, he studied the flow of water in a horizontal glass tube by injecting tracer liquid colored with a dye from a small nozzle placed along the centerline of the tube. According to his observations, there are two types of flow, as shown in Figure 2.3 (a) and (b). The tracer is observed in a form like a single string if the flow rate of the water is relatively low [Figure 2.3 (a)], and similar results are observed for tracer injected from different radial positions. This type of flow, in which a fluid behaves as though it were composed of parallel layers, is called *laminar flow*. On the other hand, if the flow rate of the water exceeds a certain critical value, the flow suddenly changes to a completely different type and many eddies are observed, as shown in Figure 2.3 (b). Under these conditions, the tracer will spread in the downstream region of the tube and finally the whole tube section is filled with the dispersed tracer. This type of flow, in which irregular motion of the fluid due to eddies is observed, is called *turbulent flow*.

Reynolds number and transition from laminar to turbulent flow: Reynolds studied the conditions under which one type of flow changes into the other and found that the critical velocity, at which laminar flow changes into turbulent flow, depends on four quantities: the diameter of the tube and the viscosity, density, and average linear velocity the liquid. Furthermore, he found that these four factors can be combined into one group and that the change in kind of flow occurs at a definite value of the group. The grouping of variables so found was:

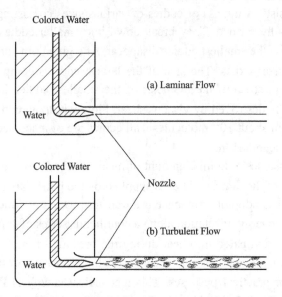

Figure 2.3   Laminar and turbulent flow, experiment by O. Reynolds

$$Re = \frac{du\rho}{\mu} \qquad\qquad (2\text{-}1)$$

Where d=diameter of tube

　　　u=average velocity of liquid

　　　μ=viscosity of liquid

　　　ρ=density of liquid

　　The dimensionless group of variables defined by Equation (2-1) is called the Reynolds number Re. Its magnitude is independent of the units used, provided the units are consistent.

　　Additional observations have shown that the transition from laminar to turbulent flow actually may occur over a wide range of Reynolds numbers. In a pipe, flow is always laminar at Reynolds numbers below 2100, but laminar flow can persist up to Reynolds numbers of several thousand under special conditions of well-rounded tube entrance and very quiet liquid in the tank. Under ordinary conditions, the flow in a pipe or tube is turbulent at Reynolds numbers above about 4000. Between 2100 and 4000 a transition region is found where the flow may be either laminar or turbulent, depending upon conditions at the entrance of the tube and on the distance from the entrance.

　　Nature of turbulence: Because of its importance in many branches of engineering, turbulent flow has been extensively investigated in recent years, and a large literature has accumulated on this subject. Refined methods of measurement have been used to follow in detail the actual velocity fluctuations of the eddies during turbulent flow, and the results of such measurements have shed much qualitative and quantitative light on the nature of turbulence.

　　Turbulence may be generated in other ways than by flow through a pipe. In general, it can result either from contact of the flowing stream with solid boundaries or from contact between two layers of fluid moving at different velocities. The first kind of turbulence is called wall turbulence and the second kind free turbulence. Wall turbulence appears when the fluid flows through closed or open channels or past solid shapes immersed in the stream. Free turbulence appears in the flow of a jet into a mass of stagnant fluid or when a boundary layer separates from a solid wall and flows through the bulk of the fluid.

　　Turbulent flow consists of a mass of eddies of various sizes coexisting in the flowing stream. Large eddies are continually formed. They break down into smaller eddies, which in turn evolve still smaller ones. Finally, the smallest eddies disappear. At a given time and in a given volume, a wide spectrum of eddy sizes exists. The size of the largest eddy is comparable with the smallest dimension of the turbulent stream; the diameter of the smallest eddies is 10 to 100μm. Smaller eddies than this are rapidly destroyed by viscous shear. Flow within an eddy is laminar. Since even the smallest eddies contain about 10^{12} molecules, all eddies are of macroscopic size, and turbulent flow is not a molecular phenomenon.

　　Any given eddy possesses a definite amount of mechanical energy, much like that of a small spinning top. The energy of the largest eddies is supplied by the potential energy of the bulk flow of the fluid. From an energy standpoint turbulence is a transfer process in which large eddies, formed from the bulk flow, pass energy of rotation along a continuous series of smaller eddies. Mechanical energy is not appreciably dissipated into heat during the breakup of large eddies into smaller and smaller ones, but such energy is not available for maintaining pressure or overcoming resistance to flow and is worthless for practical purposes. This mechanical energy is finally converted to heat when the smallest eddies are obliterated by viscous action.

一、翻译的标准

在中国翻译界，一提到翻译的标准，人们首先想到的就是清末启蒙思想家严复所提出的著名"信达雅"三字标准。所谓"信"，就是译文的思想内容忠实于原作；"达"就是译文表达通顺明白；"雅"即要求风格优美。

当代翻译界普遍认同的翻译标准为：忠实、通顺。所谓"忠实"，首先是指忠实于原文的内容。译者必须把原文的内容完整准确地表达出来，不得有篡改、歪曲、遗漏或任意删减增加。忠实还指保持原文的风格——即原文的民族风格、时代风格、语体风格以及原作者的语言风格。所谓"通顺"，指译文的语言应规范、流畅和通顺易懂。

然而，就科技英语的特点和用途而言，其翻译标准应略区别于文学翻译。科技英语的标准应该是：准确规范、通俗易懂、简洁明晰。

1. 准确规范

科技文献和情报技术资料的主要功能是论述科学事实、探讨科学问题、传授科学知识、记录科学实验、总结科学经验等，这就要求科学文献和情报技术资料的翻译标准首先必须是标准规范。所谓准确，就是忠实地、不折不扣地传达原文的全部信息内容。所谓规范，就是译文要符合所涉及的科学技术或某个专业领域的专业语言表达规范。要做到这一点，译者必须充分地理解原文所表述的内容，其中包括对原文词汇、语法、逻辑关系和科学内容的理解。科学翻译的任何错误、甚至是不准确都会给科学研究、学术交流、生产发展等带来不良影响或巨大损失，甚至是灾难，如下。

➤ Oil and gas will continue to be our chief source of fuel.

油和气体将继续是燃料的主要源泉。

该译句使人怀疑是否一切油类和气体都可以作为"燃料的主要源泉"。事实上，在翻译科技英语时，要根据上下文将某些词的含义具体化和专业化。如果不注意这一翻译特点，只是按原文句子逐词译出，就会造成误解和歧义。这里的 oil 和 gas 不是泛指油类和气体，而是特指石油和天然气。另外，"燃料的…源泉"，也不符合汉语的表达习惯。所以该句应译为：

石油和天然气将继续是燃料的主要来源。

2. 通顺易懂

所谓通顺易懂，即指译文的语言符合译语语法结构及表达习惯，容易为读者所理解和接受。也就是说，译文语言须明白晓畅、文理通顺、结构合理、逻辑关系清楚，没有死译、硬译、语言晦涩难懂的现象。请对比下列句子：

➤ Distillation involves heating the solution until water evaporates, and then condensing the vapor.

蒸馏就是加热溶液直到水蒸发，然后冷凝蒸汽。（不好）

蒸馏就是要把溶液加热，直到水蒸发，然后再使蒸汽冷凝。（较好）

> When a person sees，smells，hears or touches something，then he is perceiving.

当一个人看到某种东西、闻到某种气味、听到某个声音或触到某物时，他是在察觉。（不好）

当一个人看到某种东西、闻到某种气味、听到某个声音或触到某物时，他是在运用感觉在感受。（较好）

> A material object cannot have a speed greater than the speed of light.

一个物体不会有一个大于光的速度。（不好）

一个物体的速度绝不会超过光速。（较好）

> All bodies are known to possess weight and occupy space.

所有物体被知道具有重量并占据空间。（不好）

我们知道，所有物体都具有重量并占据空间。（较好）

以上例句中，第一条译文都是照顾原文，逐字死译，不符合汉语的表达方式和习惯。因此，在翻译时，译者要仔细斟酌译文，使其通顺易懂。

3. 简洁明晰

简洁明晰是科技文体的又一特点。同样，在翻译过程中，译文的简洁明晰也是科技英语翻译的最基本要求之一：就是译文要简短精练、一目了然，要尽量避免烦琐、冗赘和不必要的重复。请比较下列句子：

> It should be realized that magnetic forces and electric forces are not the same.

磁力和电力的不一样是应该被认识到的。（欠佳）

应该认识到，磁力和电力是不同的。（简洁）

> All living things must，by reason of physiological limitations，die.

由于生理上的局限性的原因，一切生物总是要死亡的。（欠佳）

由于生理上的局限，一切生物都要死亡的。（简洁）

> The removal of minerals from water is called softening.

从水中把矿物质去除被叫做软化。（欠佳）

去除水中的矿物质的过程叫做软化。（简洁）

从以上例句的对比中，我们可以看出，译得不好句子，往往是冗长烦琐、赘词太多、不得要领，使译文显得生硬啰嗦。

在科技英语翻译中，译文的通顺必须以准确为基础和前提。倘若准确但不通顺，则准确的意义尽失；倘若通顺而又不准确，则背离了翻译的基本原则及标准。在做到准确和通顺的基础上，如能做到简洁，则应是科技英语翻译的理想境界。

二、翻译的过程

翻译的过程是正确理解原文和创造性地运用另一种语言再现原文的过程，大体上可分为理解和表达三个阶段。

1. 理解阶段

理解是表达的前提。不能正确地理解原文，表达就无从谈起。理解主要是通过阅读原文来进行的。对原文透彻的理解是翻译工作的基础和关键。译者必须把握好原文的词汇含义、句法结构和惯用法等，对原文所涉及的事物背景、专业术语及其逻辑关系要做到心中有数。有时对某些词汇理解不透彻，差错就在所难免，如下。

> The medicinal herb **helps** a cold.

这种草药**帮助**感冒。（误译）

这种草药**可治疗**感冒。（正确）

误译是因为把 help 狭隘地理解为"帮助"，而不知道 help 还可以作"治疗"解。

2. 表达阶段

如果说理解阶段是"钻进去"把原文吃透，那么表达阶段就是"跳出来"，不受原文形式的束缚，而根据本民族语言习惯重新进行叙述。表达是理解的结果。在表达阶段，最重要的是表达手段的选择，这就涉及到了翻译的技巧，翻译的创造性劳动也就体现在这上面。有时同一个句子可能会出现几种不同的译法，即使对原文理解没有偏差，译文的表达质量也不尽相同，如下。

➢ Action is equal to reaction，but it is acts in a contrary direction.

译文一：作用力与反作用力相等，但它向着相反的方向作用。

译文二：作用力与反作用力相等，但它作用的方向相反。

译文三：作用力与反作用力大小相等，方向相反。

以上三种译文在表达愿意上大体相同，但表达方式却截然不同。译文一由于"钻进去"而没有"跳出来"，所以译文不够简练通顺；译文二的后一部分由于跳出了原文形式的框框，所以较为简练；译文三言简意赅，不落窠臼，完全摆脱了原文形式的束缚，选用了由四字词构成的对偶修辞手法"大小相等，方向相反"，因而使译文生动贴切、简洁明快。

因此，仅仅能够正确理解原文还是远远不够的，没有深厚的语言根底，同样也翻译不出质量上乘的译文。

3. 校核阶段

校核阶段是理解与表达阶段的进一步深化，是对原文内容进一步核实以及对译文语言进一步推敲的阶段。校核也是对译文能够符合"准确规范、通俗易懂、简洁明晰"的翻译标准所必不可少的一个步骤。在校核过程中，往往可以查找到理解阶段或表达阶段的疏漏之处，从而可以对译文继续修改、润色，直到译文准确流畅为止。

Unit Three   Chemical Equipment

Lesson Six   Heat Exchangers

Heat exchangers are so important and so widely used in the process industries that their design has been highly developed. Standards devised and accepted by the Tubular Exchanger Manufactures Association (TEMA) are available covering in detail materials，methods of construction，technique of design，and dimensions for exchangers.

SINGLE-PASS 1-1 EXCHANGER. The simple double-pipe exchanger shown in Figure 3.1 is inadequate for flow rates that cannot readily be handled in a few tubes. If several double pipes are used in parallel，the weight of metal required for the outer tubes becomes so large that the shell-and-tube construction，such as that shown in Figure 3.2，where one shell serves for many tubes，is more economical. This exchanger，because it has one shell-side pass and one tube-side pass，is a 1-1exchanger.

In an exchanger the shell- side and tube-side heat-transfer coefficients are of comparable importance，and both must be large if a satisfactory overall coefficient is to be attained. The velocity and turbulence of the shell-side liquid are as important as those of the tube-side fluid. To promote

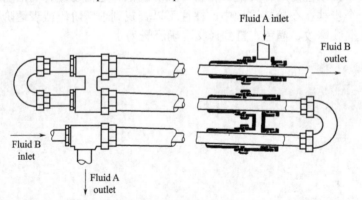

Figure 3.1   Double-pipe heat exchanger

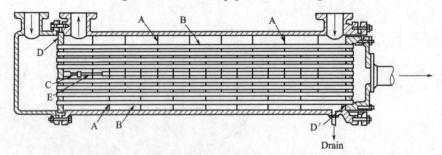

Figure 3.2   Single-pass counterflow heat exchanger
A—baffles；B—tubes；C—guide rods；D，D′—tube sheets；E—spacer tubes

crossflow and raise the average velocity of the shell-side fluid，baffles are installed in the shell. In the construction shown in Figure 3.2，the baffles A consist of circular disks of sheet metal with one side cut away. Common practice is to cut away a segment having a height equal to one-fourth the inside diameter of the shell. Such baffles are called 25 percent baffles. The baffles are perforated to receive the tubes. To minimize leakage，the clearances between baffles and shell and tubes should be small. The baffles are supported by one or more guide rods C，which are fastened between the tube sheets D and D′ by setscrews. To fix the baffles in place，short sections of tube E are slipped over the rod C between the baffles. In assembling such an exchanger，it is necessary to do the tube sheets，support rods，spacers，and baffles first and then to install the tubes.

Tubes and tube sheets Standard lengths of tubes for heat-exchanger construction are 8，12，16，and 20 feet. Tubes are arranged on triangular or square pitch. Unless the shell side tends to foul badly，triangular pitch is used，because more heat-transfer area can be packed into a shell of given diameter than in square pitch. Tubes in triangular pitch cannot be cleaned by running a brush between the rows，because no space exists for cleaning lanes. Square pitch allows cleaning of the outside of the tubes. Also，square pitch gives a lower shell- side pressure drop than triangular pitch.

TEMA standards specify a minimum center-to-center distance 1.25 times the outside diameter of the tubes for triangular pitch and a minimum cleaning lane of 0.25 inch. for square pitch.

Shell and baffles. Shell diameters are standardized. For shells up to and including 23 inch. the diameters are fixed in accordance with American Society for Testing and Materials (ASTM) pipe standards. For sizes of 25 in. and above the inside diameter is specified to the nearest inch. These shells are constructed of rolled plate. Minimum shell thicknesses are also specified.

The distance between baffles (center to center) is the baffle pitch，or baffle spacing. It should not be less than one-fifth the diameter of the shell or more than the inside diameter of the shell.

Tubes are usually attached to the tube sheets by grooving the holes circumferentially and rolling the tube ends into the holes by means of a rotating tapered mandrel，which stresses the metal of the tube beyond the elastic limit，so the metal flows into the grooves. In high-pressure exchangers，the tube are welded or brazed to the tube sheet after rolling.

New Words and Expressions

standard   ['stændəd]   *n.* 标准，水准，规范

available   [ə'veiləbl]   *a.* 可用的或可得到的

construction   [kən'strʌkʃən]   *n.* 建造，建设；建筑业

dimension   [di'menʃən]   *n.* 尺寸，度量

exchange   [iks'tʃeindʒ]   *n.* 交换，互换

inadequate   [in'ædikwit]   *a.* 不充足的,不适当的

parallel   ['pærəlel]   *a.* (指至少两条线)平行

shell   [ʃel]   *n.* (贝、卵、坚果等的)壳，外壳，框架

economical   [,ikə'nɔmikəl]   *a.* 节约的，节俭的，经济的

comparable   ['kɔmpərəbl]   *a.* 类似的，同类的，相当的，可比较的，比得上的

velocity   [vi'lɔsiti]   *n.* 速度

turbulence   ['tə:bjuləns]   *n.* 气体或水的涡流，波动

promote [prə'məut] vt. 提升，提拔

crossflow ['krɔsfləu] n. 横流式的，横向气流

baffle ['bæfl] n. 挡板；困惑

install [in'stɔ:l] vt. 安装

circular ['sə:kjulə] a. 圆形的，环形的；循环的

segment ['segmənt, seg'ment, 'segment] vi. 分割

              n. 段；部分

              vt. 分割

perforate ['pə:fəreit] vt. 穿孔于,在…上打眼

leakage ['li:kidʒ] n. 泄漏；渗漏物；漏出量

rod [rɔd] n. 竿，杆，棒

fasten ['fa:sən] vt. 系紧，拴牢

setscrew ['setskru:] n. 固定螺丝钉

assemble [ə'sembl] vt. 集合，聚集；装配；收集

         vi. 集合，聚集

spacer ['speisə] n. 分程隔板

triangular [trai'æŋgjulə] a. 三角(形)的

pitch [pitʃ] vt. 投；定位于；掷；用沥青涂；扎营；向前倾跌

    n. 沥青；程度；音高；投掷；树脂；倾斜；

    vi. 投掷；倾斜；坠落；搭帐篷

foul [faul] vt. 弄脏；犯规；淤塞；缠住，妨害

    a. 邪恶的；污秽的；犯规的；淤塞的

    vi. 犯规；缠结；腐烂

    n. 犯规；缠绕

    adv. 违反规则地，不正当地

square [skwɛə] n. 正方形

lane [lein] n. 小路，小巷

accordance [ə'cɔ:dəns] n. 一致；和谐

society [sə'saiəti] n. 社会

thickness ['θiknis] n. 厚度；层；含混不清；浓度

attach [ə'tætʃ] vt. & vi. 贴上；系；附上

groove [gru:v] n. 沟，槽

circumferential [sə,kʌmfə'renʃəl] a. 圆周的

rotate [rəu'teit] vt. & vi. (使某物)旋转[转动]，(使某人或某物) 轮流[按顺序循环]

taper ['teipə] vt. & vi. (使)一端逐渐变细；(使)成锥形；逐渐变小

mandrel ['mændrəl] n. 心轴

elastic [i'læstik] a. 有弹力的，有弹性的，可伸缩的，灵活的

weld [weld] vt. & vi. 焊接；熔接

braze [breiz] vt. 铜焊，用黄铜镀或制造

heat exchanger 换热器

double-pipe exchanger 套管式换热器

heat-transfer coefficient　传热系数
tube sheet　管板
in accordance with　与…一致
baffle spacing　挡板间距

Notes

1. Standards devised and accepted by the Tubular Exchanger Manufactures Association (TEMA) are available covering in detail materials, methods of construction, technique of design, and dimensions for exchangers. 管式换热器制造商协会（TEMA）设计和普遍使用的标准包括了使用的原料、制造的方法、设计的技术以及换热器的尺寸。devised and accepted by the Tubular Exchanger Manufactures Association (TEMA) 过去分词短语做定语修饰主语 standards, covering in detail materials, methods of construction, technique of design, and dimensions for exchangers 现在分词短语做状语。

2. If several double pipes are used in parallel, the weight of metal required for the outer tubes becomes so larger that the shell-and-tube construction, such as that shown in Figure 3.2, where one shell serves for many tubes, is more economical. 如果几个管子平行排列，外部管子的金属量的需求较大，例如图 3.2 所示一个壳程多个管子的管壳式换热器的制造是比较经济的。If 引导条件从句 several double pipes are used in parallel，required for the outer tubes 过去分词短语做定语修饰主句主语 the weight of metal，that 引导结果从句，such as that shown in Figure 3.2，where one shell serves for many tubes 是插入语。

3. Unless the shell side tends to foul badly, triangular pitch is used, because more heat-transfer area can packed into a shell of given diameter than in square pitch. 除非壳程流体易结垢，才选用三角形排列的管子，因为与正方形排列的管子相比，三角形排列管子的传热面积都集中在特定直径的壳体上。

4. Tubes are usually attached to the tube sheets by grooving the holes circumferentially and rolling the tube ends into the holes by means of a rotating tapered mandrel, which stresses the metal of the tube beyond the elastic limit, so the metal flows into the grooves. 管子是通过在管板上开圆形的凹槽，通过旋转锥形的芯棒将管子的末端旋入凹槽，这样的压力超出了管子的金属的弹性极限，最终金属管子进入了凹槽。

Exercises

1. Put the following into Chinese

　heat exchanger　　　triangular pitch　　　square pitch　　　guide rod　　　elastic limit

2. Put the following into English

　套管式换热器　　　传热系数　　　　管板
　壳体直径　　　　　管子　　　　　　折流挡板

3. Questions

　(1) How many parts does the heat exchanger consist of?

　(2) What's the baffle? What's the roles of it?

Lesson Seven   Ideal Batch Reactor

This is the classic reactor used by organic chemists. The typical volume in glassware is a few hundred milliliters. Reactants are charged to the system, rapidly mixed, and rapidly brought up to temperature so that reaction conditions are well defined. Heating is carried out with an oil bath or an electric heating mantle. Mixing is carried out with a magnetic stirrer or a small mechanical agitator. Temperature is controlled by regulating the bath temperature or by allowing a solvent to reflux.

Batch reactors are the most common type of industrial reactor and may have volumes well in excess of 100000 liters. They tend to be used for small-volume specialty products (e.g., an organic dye) rather than large-volume commodity chemicals (e.g., ethylene oxide) that are normally reacted in continuous-flow equipment. Industrial-scale batch reactors can be heated or cooled by external coils or a jacket, by internal coils, or by an external heat exchanger in a pump-around loop. Reactants are often preheated by passing them through heat exchangers as they are charged to the vessel. Heat generation due to the reaction can be significant in large vessels. Refluxing is one means for controlling the exotherm. Mixing in large batch vessels is usually carried out with a mechanical agitator, but is occasionally carried out with an external pump-around loop where the momentum of the returning fluid causes the mixing.

Heat and mass transfer limitations are rarely important in the laboratory but may emerge upon scaleup. Batch reactors with internal variations in temperature or composition are difficult to analyze and remain a challenge to the chemical reaction engineer. For now, assume an ideal batch reactor with the following characteristics.

1. Reactants are quickly charged, mixed, and brought to temperature at the beginning of the reaction cycle.

2. Mixing and heat transfer are sufficient to assure that the batch remains completely uniform throughout the reaction cycle.

A batch reactor has no input or output of mass after the initial charging. The amounts of individual components may change due to reaction but not due to flow into or out of the system. The component balance for component A, Equation is:

$$\frac{\mathrm{d}(Va)}{\mathrm{d}t} = R_{A}V \tag{3-1}$$

Together with similar equations for the other reactive components, Equation(3-1) constitutes the reactor design equation for an ideal bath reactor. Note that a and R_A have been replaced with a and R_A because of the assumption of good mixing. An ideal batch reactor has no temperature or concentration gradients within the system volume. The concentration will change with time because of the reaction, but at any time it is everywhere uniform. The temperature may also change with time, but this complication will not be discussed. The reaction rate will vary with time but is always uniform throughout the vessel. Here in this text, we make the additional assumption that the volume is constant. In a liquid-phase reaction, this corresponds to assuming constant fluid density, an assumption that is usually reasonable for preliminary calculations.

Industrial gas-phase reactions are normally conducted in flow systems rather than batch systems. When batch reactors are used，they are normally constant-volume devices so that the system pressure can vary during the batch cycle. Constant-pressure devices were used in early kinetic studies and are occasionally found in industry. The constant pressure at which they operate is usually atmospheric pressure.

New Words and Expressions

organic   [ɔːˈgænik]   *a.* 有机的；器官的；组织的；根本的

volume   [ˈvɔljuːm]   *n.* 体积；容积，容量

glassware   [ˈglɑːswɛə, ˈglæs-]   *n.* 玻璃器具类

milliliter   [ˈmili,liːtə]   *n.* 毫升

mantle   [ˈmæntl]   *n.* 套；覆盖物；幕；披风；斗篷

magnetic   [mægˈnetik]   *a.* 有吸引力的；有磁性的；地磁的

stirrer   [ˈstəːrə]   *n.* 搅拌器

mechanical   [miˈkænikəl] *a.* 机械的；呆板的；力学的；无意识的；手工操作的

continuous-flow   [流] 连续流；持续气流

agitator   [ˈædʒi,teitə]   *n.* 搅拌器

commodity   [kəˈmɔditi]   *n.* 产品

equipment   [iˈkwipmənt]   *n.* 设备；装备；配备

coil   [kɔil]   *n.* 蛇管式换热器，(一) 卷，(一) 圈；盘卷之物

jacket   [ˈdʒækit]   *n.* 夹套；保温套，绝热罩

preheat   [priːˈhiːt]   *vt.* 预先加热

significant   [sigˈnifikənt]   *a.* 重要的，重大的，可观的

exotherm   [ˈeksəu,θəːm]   *n.* [化] 放热曲线；(因释放化学能而引起的) 升温

variation   [,vɛəriˈeiʃən]   *n.* 变化，变动(的程度)

characteristic   [,kæriktəˈristik]   *a.* 特有的，典型的

individual   [,indiˈvidjuəl]   *a.* 个别的，单独的，个人的

gradient   [ˈgreidiənt]   *n.* 梯度；倾斜度；坡度
　　　　　　　　　　　　a. 倾斜的；步行的

correspond   [,kɔːriˈspɔnd]   *vi.* 符合，一致；相应；通信

density   [ˈdensiti]   *n.* 密集，稠密，[物，化]密度

calculation   [,kælkjuːleiʃən]   *n.* 计算；估计；深思熟虑；计算的结果

preliminary   [priˈliminəri]   *a.* 初步的，预备的，开端的

atmospheric   [,ætməˈsferik]   *a.* 大气的；大气层的；大气引起的

oil bath   油浴；油浴锅

electric heating mantle   电加热套

magnetic stirrer   磁力搅拌器

mechanical agitator   机械搅拌器

mass transfer   质量传递；传质

be replaced with   被替换成

Notes

1. Reactants are charged to the system, rapidly mixed, and rapidly brought up to temperature so that reaction conditions are well defined. 反应物被输送到反应器中，迅速混合，迅速达到反应温度，因而反应条件非常恒定。so that引导目的从句reaction conditions are well defined.

2. They tend to be used for small-volume specialty products (e.g., an organic dye) rather than large-volume commodity chemicals (e.g., ethylene oxide) that are normally reacted in continuous-flow equipment. 它们一般用于小批量的特殊产品的生产 (例如有机染料)，很少用于大批量的化学品的生产 (例如环氧乙烷)，这些化学品一般都在连续的设备中反应。that引导定语从句，先行词为large-volume commodity chemicals。

3. Mixing in large batch vessels is usually carried out with a mechanical agitator, but is occasionally carried out with an external pump-around loop where the momentum of the returning fluid causes the mixing. 在大型的反应器中，一般采用机械搅拌来混合反应物，偶尔也采用外部泵循环使得回流的流体具有一定的动能来混合反应物。mixing in large batch vessels动名词短语做主语。

Exercises

1. Put the following into Chinese

batch reactor   reaction rate   concentration gradient
liquid-phase reaction   constant-volume device

2. Put the following into English

油浴   磁力搅拌器   有机染料
环氧乙烷   温度梯度   恒压设备   常压

3. Question

(1) What's the properties of an ideal batch reactor?

(2) How does the temperature of an ideal batch reactor change?

Reading Material: Drying Equipment

Of the many types of commercial dryers available, only a small number of important types will be considered here.

Dryers for Solids and Pastes

Typical dryers for solids and pastes include tray and screen-conveyor dryers for materials that cannot be agitated and tray, screw-conveyor, tower dryers where agitation is permissible. In the following treatment these types are ordered, as far as possible, according to the degree of agitation and the method of exposing the solid to the gas or contacting it with a hot surface. The ordering is complicated, however, by the fact that some types of dryers may be either adiabatic or nonadiabatic or a combination of both.

Tray Dryers. A typical batch tray dryer is illustrated in Figure 3.3. It consists of a rectangular chamber of sheet metal containing two trucks that support racks H. Each rack carries a number of shallow trays, perhaps 750 mm (30 in.) square and 50 to 150 mm (2 to 6 in.) deep, that are loaded with the material to be dried. Heated air is circulated at 2 to 5 m/s (7 to 15 ft/s) between the trays by fan C and motor D and passes over heaters E. Baffles G distribute the air uniformly over the stack of trays. Some moist air is continuously vented through exhaust duct B; makeup fresh air enters through inlet A. The racks are mounted on truck wheels I, so that at the end of the drying cycle the trucks can be pulled out of the chamber and taken to a tray-dumping station.

Tray dryers are useful when the production rate is small. They can dry almost anything, but because of the labor required for loading and unloading, they are expensive to operate. They find most frequent application on valuable products like dyes and pharmaceuticals. Drying by circulation of air across stationary layers of solid is slow, and drying cycles are long: 4 to 48 h per batch. Occasionally through-circulation drying is used, but this is usually neither economical nor necessary in batch dryers because shortening the drying cycle does not reduce the labor required for each batch. Energy saving may be significant, however.

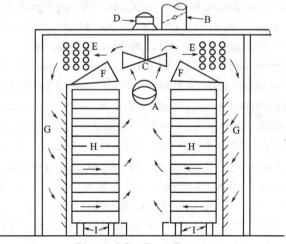

Figure 3.3   Tray Dryer

Tray dryers may be operated under vacuum, often with indirect heating. The trays may rest on hollow metal plates supplied with steam or hot water or may themselves contain spaces for a heating fluid. Vapor from the solid is removed by an ejector or vacuum pump. Freeze-drying is the sublimation of water from ice under high vacuum temperatures below 0°C. This is done in special vacuum tray dryers for drying vitamins and other heat-sensitive products.

Screen-Conveyor Dryers. A typical through-circulation screen-conveyor dryer is shown in Figure 3.4. A layer 25 to150 mm (1 to 6 in.) thick of material to be dried is slowly carried on a traveling metal screen through a long drying chamber or tunnel. The chamber consists of a series of separate sections, each with its own fan and air heater. At the inlet end of the dryer the air usually passes upward through the screen and the solids; near the discharge end, where the material is dry and may be dusty, air is passed downward through the screen. The air temperature and humidity may differ in the various sections, to give optimum conditions for drying at each point.

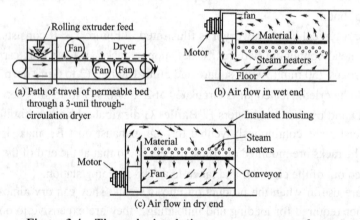

Figure 3.4　Through circulation screen-conveyor dryer

Screen-conveyor dryers are typically 2m (6 ft) wide and 4 to 50m (12 to150 ft) long, giving drying times of 5 to 120 min. The minimum screen size is about 30-mesh. Coarse granular, flaky, or fibrous material can be dried by through circulation without any pretreatment and without loss of material through the screen. Pastes and filter cakes of fine particles, however, must be preformed before they can be handled on a screen-conveyor dryer. The aggregates usually retain their shape while being dried and do not dust through the screen except in small amounts. Provision is sometimes made for recovering any fines that do sift through the screen.

Screen-conveyor dryers handle a variety of solids continuously and with a very gentle action; their cost is reasonable, and their steam consumption is low, typically 2 kg of steam per kilogram of water evaporated. Air may be recirculated through, and vented from, each section separately or passed from one section to another countercurrently to the solid. These dryers are particularly applicable when the drying conditions must be appreciably changed as the moisture content of the solid is reduced.

Tower Dryers.   A tower dryer contains a series of circular trays mounted one above the other on a central rotating shaft. Solid feed dropped on the topmost tray is exposed to a stream of hot air or gas that passes across the tray. The solid is then scraped off and dropped to the tray below. It travels in this way through the dryer, discharging as dry product from the bottom of the tower. The flow of solids and gas may be either parallel or countercurrent.

The turbodryer illustrated in Figure 3.5 is a tower dryer with internal recirculation of the heating gas. Turbine fans circulate the air or gas outward between some of the trays, over heating elements, and inward between other trays. Gas velocities are commonly 0.6 to 2.4 m/s (2 to 8 ft/s). The bottom two trays of the dryer shown in Figure 3.5 constitute a cooling section for dry solids. Preheated air is usually drawn in the bottom of the tower and discharged from the top, giving countercurrent flow. A turbodryer functions partly by cross-circulation drying, as in a tray dryer, and partly by showering the particles through the hot gas as they tumble from one tray to another.

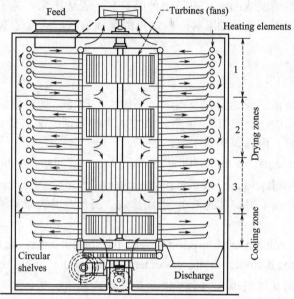

Figure 3.5   Turbodryer

科技英语翻译三　翻译的一般方法

要把一种语言文字所表达的意义用另一种语言文字表达出来，除了有较高的语言文字水平以及文化、专业知识外，还必须掌握一些常见的翻译方法，这就是本节所要讨论的内容。

一、直译和意译

1. 直译

直译就是基本保持原文表达形式及内容，不做大的改动，同时要求语言通顺易懂，表达清楚明白。直译所强调的是"形似"，主张将原文内容按照原文的形式（包括词序、语序、语气、结构、修辞方法等）用译语表达出来，如下。

➢ Most of the liquid passes through the medium (e.g., a filter) to form the filtrate, and the solids and some entrained liquid are retained on the filter to form the filter cake.

大部分液体通过介质（例如过滤器），形成滤液，固体和其夹带的液体被截留在过滤器上形成滤饼。

➢ In an absorption column or absorption tower, the solvent enters the top of a column, flows down, and emerges at the bottom, and the gas enters at the bottom, flows up, and leaves at the top.

在吸收塔中，溶剂从塔顶进入，向下流动，从塔底采出；气体从塔底进入，向上流动，从塔顶采出。

2. 意译

所谓意译，是将原文所表达的内容以一种释义性的方式用译语将其意义表达出来。意译强调的是"神似"，也就是不拘泥于原文的词序、语序、语法结构等方面的形式，用译语的习惯表达方式将原文的本意（真正含义）翻译出来，如下。

➢ We can get more current from cells connected in parallel.
电池并联时提供的电流更大。

➢ The law of reflection holds good for all surfaces.
反射定律对一切表面都适用。

➢ Over the course of several days, atmospheric methanol is oxidized with the help of sunlight to carbon dioxide and water.

过了几天，大气中的甲醇在阳光的作用下被氧化为二氧化碳和水。

在翻译实践中，直译与意译不是两种完全孤立的翻译方法，译者不应该完全拘泥于其中的某一种，必须学会将直译与意译有机地结合起来。要以完整、准确、通顺地表达出原文的意义为翻译的最终目的。

二、合译和分译

英语句子从结构上看，可以分为 3 种类型：简单句、并列句和复合句。如果句子只包含一个主谓结构，而句子各个成分都只由单词或短语表示，它就是简单句（不管句子是长还是短)，有时两个或更多的主语共用一个谓语，两个或更多谓语共用一个主语，有时甚至可以有两个主语和两个谓语，但是主语和谓语互相依从，这样的句子仍然是简单句，如下。

➢ The teachers and the students all liked the place and wanted to stay there a little longer. (两个主语和两个谓语)

老师和学生都喜欢这个地方，想在那儿多待一会儿。

如果句子有两个或更多互不依从的主谓结构，就是并列句。并列句中的分词通常用一个并列连词来连接，如下。

➢ The camera-work is perfect and the cast is good.

电影拍摄的好极了，演员也很强。

复合句中包含有两个或更多的主谓结构，其中有一个（或更多）的主谓结构充当句子的某一成分，如主语、宾语、表语、定语、状语、同位语等，如下。

➢ What I want to emphasize is this.

我想强调的是这一点。

翻译英语句子时，有时我们可以把原文的结构保留下来，并在译文中体现出来。但不少情况下，我们则必须对句子的结构作较大的改变，合译法和分译法就是改变原文句子结构的两种常用的方法。

1. 合译

合译就是把原文两个或两个以上的简单句或复合句，在译文中用一个单句来表达，如下。

➢ Leaves are to the plant what lungs are to the animal.
植物叶子的作用好比动物的肺一样。

➢ There are some metals which possess the power to conduct electricity and ability to be magnetized.
某些金属具有导电和被磁化的能力。

➢ The most important of the factors affecting plant growth is that it requires the supply of water.
植物生长的各因素中最重要的是水的供应。

2. 分译

所谓分译就是把原文的一个简单句中的一个词、词组或短语译成汉语的一个句子，这样，原文的一个简单句就被译成了汉语的两个或两个以上的句子，如下。

➢ With the same number of protons, all nuclei of given element may have different numbers of neutrons.
虽然某个元素的所有原子核都含有相同数目的质子，但它们含有的中子数可以不同。

➢ The doctor analyzed the blood sample for anemia.
医生对血样做了分析，看是不是贫血症。

➢ Manufacturing processes may be classified as unit production with small quantities being made and mass production with large numbers of identical parts being produced.
制造过程可以分为单件生产和大量生产。前者指的是生产少量的零件，后者则是指生产大量相同的零件。

汉语习惯于用短语表达，而英语使用长句较多，由于英汉两种语言的句型结构的这种差异，在科技英语翻译过程中，要把原文句子中复杂的逻辑关系表述清楚，经常采用分译法。

三、增译和省译

英语与汉语在表达上有很大的差异。在汉译过程中，如果按原文一对一的翻译，译文则很难符合汉语的表达习惯，会显得生搬硬套、牵强附会。在翻译过程中，译者应遵循汉语的习惯表达方式，在忠实原文的基础上，适合地进行增译或省译。

1. 增译

所谓增译，就是在译文中增加英语原文省略、或原文中无其词而有其意的词语，使译文既能准确地表达原文含义，又更符合汉语的表达习惯和修辞需要，如下。

> Oily soil is removed by the combined action of surfactants and enzymes.

油垢的去除是表面活性剂和酶共同作用的**结果**。（增译了名词"结果"）

> Renewable energy and energy efficiency.

可再生能源和能源**利用**效率。（增译了动词"利用"）

2. 省译

严格地来说，翻译时不允许对原文的内容有任何删略，但由于英汉两种语言表达方式不同，英语句子中有些词语如果硬是要译成汉语，反而会使得译文晦涩难懂。为使译文通顺、准确地表达出原文的思想内容，有时需将一些词语省略不译，如下。

> Ammonia is synthesized by reacting hydrogen with nitrogen at **a** molar ratio of 3 to 1.

氢气和氮气以3比1的摩尔比反应合成氨气。（省译了不定冠词a）

> For the **purpose** of our discussion，let us neglect the friction.

为了便于讨论，我们将摩擦力忽略不计。（省译了名词purpose）

> Little information **is given** about the origin of life.

关于生命起源方面的资料很少。（省译了谓语动词is given）

> Generally speaking, the amount of waste generated by batch processing is higher than **it** is in the case of continuous processing.

一般来说，间歇生产产生的废物量比连续生产的多。(省译了代词it)

从以上例句中不难看出，不但介词、冠词等可以增译或省译，动词、名词等实义词有时也可增译或省译。但是，无论是增译还是省译，都必须以完整、准确地表达原文，以符合译语的表达习惯为准则，来进行适当的增译或省译，切不可随意使用。

四、顺译和倒译

1. 顺译

所谓顺译就是按照原文相同或相似的语序进行翻译。顺译可以是完整顺译，也可以是基本顺译。基本顺译是指为了表达准确和通顺而进行个别语序的调整，如下。

> Part of the condensate is withdrawn as the product，and the remainder is returned to the top of the column.

部分冷凝液作为产品被采出，剩余的冷凝液返回到蒸馏塔的顶部。

2. 倒译

有时完全按照原文的词序来翻译是很困难的，为了使译文更加顺畅，更符合汉语的表达习惯，须采用完全不同于原文词语顺序的方法来翻译，我们称之为倒译，如下。

> Too large a current must not be used.

不得使用过大的电流。

> Man can't live without air.

没有空气人就不能存活。

➤ It's important to learn when the environment is not good for plants and animals，it is not good for man.

懂得当环境不利于动植物时也不利于人类这一点是很重要的。

在翻译实践中，顺译与倒译的使用不可能是完全孤立的，很多情况下，不可能完全顺译，也不可能完全倒译，译者需要根据具体情况将两种方法有机地结合起来灵活使用。

以上我们所介绍的各种翻译方法须灵活使用，无论是采用哪一种方法，其目的都是为了能准确、通顺地用译文表达原文的思想内容。事实上，在翻译实践中，我们不会也不可能完全孤立地使用一种方法。译者需要将各种译法融会贯通，有机结合使用，力求使译文达到理想的翻译标准：准确规范、通顺易懂、简洁明晰。

Unit Four   Inorganic Chemical Engineering

Lesson Eight   Ammonia Synthesis

Anhydrous ammonia is synthesized by reacting hydrogen with nitrogen at a molar ratio of 3 to 1, then compressing the gas and cooling it to $-33℃$. Nitrogen is obtained from the air, while hydrogen is obtained from either the catalytic steam reforming of natural gas (methane [CH_4]) or naphtha. In the U. S., about 98 percent of synthetic ammonia is produced by catalytic steam reforming of natural gas. Figure 4.1 shows a general process flow diagram of a typical ammonia plant.

Six process steps are required to produce synthetic ammonia using the catalytic steam reforming method: (1) natural gas desulfurization, (2) catalytic steam reforming, (3) carbon monoxide (CO) shift, (4) carbon dioxide (CO_2) removal, (5) methanation, and (6) ammonia synthesis. The first, third, fourth, and fifth steps remove impurities such as sulfur, CO, CO_2 and water (H_2O) from the feedstock, hydrogen, and synthesis gas streams. In the second step, hydrogen is manufactured and nitrogen (air) is introduced into this 2-stage process. The sixth step produces anhydrous ammonia from the synthetic gas. While all ammonia plants use this basic process, details such as operating pressures, temperatures, and quantities of feedstock vary from plant to plant.

1. Natural Gas Desulfurization

In this step, the sulfur content (as hydrogen sulfide [H_2S]) in natural gas is reduced to below 280 micrograms per cubic meter ($\mu g/m^3$) to prevent poisoning of the nickel catalyst in the primary reformer. Desulfurization can be accomplished by using either activated carbon or zinc oxide.

2. Catalytic Steam Reforming

Natural gas leaving the desulfurization tank is mixed with process steam and preheated to $540℃$. The mixture of steam and gas enters the primary reformer, which is filled with a nickel-based reforming catalyst. Approximately 70 percent of the CH_4 is converted to hydrogen and CO_2. An additional amount of CH_4 is converted to CO. This process gas is then sent to the secondary reformer, where it is mixed with compressed air that has been preheated to about $540℃$. Sufficient air is added to produce a final synthesis gas having a hydrogen-to-nitrogen mole ratio of 3 to 1. The gas leaving the secondary reformer is then cooled to 360℃ in a waste heat boiler.

3. Carbon Monoxide Shift

After cooling, the secondary reformer effluent gas enters a high temperature CO shift converter which is filled with chromium oxide initiator and iron oxide catalyst. The following reaction takes place in the carbon monoxide converter:

$$CO + H_2O \longrightarrow CO_2 + H_2$$

The exit gas is then cooled in a heat exchanger.

4. Carbon Dioxide Removal

In this step, CO_2 in the final shift gas is removed. CO_2 removal can be done by using 2 methods: monoethanolamine ($C_2H_4NH_2OH$) scrubbing and hot potassium scrubbing. Approximately 80 percent of the ammonia plants use monoethanolamine (MEA) to aid in removing CO_2. The CO_2 gas is passed upward through an absorption tower countercurrent to a 15 to 30 percent solution of MEA in water. After absorbing the CO_2, the amine solution is preheated and regenerated (carbon dioxide regenerator) in a reactivating tower. This reacting tower removes CO_2 by steam stripping and then by heating. The CO_2 gas (98.5 percent CO_2) is either vented to the atmosphere or used for chemical feedstock in other parts of the plant complex. The regenerated MEA is pumped back to the absorber tower after being cooled in a heat exchanger and solution cooler.

5. Methanation

Residual CO_2 in the synthesis gas is removed by catalytic methanation which is conducted over a nickel catalyst at temperatures of 400 to 600℃ and pressures up to 3000 kPa according to the following reactions:

$$CO_2 + H_2 \longrightarrow CO + H_2O$$

$$CO + 3H_2 \longrightarrow CH_4 + H_2O$$

$$CO_2 + 4H_2 \longrightarrow CH_4 + 2H_2O$$

Exit gas from the methanator, which has a 3:1 mole ratio of hydrogen and nitrogen, is then cooled to 38℃.

6. Ammonia Synthesis

In the synthesis step, the synthesis gas from the methanator is compressed at pressures ranging from 13800 to 34500 kPa, mixed with recycled synthesis gas, and cooled to 0℃. Condensed ammonia is separated from the unconverted synthesis gas in a liquid-vapor separator and sent to a let-down separator.

Ammonia in the let-down separator is flashed to 100 kPa at −33℃ to remove impurities from the liquid. The flash vapor is condensed in the let-down chiller where anhydrous ammonia is drawn off and stored at low temperature (Figure 4.1).

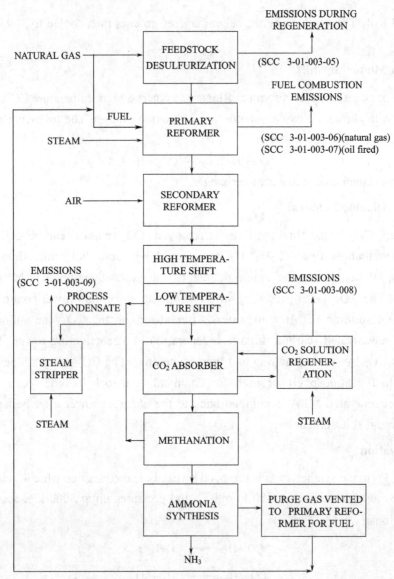

Figure 4.1   A general process flow diagram of a typical ammonia plant

New Words and Expressions

anhydrous   [æn'haidrəs]   *a.* [化]无水的

hydrogen   ['haidrədʒen]   *n.* 氢

nitrogen   ['naitrədʒen]   *n.* [化]氮

catalytic   [kætə'litik]   *a.* 接触反应的；起催化作用的

naphtha   ['næfθə, 'næp-]   *n.* 石脑油；挥发油；粗汽油

synthetic   [sin'θetik]   *a.* 综合的；合成的，人造的

desulfurization   [diːsʌlfjurai'zeiʃ ən, -ri'z-]   *n.* 脱硫作用；直接脱硫

dioxide   [dai'ɔksaid]   *n.* [化]二氧化物

removal   [ri'muːvəl]   *n.* 免职；移动；排除；搬迁

methanation   [ˌmeθəˈneiʃən]   *n.* [化]甲烷化；甲烷化作用

impurities   [imˈpjuəritis]   *n.* 杂质（impurity 的复数）

feedstock   [ˈfiːdstɔk]   *n.* 原料；给料（指供送入机器或加工厂的原料）

manufacture   [ˌmænjuˈfæktʃə]   *vt.* 制造；加工；捏造

vary   [ˈvɛəri]   *vi.* 变化；[生]变异

sulfide   [ˈsʌlfaid]   *n.* [化]硫化物

microgram   [ˈmaikrəugræm]   *n.* 微克；微观图，显微照片

poison   [ˈpɔizən]   *vt.* 污染；使中毒，放毒于；败坏

nickel   [ˈnikəl]   *n.* 镍；镍币；五分镍币

　　　　　　　　　　vt. 镀镍于

activated   [ˈæktiveitid]   *a.* 活性化的；活泼的

　　　　　　　　　　v. 使活动起来；使激活；有生气

primary   [ˈpraiməri]   *a.* 主要的；初级的；基本的

reformer   [riˈfɔːmə]   *n.* 转化器；改革运动者；改革家；改良者

zinc   [ziŋk]   *n.* 锌

sufficient   [səˈfiʃnt]   *a.* 足够的；充分的

boiler   [ˈbɔilə]   *n.* 锅炉；烧水壶，热水器；盛热水器

effluent   [ˈefluənt]   *n.* 污水；流出物；废气

　　　　　　　　　　a. 流出的，发出的

chromium   [ˈkrəumjəm]   *n.* [化]铬（24 号元素，符号 Cr）

initiator   [iˈniʃieitə]   *n.* [化]引发剂；发起人，创始者；启动程序；引爆器

converter   [kənˈvəːtə]   *n.* 转化器；变流器，整流器

exchanger   [iksˈtʃeindʒə]   *n.* 交换器；交易所；交换程序

monoethanolamine   [ˈmɔnəuˌeθənəˈlæmiːn]   *n.* [化]单乙醇胺

scrubbing   [skrʌbliŋ]   *n.* 洗涤

potassium   [pəˈtæsjəm]   *n.* 钾

amine   [əˈmiːn, ˈæmin]   *n.* 胺

regenerate   [riˈdʒenəreit, riː-]   *vt.* 使再生；革新

　　　　　　　　　　vi. 再生；革新

　　　　　　　　　　a. 再生的；革新的

vent   [vent]   *vi.* 放出

　　　　　　　　　　n. 出口；通风孔

chiller   [ˈtʃilə]   *n.* 冷却装置

stripping   [ˈstripiŋ]   *n.* 剥离；剥脱；拆封

　　　　　　　　　　v. 剥去；脱掉；拆除

catalytic steam reforming   催化蒸汽转化

steam stripping   汽提；蒸汽脱附

be purged to   清除

let-down separator   让式分离器

Notes

1. An additional amount of CH₄ is converted to CO.其余的甲烷转化为一氧化碳。形容词 additional有附加的、追加的和另外的意思，这里根据上下文译为"其余的"比较恰当。

2. Sufficient air is added to produce a final synthesis gas having a hydrogen-to-nitrogen mole ratio of 3 to 1.填加充足的空气是为了最终产生氢气和氮气的摩尔比为3:1的合成气。having a hydrogen-to-nitrogen mole ratio of 3 to 1是现在分词短语做定语修饰synthesis gas。形容词final 转译为副词"最终"。

3. The CO₂ gas is passed upward through an adsorption tower countercurrent to a 15 to 30 percent solution of MEA in water.二氧化碳（从下）向上通过吸收塔与浓度为15%～30%的单乙醇胺水溶液逆流（接触）。该句增译了副词"从下"和动词"接触"，这样使译文能更准确清晰。

4. Residual CO₂ in the synthesis gas is removed by catalytic methanation which is conducted over a nickel catalyst at temperatures of 400 to 600℃ and pressures up to 3000 kPa according to the following reactions:通过催化甲烷化作用祛除残余的CO₂，该作用使用镍催化剂，温度是 400～600℃，压力是3000 kPa，按照下面的反应实现的：该句是由一个主句，一个定语从句构成。采用的是分译法。副词over转译为动词"使用"。

Exercises

1. Put the following into Chinese

anhydrous ammonia	natural gas
natural gas desulfurization	catalytic steam reforming
carbon monoxide (CO) shift	carbon dioxide (CO₂) removal
methanation	ammonia synthesis.

2. Put the following into English

初级转化器	活性炭
二级转化器	高温一氧化碳变换器
合成气	气液分离器

3. Questions

How many process steps are required to produce synthetic ammonia using the catalytic steam reforming method? What are they?

Lesson Nine   Sulfuric Acid

Sulfuric acid (H_2SO_4), chemical compound, is a colorless, odorless, extremely corrosive, oily liquid. It is sometimes called "oil of vitriol". Sulfuric acid is one of the most important industrial chemicals. More of it is made each year than any other manufactured chemical; more than 40 million tons were produced in the United States in 1990. It has widely varied uses and takes some part in the production of nearly all manufactured goods.

There are two major processes (lead chamber and contact) for production of sulfuric acid, and it is available commercially in a number of grades and concentrations. The lead chamber process, the older of the two processes, is used to produce much of the acid used to make fertilizers; it produces a relatively dilute acid ($62\%\sim78\%$ H_2SO_4). The contact process produces a purer, more concentrated acid but requires purer raw materials and the use of expensive catalysts. In both processes surlfur dioxide is oxidized and dissolved in water. The sulfur dioxide is obtained by burning sulfur, by burning pyrites (iron sulfides), or by burning hydrogen sulfide gas. Some sulfuric acid is also made from ferrous sulfate waste solutions from pickling iron and steel and from waste acid sludge from oil refineries.

Lead Chamber Process

In the lead chamber process hot sulfur dioxide gas enters the bottom of a reactor called a Glover tower where it is washed with nitrous vitriol (sulfuric acid with nitric oxide, NO, and nitrogen dioxide, NO_2, dissolved in it) and mixed with nitric oxide and nitrogen dioxide gases; some of the sulfur dioxide is oxidized to sulfur trioxide and dissolved in the acid wash to form tower acid or Glover acid (about 78% H_2SO_4). From the Glover tower a mixture of gases (including sulfur dioxide and trioxide, nitrogen oxides, nitrogen, oxygen, and steam) is transferred to a lead-lined chamber where it is reacted with more water. The chamber may be a large, boxlike room or an enclosure in the form of a truncated cone. Sulfuric acid is formed by a complex series of reactions; it condenses on the walls and collects on the floor of the chamber. There may be from three to twelve chambers in a series; the gases pass through each in succession. The acid produced in the chambers, often called chamber acid or fertilizer acid, contains 62% to 68% H_2SO_4. After the gases have passed through the chambers they are passed into a reactor called the Gay-Lussac tower where they are washed with cooled concentrated acid (from the Glover tower); the nitrogen oxides and unreacted sulfur dioxide dissolve in the acid to form the nitrous vitriol used in the Glover tower. Remaining waste gases are usually discharged into the atmosphere.

Contact Process

In 1831, the Contact Process was patented by Peregrine Phillips, a British vinegar merchant, although serious production using the contact process did not occur until the 1880s onwards. The Contact Process has been the dominant process used to manufacture sulphuric acid for most of the past 100 years. In this process, sulphur dioxide is oxidised to sulphur trioxide using a platinum catalyst, and the sulphur trioxide is then reacted with water.

In the contact process, purified sulfur dioxide and air are mixed, heated to about 450℃, and passed over a catalyst; the sulfur dioxide is oxidized to sulfur trioxide. The catalyst is usually platinum on a silica or asbestos carrier or vanadium pentoxide on a silica carrier. The sulfur trioxide is cooled and passed through two towers. In the first tower it is washed with oleum (fuming sulfuric acid, 100% sulfuric acid with sulfur trioxide dissolved in it). In the second tower it is washed with 97% sulfuric acid; 98% sulfuric acid is usually produced in this tower. Waste gases are usually discharged into the atmosphere. Acid of any desired concentration may be produced by mixing or diluting the products of this process.

New Words and Expressions

sulfuric [sʌlˈfjuərik] *a.* 硫黄的；含多量硫黄的；含（六价）硫的

colorless [ˈkʌləlis] *a.* 无色的；无趣味的；苍白的；

odorless [ˈəudəlis] *a.* 没有气味的

corrosive [kəˈrəusiv] *a.* 腐蚀的；侵蚀性的

　　　　　　　　　　　n. 腐蚀物

vitriol [ˈvitriəl] *n.* 硫酸，硫酸盐

chamber [ˈtʃeimbə] *n.* （身体或器官内的）室，腔；房间；会所

commercially [kəˈməːʃəli] *adv.* 工业上；商业上；通商上

fertilizer [ˈfəːtilaizə] *n.* 肥料

dilute [daiˈljuːt, di-] *a.* 稀释的；淡的

pyrite [ˈpairait] *n.* [矿]黄铁矿

ferrous [ˈferəs] *a.* [化]亚铁的；铁的，含铁的

pickling [ˈpikliŋ] *n.* 酸洗；浸酸

sludge [slʌdʒ] *n.* 烂泥；泥泞；泥状雪；沉淀物

nitrous [ˈnaitrəs] *a.* 氮的；硝石的；含氮的

boxlike [ˈbɔkslaik] *a.* 像箱子一样的

enclosure [inˈkləuʒə] *n.* 附件；围墙；围场

truncated [trʌŋˈkeitid, ˈtrʌŋk-] *a.* 缩短了的；被删节的；切去顶端的

cone [kəun] *n.* 圆锥体，圆锥形；球果

patent [ˈpeitənt] *vt.* 授予专利；取得…的专利权

vinegar [ˈvinigə] *n.* 醋

merchant [ˈməːtʃənt] *n.* 商人，批发商；店主

onwards [ˈɔnwədz] *adv.* 向前；在前面

dominant [ˈdɔminənt] *a.* 显性的；占优势的；支配的，统治的

oxidise [ˈɔksidaiz] *vt.* 使氧化；使生锈

platinum [ˈplætinəm] *n.* 铂；白金

silica [ˈsilikə] *n.* 二氧化硅；硅土

asbestos [æzˈbestɔs] *n.* [矿]石棉

carrier [ˈkæriə] *n.* 载体

vanadium [vəˈneidiəm] *n.* [化]钒

pentoxide [penˈtɔksaid,-sid] *n.* [化]五氧化物

oleum [ˈəuliəm] *n.* 发烟硫酸

fuming [fjumiŋ] *a.* 熏的；冒烟的

lead chamber process 铅室法

dilute acid 稀酸

Glover tower 格洛弗塔；喷淋式气体洗涤塔

lead-lined chamber 衬铅室

in succession 接连地，连续地

Gay-Lussac tower [化]盖-吕萨克塔

be discharged into 被排入

contact process [化]接触过程；接触法

Notes

1. There are two major processes (lead chamber and contact) for production of sulfuric acid, and it is available commercially in a number of grades and concentrations. 硫酸生产有两种主要方法（铅室法和接触法），（通过这两种方法）可以获得不同等级和浓度的工业硫酸。增译了"通过这两种方法"。副词commercially转译为形容词"商业化的"。

2. Some sulfuric acid is also made from ferrous sulfate waste solutions from pickling iron and steel and from waste acid sludge from oil refineries.从酸洗钢铁的硫酸亚铁废液中，或者石油炼制（产生的）废酸淤泥中也能生产硫酸。

3. There may be from three to twelve chambers in a series; the gases pass through each in succession.有串联的3～12个铅室，气体连续地通过每一个铅室。

4. In 1831, the Contact Process was patented by Peregrine Phillips, a British vinegar merchant, although serious production using the contact process did not occur until the 1880s onwards. 虽然1831年英国醋商Peregrine Phillips就已经申请了接触法的专利，但这种重要的生产方法直到19世纪80年代前才被工业生产采用。该句由一个主句和一个让步状语从句组成。not …until 直到…才。省译了动词occur。

Exercises

1. Put the following into Chinese

sulfuric acid   chemical compound

make fertilizers   dilute acid

2. Put the following into English

接触法   铅室法

二氧化硫   三氧化硫

3. Questions

How many major processes are there for production of sulfuric acid? What are they?

Reading Material: Sodium Carbonate

Sodium carbonate or called claimed soda, is a white powdery compound, used in the manufacture of baking soda, sodium nitrate, glass, ceramics, detergents, and soap. It is soluble in water and very slightly soluble in alcohol. Pure sodium carbonate is a white, odorless powder that absorbs moisture from the air, has an alkaline taste, and forms a strongly alkaline water solution. It is one of the most basic industrial chemicals. Sodium carbonate decahydrate, $Na_2CO_3 \cdot 10H_2O$, is a colorless, transparent crystalline compound commonly called sal soda or washing soda. Because seaweed ashes were an early source of sodium carbonate, it is often called soda ash or, simply, soda. The Solvay process provides most sodium carbonate for industrial use. It is found in large natural deposits and is mined in Wyoming; it is also recovered (with other chemicals) from lake brines in California. The principal uses of sodium carbonate are in the manufacture of glass and the production of chemicals. It is also used in processing wood pulp to make paper, in making soaps and detergents, in refining aluminum, in water softening, and in many other applications. The Leblanc process, the first successful commercial process for making soda, is no longer used in the United States but played a major role in the Industrial Revolution.

Uses

Sodium carbonate is used in the manufacture of glass, pulp and paper, detergents, and chemicals such as sodium silicates and sodium phosphates. It is also used as an alkaline agent in many chemical industries. Domestically it is used as a water softener during laundry. It competes with the ions magnesium and calcium in hard water and prevents them from bonding with the detergent being used. Without using washing soda, additional detergent is needed to soak up the magnesium and calcium ions. Called washing soda in the detergent section of stores, it effectively removes oil, grease, and alcohol stains. Sodium carbonate is also used in a photographic process known as reticulation. A film negative can be placed in a hot bath of sodium carbonate which may cause the metallic silver to clump and the emulsion to separate from the base of the film, producing a cracked and abstracted image. It is also commonly used as a buffering agent in photographic developers. Sodium carbonate is also used by the brick industry as a wetting agent to reduce the amount of water needed to extrude the clay.

Production

In 1791, the French chemist Nicolas Leblanc patented a process for producing sodium carbonate from salt, sulphuric acid, limestone, and coal. First, sea salt (sodium chloride) was boiled in sulphuric acid to yield sodium sulphate and hydrochloric acid gas, according to the chemical equation

$$2\,NaCl + H_2SO_4 \longrightarrow Na_2SO_4 + 2\,HCl$$

Next, the sodium suphate was blended with crushed limestone (calcium carbonate) and coal, and the mixture was burnt, producing sodium carbonate along with carbon dioxide and calcium sulphide.

$$Na_2SO_4 + CaCO_3 + 2\,C \longrightarrow Na_2CO_3 + 2\,CO_2 + CaS$$

The sodium carbonate was extracted from the ashes with water, and then collected by allowing the water to evaporate. The hydrochloric acid produced by the Leblanc process was a major source of air pollution, and the calcium sulphide byproduct also presented waste disposal issues. However, it remained the major production method for sodium carbonate until the late 1880s.

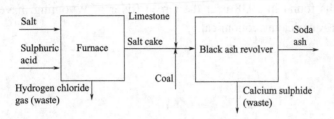

Solvay process

In 1861, the Belgian industrial chemist Ernest Solvay developed a method to convert sodium chloride to sodium carbonate using ammonia. The Solvay process centered around a large hollow tower. At the bottom, calcium carbonate (limestone) was heated to release carbon dioxide:

$$CaCO_3 \longrightarrow CaO + CO_2$$

At the top, a concentrated solution of sodium chloride and ammonia entered the tower. As the carbon dioxide bubbled up through it, sodium bicarbonate precipitated:

$$NaCl + NH_3 + CO_2 + H_2O \longrightarrow NaHCO_3 + NH_4Cl$$

The sodium bicarbonate was then converted to sodium carbonate by heating it, releasing water and carbon dioxide:

$$2\,NaHCO_3 \longrightarrow Na_2CO_3 + H_2O + CO_2$$

Meanwhile, the ammonia was regenerated from the ammonium chloride byproduct by treating it with the lime (calcium hydroxide) left over from carbon dioxide generation:

$$CaO + H_2O \longrightarrow Ca(OH)_2$$
$$Ca(OH)_2 + 2\,NH_4Cl \longrightarrow CaCl_2 + 2\,NH_3 + 2\,H_2O$$

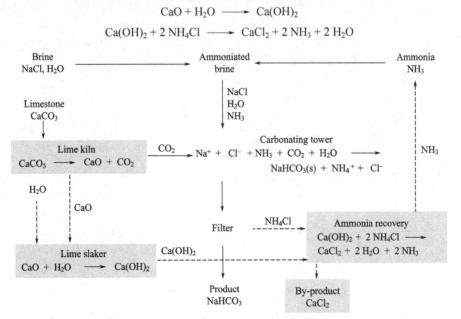

Because the Solvay process recycled its ammonia, it consumed only brine and limestone, and had calcium chloride as its only waste product. This made it substantially more economical than the Leblanc process, and it soon came to dominate world sodium carbonate production. By 1900, 90% of sodium carbonate was produced by the Solvay process, and the last Leblanc process plant closed in the early 1920s.

Sodium carbonate is still produced by the Solvay process in much of the world today. However, large natural deposits found in 1938 near the Green River in Wyoming, have made its industrial production in North America uneconomical.

科技英语翻译四 词性转换法

由于英汉两种语言结构与表达方式不同，有些句子在汉译时不能逐词对译。为了更好地表达原文的思想内容，使译文更符合汉语的表达习惯，更加通顺自然，在翻译时，常需进行词类转换，即英语中的某一词类，并不一定译成汉语中的相应的词类，而要作适当的转换。词类转换主要有以下4种情况。

一、转译为动词

英语与汉语相比，英语句子中往往只有一个谓语动词，而汉语句子中动词用得比较多，几个动词或动词性结构一起连用的情况比较常见。根据需要，英语中的名词、形容词、副词、动名词和介词在翻译时可转换为汉语的动词。

1. 名词转译为动词

➤ Despite all the **improvements**, rubber still has a number of limitations.

尽管**改进**了很多，但合成橡胶仍有一些缺陷。（名词 improvements 转译为动词）

2. 形容词转译为动词

一些表示心理活动、心理状态的形容词作表语时，通常可以转译为动词。有些具有动词意义的形容词也可以转译为汉语的动词，如下。

➤ Electrical energy is **available** from a simple cell.

就从一节电池中便可**得到**电能。（形容词 available 转译为动词）

➤ The circuits are connected in parallel in the interest of a **small** resistance.

将电路并联是为了**减小**电阻。（形容词 small 转译为动词）

3. 副词转译为动词

英语中很多副词在古英语中曾是动词。在翻译时常常可以将副词转译成汉语的动词，尤其当它们在原文句子中作表语或状语时，如下。

➤ If one generator is out of order, the other will produce electricity **instead**.

如果一台发电机发生故障，另一台便**代替**它发电。（副词 instead 转译为动词）

➤ The fatigue life test is **over**.

疲劳寿命试验**结束**了。（副词 over 转译为动词）

4. 介词转译为动词

英语中很多介词在古英语中曾是动词，在翻译时也常可以将介词转译成汉语的动词，如下。

➤ Batch reactors are the most common type of industrial reactor and may have volumes well **above** 100000 liters.

间歇反应器是工业反应器中最常见的一种，其容积远远**超过** 100000L。（介词 above 转译为动词）

➤ This type of film develops **in** twenty minutes.

冲洗此类胶卷**需要** 20min。（介词 in 转译为动词）

二、转译为名词

英语中的动词、代词和形容词等也可以转译为汉语的名词。

1. 动词转译为名词

➤ Boiling point is **defined** as the temperature at which the vapor pressure is equal to that of the atmosphere.

沸点的**定义**就是蒸汽的气压等于大气压时的温度。（动词 defined 转译为名词）

➤ Black holes **act** like huge drains in the universe.

黑洞的**作用**像宇宙中巨大的吸管。（动词 act 转译为名词）

➤ In practice, oily soil is **removed** by the combined action of surfactants and enzymes.

事实上，油垢的**去除**是表面活性剂和酶共同作用的结果。（动词 removed 转译为名词）

2. 代词转译为名词

所谓的代词转译为名词，实际上就是将代词所代替的名词翻译出来，我们也可称之为"还原"，如下。

➤ The radioactivity of the new element is much stronger than **that** of uranium.

这种新元素的放射性比铀的**放射性**强得多。（代词 that 还原为名词放射性）

➤ If the bearings were not lubricated, **they** would rapidly overheat.

假如轴承未加润滑油，轴承很快就会过热。（代词 they 还原为名词轴承）

3. 形容词转译为名词

➤ Television is **different** from radio in that it sends and receives a picture.

电视和无线电的**区别**在于电视发送和接收的是图像。（形容词 different 转译为名词）

➤ The steam engine is only about 20 per cent **efficient**.

这种蒸汽机的**效率**只有20%。（形容词 efficient 转译为名词）

4. 副词转译为名词

除了动词、代词和形容词可以转译为名词外，有时副词、介词甚至连词也可以转译为名词，如下。

➤ Oxygen is one of the important elements in the physical world, it is very active **chemically**.

氧是物质世界的重要元素之一，它的**化学性质**很活泼。（副词 chemically 转译为名词）

➤ These parts must be **proportionally** correct.

这些零件的**比例**必须准确无误。（副词 proportionally 转译为名词）

三、转译为形容词

1. 名词转译为形容词

➤ **Shell** diameters are standardized.

壳体的直径是标准的。（名词 Shell 转译为形容词）

➤ The law of thermodynamics is of great **importance** in the study of heat.

热力学定律在研究热方面是很**重要的**。（名词 importance 转译为形容词）

2. 副词转译为形容词

当英语动词转译为汉语的名词时，修饰该英语动词的副词往往随之转译为汉语的形容词，如下。

➤ Heat exchangers are so **widely** used in the process industries that their design has been highly developed.

换热器在工业发展中得到了**广泛的**应用，使得它们的设计类型快速发展。（副词 widely 转译为形容词）

为了使用译文通顺，在汉译时，有时可把修饰性形容词的副词转译为汉语的形容词。

➤ Sulphuric acid is one of **extremely** reactive agents.

强酸是**强烈的**反应试剂之一。（副词 extremely 转译为形容词）

3. 动词转译为形容词

➤ Light waves **differ** in frquency just as sound waves do.

同声波一样，光波也有**不同的**频率。（动词 differ 转译为形容词）

四、转译为副词

1. 形容词转译为副词

英语中能转译成汉语副词的主要是形容词。形容词转译为副词有以下 3 种情况。

（1）当英语中的名词转译成汉语的动词时，原来修饰名词的英语形容词就相应的转译为汉语的副词，如下。

➤ With **slight** repairs the old type of engine can be used.

只要**稍加**修理，这台老式发动机就可使用。（形容词 slight 转译为副词）

（2）在系动词+表语的句型结构中，作表语的名词转译为汉语的形容词时，原来修饰名词的英语形容词就相应地转译为汉语的副词，如下。

➤ Heat exchangers are of **great** importance in the process industries.

在工业生产中换热器是**非常**重要的。（形容词 great 转译为副词）

（3）除了以上两种形式外，其他形式的形容词也可转译为副词。

➤ Batch reactors with internal variations in temperature or composition are **difficult** to analyze.

间歇反应器的内部温度和组成的变化**很难**分析。（形容词 difficult 转译为副词）

2. 动词转译为副词

当英语句子中的谓语动词后面的不定式短语或分词转译为汉语句子中的谓语时，原来的谓语动词就相应的转译为汉语的副词，如下。

➤ Rapid evaporation **tends** to make the steam wat.

快速蒸发**往往**使蒸汽的湿度加大。（动词 tends 转译为副词）

从以上的例句中可以看出，不同词类之间的相互转译现象还是很普遍的，并且是多种多样的，不仅仅局限于以上介绍的几种。词类是否转译或转译为何种词类，由于处理方法的不同，也可能有不同的转译方法，译者可以根据对专业技术的理解，以及汉语语言的表达习惯灵活使用。

Unit Five　Organic Chemical Engineering

Lesson Ten　Methanol Synthesis

Methanol, also known as methyl alcohol, wood alcohol, wood naphtha or wood spirits, is a chemical with formula CH_3OH (often abbreviated MeOH). It is the simplest alcohol, and is a light, volatile, colorless, flammable, liquid with a distinctive odor that is very similar to but slightly sweeter than ethanol (drinking alcohol).

Methanol is one of the most important organic chemicals. At room temperature it is a polar liquid and is used as an antifreeze, solvent, fuel, and as a denaturant for ethanol.It is also used as an intermediate for production of formaldehyde, methyl tert-butyl ether (MTBE), acetic acid, amines, and others.

Methanol is produced naturally in the anaerobic metabolism of many varieties of bacteria, and is ubiquitous in the environment. As a result, there is a small fraction of methanol vapor in the atmosphere. Over the course of several days, atmospheric methanol is oxidized with the help of sunlight to carbon dioxide and water.

Methanol is produced industrially from synthesis gas according to the following stoichiometry:

$$CO + 2H_2 \longrightarrow CH_3OH$$

Today synthesis gas is most commonly produced from the methane component in natural gas rather than from coal. Three processes are commercially practiced. At moderate pressures of 4 MPa (40 atm) and high temperatures (around 850℃), methane reacts with steam on a nickel catalyst to produce syngas according to the chemical equation:

$$CH_4 + H_2O \longrightarrow CO + 3\,H_2$$

This reaction, commonly called steam-methane reforming or SMR, is endothermic and equilibrium-limited.

Methane can also undergo partial oxidation with molecular oxygen to produce syngas, as the following equation shows:

$$2\,CH_4 + O_2 \longrightarrow 2\,CO + 4\,H_2$$

This reaction is exothermic and the heat given off can be used in-situ to drive the steam-methane reforming reaction. When the two processes are combined, it is referred to as autothermal reforming. The ratio of CO and H_2 can be adjusted to some extent by the water-gas shift reaction:

$$CO + H_2O \longrightarrow CO_2 + H_2$$

to provide the appropriate stoichiometry for methanol synthesis.

The carbon monoxide and hydrogen then react on a catalyst to produce methanol. Today, the most widely used catalyst is a mixture of copper, zinc oxide, and alumina first used by ICI in 1966.

At 5~10 MPa (50~100 atm) and 250℃, it can catalyze the production of methanol from carbon monoxide and hydrogen with high selectivity:

$$CO + 2 H_2 \longrightarrow CH_3OH$$

It is worth noting that the production of synthesis gas from methane produces 3 moles of hydrogen gas for every mole of carbon monoxide, while the methanol synthesis consumes only 2 moles of hydrogen gas for every mole of carbon monoxide. One way of dealing with the excess hydrogen is to inject carbon dioxide into the methanol synthesis reactor, where it reacts to form methanol according to the equation:

$$CO_2 + 3 H_2 \longrightarrow CH_3OH + H_2O$$

Although natural gas is the most economical and widely used feedstock for methanol production, many other feedstocks can be used to produce syngas via steam reforming. Coal is increasingly being used as a feedstock for methanol production, particularly in China. In addition, mature technologies available for biomass gasification are being utilized for methanol production. For instance, woody biomass can be gasified to water gas (a hydrogen-rich syngas), by introducing a blast of steam in a blast furnace. The water-gas / syngas can then be synthesized to methanol using standard methods.

$$2 C_{16}H_{23}O_{11} + 19 H_2O + O_2 \longrightarrow 42 H_2 + 21 CO + 11 CO_2 \longrightarrow 21 CH_3OH + 11 CO_2$$

New Words and Expressions

methanol ['meθənɔl] *n.* 甲醇

methyl ['miːθail, 'miθil] *n.* 甲基；木精

flammable ['flæməbl] *a.* 易燃的；可燃的；可燃性的
　　　　　　　　　　　n. 易燃物

distinctive [dis'tiŋktiv] *a.* 有特色的，与众不同的

polar ['pəulə] *a.* 极性的；极地的；两极的；正好相反的

antifreeze ['æntifriːz] *n.* 防冻剂

denaturant [diː'neitʃərənt] *n.* 变性剂

formaldehyde [fɔː'mældihaid] *n.* [化]蚁醛，甲醛

tert-butyl [təːt-'bjuːtil] *n.* [化] 叔丁基

ether ['iːθə] *n.* 乙醚；以太；苍天；天空醚

acetic [ə'siːtik] *a.* 醋的，乙酸的

anaerobic [,ænɛə'rəubik] *a.* 厌氧的，厌气的；没有气而能生活的

metabolism [mi'tæbəlizəm, me-] *n.* 新陈代谢

bacteria [bæk'tiəriə] *n.* 细菌

ubiquitous [juː'bikwitəs] *a.* 普遍存在的；无所不在的

moderate ['mɔdərət, 'mɔdəreit] *a.* 温和的；适度的，中等的；有节制的

syngas ['singæs] *n.* 合成气（指一氧化碳和氢的混合物，尤指由低级煤生产的可燃性气体，
　　　　　　　　　　主要用于化学和生物加工以及甲醇的生产）

equation [i'kweiʒən, -ʃən] *n.* 方程式，等式；相等；反应式

reforming [ri'fɔːmiŋ] n. 变换；重整；改进

endothermic [ˌendəu'θəːmik,-məl] a. [化]吸热的

partial ['paːʃəl] a. 局部的；部分的

exothermic [ˌeksəu'θəːmik,-'θəːməl] a. 发热的；放出热量的

in-situ [in'sitjuː] n. 原位；现场

appropriate [ə'prəuprieit, ə'prəupriət] a. 适当的

alumina [ə'ljuːminə] n. [无化]氧化铝；矾土

catalyze ['kætəlaiz] vt. [化]催化；刺激，促进

consume [kən'sjuːm] vt. 消耗，消费；使…着迷；挥霍

inject [in'dʒekt] vt. 注入；注射

via ['vaiə] prep. 取道，通过；经由

increasingly [in'kriːsiŋli] adv. 越来越多地；渐增地

mature [mə'tjuə] a. 成熟的；充分考虑的；到期的；成年人的

technology [tek'nɔlədʒi] n. 技术；工艺；术语

available [ə'veiləbl] a. 有效的，可得的；可利用的；空闲的

biomass ['baiəumæs] n. 生物质

blast [blæst] n. 一阵；爆炸；冲击波

woody ['wudi] a. 木质的；多树木的；木头似的

known as   被认为是，被称为；以…而著称

as a result   结果

a small fraction of   一小部分

rather than   而不是

give off   发出（光等）；长出（枝、杈等）

be referred to as   被称为…

autothermal reforming   自热转化

to some extent   在一定程度上；在某种程度上

ICI abbr.   英国化学工业公司（Imperial Chemical Industries Ltd.）

deal with   处理；涉及；做生意

in addition   另外，此外

for instance   例如

blast furnace   鼓风炉，高炉

standard method   标准方法；标准措施

inject into   把…注入

Notes

1. Three processes are commercially practiced.（合成气）的商业生产需要三步。本句根据上下文的内容，采用了意译的翻译方法。增译了"合成气"。副词commercially转译为名词"商业"。 在译文中由"生产需要"表达了Practiced要表达的意思。

2. This reaction is exothermic and the heat given off can be used in-situ to drive the steam-methane reforming reaction.这是一个放热反应，所释放出来的热量被原位利用来驱动蒸

汽-甲烷转化反应。本句是由两个并列分句构成的复合句。given off是过去分词短语做后置定语修饰the heat。

3. Today, the most widely used catalyst is a mixture of copper, zinc oxide, and alumina first used by ICI in 1966.目前，最广泛使用的催化剂是铜、氧化锌和铝的混合物，该催化剂在1966年由英国化学工业公司首次使用。这是一个简单句，采用的是分译法。句中出现两个used，都是过去分词做定语，前一个是前置定语，后一个是后置定语。

4. In addition, mature technologies available for biomass gasification are being utilized for methanol production.另外，采用生物质汽化法生产甲醇的工艺越来越成熟。该句省译了形容词available。

Exercises

1. Put the following into Chinese

methanol synthesis   a distinctive odor

at room temperature   a polar liquid

many varieties of bacteria   steam-methane reforming

2. Put the following into English

所释放的热量   自热转化反应

成熟的工艺   在光照的作用下

部分氧化   镍催化剂

3. Questions

How many processes are there for the production of synthesis gas($CO + 2H_2$) ? what are they?

Lesson Eleven   Production of Phenol

Phenol, C_6H_5OH (hydroxybenzene), is produced from cumene by a two-step process. In the first step, cumene is oxidized with air to cumene hydroperoxide. The reaction conditions are approximately $100\sim130°C$ and $2\sim3$ atmospheres in the presence of a metal salt catalyst:

$$CH_3CHCH_3 \qquad (CH_3)_2COOH$$

$$\text{(benzene)} + O_2 \longrightarrow \text{(benzene)} \qquad \Delta H = -116kJ/mol$$

In the second step, the hydroperoxide is decomposed in the presence of an acid to phenol and acetone. The reaction conditions are approximately $80°C$ and slightly below atmospheric:

$$(CH_3)_2COOH \qquad OH$$

$$\text{(benzene)} \xrightarrow{H^+} \text{(benzene)} + CH_3\overset{O}{\overset{\|}{C}}CH_3$$

In this process (Figure 5.1), cumene is oxidized in the liquid phase. The oxidation product is concentrated to 80% cumene hydroperoxide by vacuum distillation. To avoid decomposition of the hydroperoxide, it is transferred immediately to the cleavage reactor in the presence of a small amount of H_2SO_4. The cleavage product is neutralized with alkali before it is finally purified.

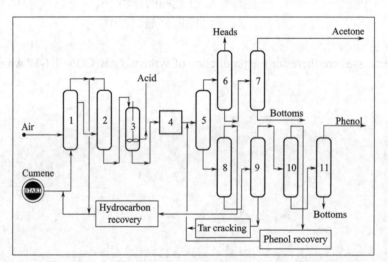

Figure 5.1   The Mitsui Petrochemical Industries process for producing phenol and acetone from cumene
1—autooxidation reactor; 2—vacuum tower; 3—cleavage reactor; 4—neutralizer; 5~11—purification train

After an initial distillation to split the coproducts phenol and acetone, each is purified in separate distillation and treating trains. An acetone finishing column distills product acetone from an acetone/water/oil mixture. The oil, which is mostly unreacted cumene, is sent to cumene recovery. Acidic impurities, such as acetic acid and phenol, are neutralized by caustic injection.

Previously, phenol was produced from benzene by sulfonation followed by caustic fusion to sodium phenate. Phenol is released from the sodium salt of phenol by the action of carbon dioxide or sulfur dioxide.

$$C_6H_5SO_3H + 2\,NaOH \longrightarrow C_6H_5OH + Na_2SO_3 + H_2O$$

Direct hydroxylation of benzene to phenol could be achieved using zeolite catalysts containing rhodium, platinum, palladium, or irridium. Phenol is also produced from chlorobenzene and from toluene via a benzoic acid intermediate.

Properties and Uses of Phenol

Phenol, a white crystalline mass with a distinctive odor, becomes reddish when subjected to light. It is highly soluble in water, and the solution is weakly acidic.

Phenol was the 33rd highest-volume chemical. The 1994 U.S. production of phenol was approximately 4 billion pounds. The current world capacity is approximately 15 billion pounds. Many chemicals and polymers derive from phenol. Approximately 50% of production goes to phenolic resins. Phenol and acetone produce bis-phenol A, an important monomer for epoxy resins and polycarbonates. It is produced by condensing acetone and phenol in the presence of HCl, or by using a cation exchange resin.

Important chemicals derived from phenol are salicylic acid; acetylsalicyclic acid (aspirin); 2,4-dichlorophenoxy acetic acid (2,4-D), and 2,4,5-triphenoxy acetic acid (2,4,5-T), which are selective herbicides; and pentachlorophenol, a wood preservative:

| Salicyclic acid | Aspirin | 2,4,5-T |

In addition, halophenols are miticides, bactericides, and leather preservatives. Halophenols account for about 5% of phenol uses.

About 12% of phenol demand is used to produce caprolactam, a monomer for nylon 6. The main source for caprolactam, however, is toluene.

Phenol can be alkylated to alkylphenols. These compounds are widely used as nonionic surfactants, antioxidants, and monomers in resin polymer applications:

An alkylphenol

Phenol is also a precursor for aniline. Ammonolysis of phenol occurs in the vapor phase. Aniline produced this way should be very pure. The largest application of aniline is for the preparation of methylene diphenyl diisocyanate (MDI). Other uses include rubber processing chemicals (9%), herbicides (2%), and dyes and pigments (2%).

New Words and Expressions

phenol ['fiːnɔl, fi'n-] *n.* [化] 苯酚，石炭酸

hydroxybenzene [hai,drɔksi'benziːn] *n.* [化]酚；[化]羟基苯

cumene ['kjuːmin] *n.* 异丙基苯，枯烯

oxidize ['ɔksidaiz] *vt.* 使生锈；使氧化

                  vi. 氧化

hydroperoxide [,haidrəupə'rɔksaid] *n.* 氢过氧化物

acetone ['æsitəun] *n.* [化]丙酮

vacuum ['vækjuəm] *n.* 真空

                a. 真空的

decomposition [,diːkɔmpə'ziʃən] *n.* 分解

cleavage ['kliːvidʒ] *n.* [化]裂解；劈开，分裂

neutralize ['njuːtrəlaiz] *vt.* 使…中和；使…无效；使…中立

alkali ['ælkəlai] *n.* 碱；可溶性无机盐

              a. 碱性的

coproduct ['kəu,prɔdəkt] *n.* 副产物

split [split] *vt.* 分离；使分离；劈开；离开

purify ['pjuərifai] *vt.* 净化；使纯净

             vi. 变纯净；净化

distill [dis'til] *vt.* 蒸馏；提取；使滴下

             vi. 滴下；蒸馏；作为精华产生

benzene ['benziːn] *n.* [化]苯

caustic ['kɔːstik] *a.* [化]腐蚀性的；[化] 苛性的；刻薄的；焦散的

injection [in'dʒekʃən] *n.* 注射；注射剂；充血；射入轨道

sulfonation [,sʌlfθ'neiʃən] *n.* [有化]磺化，磺酸盐

             vt. 使…磺化

fusion ['fjuːʒən] *n.* 融合；熔化；熔接；融合物

phenate ['fiːneit, 'fe-] *n.* 石炭酸盐；苯酚盐

hydroxylation [haidrɔksi'leiʃən] *n.* [有化]羟基化

zeolite ['ziːəlait] *n.* 沸石

rhodium ['rəudiəm] *n.* [化学]铑（一种元素）

palladium [pə'leidiəm] *n.* [化学]钯

iridium [ai'ridiəm, i'ri-] *n.* [化学]铱（Ir）

chlorobenzene [,klɔːrəu'benziːn] *n.* [有化]氯苯

toluene ['tɔljuiːn] *n.* [有化]甲苯

benzoic [ben'zəuik] *a.* 安息香的

intermediate [,intə'miːdjət, -dieit] *n.* [化学]中间产物；中间物；媒介

crystalline ['kristəlain] *a.* 透明的；水晶般的；水晶制的；晶体的，结晶的

odor   ['əudə]   *n.* 气味；名声

reddish   ['rediʃ]   *a.* 微红的；略带红色的

phenolic   [fi'nɔlik]   *a.* [有化]酚的；[胶黏]酚醛树脂的；石炭酸的

　　　　　　　　　　n. [胶黏]酚醛树脂

resin   ['rezin]   *n.* 树脂；松香

epoxy   [ep'ɔksi]   *a.* 环氧的

　　　　　　　n. 环氧基树脂

polycarbonate   [ˌpɔli'kɑ:bə,neit, -nit]   *n.* [高分子]聚碳酸酯

cation   ['kætaiən]   *n.* [化]阳离子；[化]正离子

salicylic   [ˌsæli'silik]   *a.* 水杨酸的；得自水杨酸的

acetylsalicylic   [ə'si:til,sæli'silik]   *a.* 乙酰水杨酸的

herbicide   ['hə:bisaid, 'ə:-]   *n.* [农药]除草剂

pentachlorophenol   [ˌpentə,klɔ:rə'fi:nəul]   *n.* [有化][农药]五氯苯酚

preservative   [pri'zə:vətiv]   *n.* 防腐剂；预防法；防护层

　　　　　　　　　　　　a. 防腐的；有保护性的

miticide   ['mitisaid]   *n.* [农药]杀螨药

bactericide   [bæk'tiəri,said]   *n.* [药]杀菌剂

caprolactam   [ˌkæprəu'læktəm]   *n.* [有化]己内酰胺

nylon   ['nailɔn]   *n.* 尼龙，[纺]聚酰胺纤维；尼龙袜

alkylate   ['ælkilət, 'ælkileit]   *vt.* 使烷基化

nonionic   [ˌnɔnai'ɔnik]   *a.* 在溶液中不分解成离子的

　　　　　　　　　n. 非离子物质

antioxidant   [ˌænti'ɔksidənt]   *n.* 抗氧化剂；硬化防止剂；防老化剂

salicylic acid   水杨酸；柳酸

methylene diphenyl diisocyanate   甲基二苯二异氰酸酯

Notes

1. After an initial distillation to split the coproducts phenol and acetone, each is purified in separate distillation and treating trains. 初次精馏把共产物苯酚和丙酮分开，之后它们去各自的精馏和处理装置。根据上下文的内容，把train译成"装置"比较恰当。

2. An acetone finishing column distills product acetone from an acetone/water/oil mixture. 丙酮的最后一个（精馏）塔从丙酮、水和油的混合物中提取丙酮。

3. Phenol was the 33rd highest-volume chemical.苯酚产量曾经位居第33位。增译时态词"曾经"。

4. Approximately 50% of production goes to phenolic resins.大约苯酚产量的50%用来（生产）酚醛树脂。增译动词"生产"。

5. These compounds are widely used as nonionic surfactants, antioxidants, and monomers in resin polymer applications.这些化合物被广泛用来（生产）非离子表面活性剂、抗氧剂和用做

聚合物的单体。增译动词"生产"。本课中多次出现增译"生产"的现象。

Exercises

1. Put the following into Chinese

phenolic resins   bis-phenol A

epoxy resins   a cation exchange resin

selective herbicides   leather preservatives

2. Put the following into English

苯酚的生产   过氧化异丙苯

真空精馏   除草剂

杀螨剂   杀菌剂

3. Questions

How many steps are there for the production of phenol from cumene ? What are they?

Reading Material: Development of Organic Synthesis

The well-being of modern society is unimaginable without the myriad products of industrial organic synthesis. Our quality of life is strongly dependent on the products of the pharmaceutical industry, such as antibiotics for combating disease and analgesics or anti-inflammatory drugs for relieving pain. The origins of this industry date back to 1935, when Domagk discovered the antibacterial properties of the red dye, prontosil, the prototype of a range of sulfa drugs that quickly found their way into medical practice. The history of organic synthesis is generally traced back to Wohler's synthesis of the natural product urea from ammonium isocyanate in 1828. This laid to rest the *vis vitalis* (vital force) theory, which maintained that a substance produced by a living organism could not be produced synthetically. The discovery had monumental significance, because it showed that, in principle, all organic compounds are amenable to synthesis in the laboratory.

The next landmark in the development of organic synthesis was the preparation of the first synthetic dye, mauveine (aniline purple) by Perkin in 1856, generally regarded as the first industrial organic synthesis. It is also a remarkable example of serendipity. Perkin was trying to synthesize the anti-malarial drug quinine by oxidation of *N*-allyl toluidine with potassium dichromate. This noble but naive attempt, bearing in mind that only the molecular formula of quinine ($C_{20}H_{24}N_2O_2$) was known at the time, was doomed to fail. In subsequent experiments with aniline, fortuitously contaminated with toluidines, Perkin obtained a low yield of a purple-colored product. Apparently, the young Perkin was not only a good chemist but also a good businessman, and he quickly recognized the commercial potential of his finding. The rapid development of the product, and the process to make it, culminated in the commercialization of mauveine, which replaced the natural dye, Tyrian purple. At the time of Perkin's discovery Tyrian purple, which was extracted from a species of Mediterranean snail, cost more per kg than gold. This serendipitous discovery marked the advent of the synthetic dyestuffs industry based on coal tar, a waste product from steel manufacture.

The development of mauveine was followed by the industrial synthesis of the natural dyes alizarin and indigo by Graebe and Liebermann in 1868 and Adolf Baeyer in 1870, respectively. The commercialization of these dyes marked the demise of their agricultural production and the birth of a science-based, predominantly German, chemical industry. By the turn of the 20th century the germ theory of disease had been developed by Pasteur and Koch, and for chemists seeking new uses for coal tar derivatives which were unsuitable as dyes, the burgeoning field of pharmaceuticals was an obvious one for exploitation. A leading light in this field was Paul Ehrlich, who coined the term chemotherapy. He envisaged that certain chemicals could act as 'magic bullets' by being extremely toxic to an infecting microbe but harmless to the host. This led him to test dyes as chemotherapeutic agents and to the discovery of an effective treatment for syphilis. Because Ehrlich had studied dye molecules as 'magic bullets' it became routine to test all dyes as chemotherapeutic agents, and this practice led to the above-mentioned discovery of prontosil as an antibacterial agent. Thus, the modern pharmaceutical industry was born as a spin-off of the manufacture of synthetic dyestuffs from coal tar.

The introduction of the sulfa drugs was followed by the development of the penicillin antibiotics. Fleming's chance observation of the anti-bacterial action of the penicillin mold in 1928 and the subsequent isolation and identification of its active constituent by Florey and Chain in 1940 marked the beginning of the antibiotics era that still continues today. At roughly the same time, the steroid hormones found their way into medical practice. Cortisone was introduced by the pharmaceutical industry in 1944 as a drug for the treatment of arthritis and rheumatic fever. This was followed by the development of steroid hormones as the active constituents of the contraceptive pill. The penicillins, the related cephalosporins, and the steroid hormones represented considerably more complicated synthetic targets than the earlier mentioned sulfa drugs. Indeed, as the target molecules shifted from readily available natural compounds and relatively simple synthetic molecules to complex semi-synthetic structures, a key factor in their successful introduction into medical practice became the availability of a cost-effective synthesis. For example, the discovery of the regio and enantiospecific microbial hydroxylation of progesterone to 11α-hydroxyprogesterone by Peterson and Murray at the Upjohn Company led to a commercially viable synthesis of cortisone that replaced a 31-step chemical synthesis from a bile acid and paved the way for the subsequent commercial success of the steroid hormones. According to Peterson, when he proposed the microbial hydroxylation, many outstanding organic chemists were of the opinion that it couldn't be done. Peterson's response was that the microbes didn't know that. Although this chemistry was invented four decades before the term Green Chemistry was officially coined, it remains one of the outstanding applications of Green Chemistry within the pharmaceutical industry.

This monumental discovery marked the beginning of the development, over the following decades, of drugs of ever-increasing molecular complexity. In order to meet this challenge, synthetic organic chemists aspired to increasing levels of sophistication. A case in point is the anticancer drug, Taxol, derived from the bark of the Pacific yew tree, *Taxus brevifolia,* and introduced into medical practice in the 1990s. The breakthrough was made possible by Holton's invention of a commercially viable and sustainable semi-synthesis from 10-deacetylbaccatin III, a constituent of the needles of the English yew, *Taxus baccata.* The Bristol-Myers Squibb Company subsequently developed and commercialized a fermentation process that avoids the semi-synthetic process.

In short, the success of the modern pharmaceutical industry is firmly built on the remarkable achievements of organic synthesis over the last century. However, the down side is that many of these time-honored and trusted synthetic methodologies were developed in an era when the toxic properties of many reagents and solvents were not known and the issues of waste minimization and sustainability were largely unheard of.

科技英语翻译五　增词省词译法

一、增词译法

所谓增词译法是指译者在英译汉时，为使译文通顺达意，在译文中增补某些必要的词。运用增补法应遵循的一条基本原则是：所增补的词必须是在修辞上、语言结构上或语义上必不可少的，绝不可随心所欲地任意增补。译者首先要理解原句的内容与结构，并结合专业技术术语的表达规范，用符合汉语表达习惯的语言完整、准确、流畅地将原文的意思翻译出来。

1. 增补一些附加性的名词

> From the evaporation of water people know that liquid can turn into gases under certain conditions.

从水的蒸发**现象**，人们知道液体在一定条件下能转变为气体。

> In practice, oily soil is removed by the combined action of surfactants and enzymes.

事实上，油垢的去除是表面活性剂和酶共同作用的**结果**。

2. 在某些名词、动名词前增补动词

> Approximately 50% of phenol goes to phenolic resins.

大约50%的苯酚用于**生产**酚醛树脂。

3. 增补一些解释性的形容词

根据原文所需要表达的含义，结合上下文，在部分名词后适当的增译形容词，使译文能更加确切地表达原意，如下。

> Polyethylene is classified into several different categories based on its density and branching.

根据聚乙烯的密度**大小**和支化度**高低**，把它们分为几个不同的种类。

> Speed and reliability are the chief advantages of the electronic computer.

速度**快**、可靠性**高**是电子计算机的主要优点。

4. 增补代词

增补代词是指通过在句首增译"人们"、"有人"、"我们"等泛指代词，将英语的被动句翻译为汉语的主动句。有时，翻译英语的主动句时也增译动词，这完全是为了遵循汉语的表达习惯，如下。

> Hydrogen is known to be the lightest element.

人们知道氢是最轻的元素。

5. 增补量词

英语中的量词是很有限的，表示数量概念时往往是数词或不定冠词（a/an）与可数名词连用；而汉语却习惯于根据事物的形状、特征或材料，用不同的量词来表示不同的事物数量概念。因此，翻译时应根据汉语的表达习惯，增补适当的量词，如下。

> An oil pump　一**台**油泵

> The initiator is an organic material.

引发剂是一**种**有机物。

6. 增补表示名词复数的词

如果英语原句中的名词为复数，汉译时，可根据具体情况增译适当的表示复数概念的词：

"们"、"各种"、"种种"、"许多"、"大量"、"几个"、"一些"等，如下。

> The mechanical properties of PE depend on its variables.

聚乙烯的力学性能取决于它的**多种**参数。

> The cracked product is charged to a fractionating column where it is separated into fractions。

裂解产物被送到分馏塔，在那里它被分离成**各种**馏分。

7．增补时态词

英语的时态是通过动词词形的变化来体现的，而汉语则是通过增加表示时态的助词或表示时间的副词来完成的。因此，在翻译英语的进行时态时，往往增译"正在"、"在"、"不断"、"着"等词语；翻译将来时态时，增译为"将"、"要"、"便"、"会"等；翻译过去时态时，增译"曾经"、"当时"、"以前"、"过去"等；翻译英语的完成时态时，增译"已经"、"历来"、"了"等，如下。

> The Contact Process **was patented** by a British vinegar merchant.

当时，一位英国醋商申请了接触法的专利。（用"当时"表示过去时态）

> The Contact Process **has been** the dominant process used to manufacture sulphuric acid for most of the past 100 years.

在过去的一百多年里，接触法**一直**是生产硫酸的主要工艺。（用"一直"表示现在完成时态）

> Phenol **was** the 33rd highest-volume chemical.

苯酚的产量**曾经**位居第 33 位。（用"曾经"表示过去时态）

8．增译概括性的词

所谓概括词，就是指类似"两种"、"三类"、"双方"、"等等"、"种种"等词语。增译概括性的词就是将所罗列的事物用概括性的词语进行总结概括，使译文更加清晰明了。如：

> Proteins are composed of carbon, hydrogen ,oxygen and nitrogen.

蛋白质是由碳、氢、氧和氮**等四种**元素组成。

9．增译连接词

为了使译文更富有逻辑、更符合汉语的表达习惯、更加通顺流畅，可以适当地在译文中增加一些表示原因、条件、目的、结果、让步、假设等连接词，如下。

> The ratio of CO and H_2 can be adjusted by the water-gas shift reaction to provide the appropriate stoichiometry for methanol synthesis.

通过水煤气转化反应能够调整CO和 H_2 的比例，**以便**为甲醇的合成提供适宜的计量比。

10．增译转折词

当英语原句子中没有转折词，但是在翻译时，为了使译文的语句通顺、符合汉语的表达方式，可在译文中适当地增译转折词。这种增译不是依据句法结构，而是根据语义要求来进行的，如下。

> The lead chamber process is used to produce much of the acid used to make fertilizers; it produces a relatively dilute acid (62%～78% H_2SO_4).

铅室法被大量用来生产肥料用的酸，**但**它生产的酸浓度相对较低。

> The "reactor" no longer functions as a reactor; it merely serves as a holding vessel for the cyclones.

"反应器"不再起到反应器的作用；**而是**仅仅起到旋风器的作用。

二、省词译法

省译是指把原文中的某个（些）词不译出来。由于英语和汉语在句法结构、用词造句上的不同，英语中需要的词，汉语句子中并不一定需要。根据省词不省意的原则，可把它们省译。如果将其译出，反而会使得译文晦涩难懂；如果不译出来，则会使译文更能通顺、准确地表达出原文的思想内容。因此，省译法是科技英语翻译时常用的重要技巧。

1．省译冠词

英语中有冠词，而汉语中没有冠词。另外，英语句子使用冠词往往是出于句法结构的需要。因此，汉英时冠词常常可以省去不译，如下。

➢ Ammonia is synthesized by reacting hydrogen with nitrogen at **a** molar ratio of 3 to 1.

氢气与氮气以 1:3 的摩尔比反应合成氨气。（省译冠词 a）

➢ **The** initiator is an organic material.

引发剂是一种有机物。（省译定冠词 The）

2．省译代词

英语的特点之一就是代词多，但译成汉语时，无须保留全部代词，可以根据情况省译一些，如下。

➢ If **you** know that 1500 kg of sulfur is contained in the coal burned each day in the furnace, **you** do not have to analyze the ash and stack gases to know that on the average of 1500 kg sulfur per day leaves the furnace.

如果已知锅炉中每天燃烧的煤中含硫 1500 kg，那么就没有必要分析灰分和放出的气体，就可以知道每天离开燃烧炉的硫的平均数量是 1500 kg。（省译代词 you）

3．省译介词

大量使用介词是英语的又一大特点，汉译时一些介词常常可以省略不译，如下。

➢ Methanol is a chemical **with** formula CH$_3$OH.

甲醇是一种化学品，分子式为 CH$_3$OH。（省译介词 with）

4．省译连词

英语句子中的连词，包括并列连词和从属连词的使用较多，但汉语却比较少。因此在翻译时，英语原文中的连词常常可以省译，如下。

➢ It takes time **before** ozone-depleting chemicals can be totally eliminated.

要彻底清除消耗臭氧的化学品还需要时间。（省译连词 before）

5．省译动词

英语的句子必须由动词来做谓语，而汉语则不然，句子中除了动词作谓语，形容词、名词或词组都可以作谓语。这样的特点使我们在翻译时常常可以省译原文中的动词。被省译的动词通常是英语中的某些系动词或行为动词。

➢ All of the catalyst is regenerated in situ during routine catalyst regeneration shutdowns which **occur** approximately once each 6 to 24 months.

在常规的催化剂再生停车期间，所有催化剂现场再生，大约每 6～12 个月停车一次。（省译动词 occur）

6. there be 句型中的省译现象

There be 句型是英语所特有的句型结构，汉译带有 there be 的科技英语句子的方法有多种，其中常见是一种方法就是省译 there be 本身的含义，即不把"有"翻译出来，如下。

➢ **There are** a good many chemical reactions that occur in the presence of a catalyst.

在催化剂作用下发生了很多化学反应。

Unit Six Petroleum Chemical Engineering

Lesson Twelve Cracking

Cracking is a petroleum refining process in which heavy-molecular weight hydrocarbons are broken up into light hydrocarbon molecules by the application of heat and pressure, with or without the use of catalysts, to derive a variety of fuel products. Cracking is one of the principal ways in which crude oil is converted into useful fuels such as motor gasoline, jet fuel, and home heating oil.

Thermal Cracking

Thermal cracking is a refining process in which heat (~800℃) and pressure (~700 kPa) are used to break down, rearrange, or combine hydrocarbon molecules. The first thermal cracking process was developed around 1913. Heavy oils were heated under pressure in large drums until they cracked into smaller molecules with better antiknock characteristics. However, this method produced large amounts of solid, unwanted coke.

Catalytic Cracking

Catalytic cracking breaks complex hydrocarbons into simpler molecules in order to increase the quality and quantity of lighter, more desirable products and decrease the amount of residuals. This process rearranges the molecular structure of hydrocarbon compounds to convert heavy hydrocarbon feedstock into lighter fractions such as kerosene, gasoline, liquified petroleum gas (LPG), heating oil, and petrochemical feedstock.

Catalytic cracking is similar to thermal cracking except that catalysts facilitate the conversion of the heavier molecules into lighter products. Use of a catalyst (a material that assists a chemical reaction but does not take part in it) in the cracking reaction increases the yield of improved-quality products under much less severe operating conditions than in thermal cracking. Typical temperatures are from 850~950°F at much lower pressures of 10~20 psi. The catalysts used in refinery cracking units are typically solid materials (zeolite, aluminum hydrosilicate, treated bentonite clay, bauxite, and silica-alumina) that come in the form of powders, beads, pellets or other shaped materials.

There are three basic functions in the catalytic cracking process:

- Reaction: Feedstock reacts with catalyst and cracks into different hydrocarbons;
- Regeneration: Catalyst is reactivated by burning off coke;
- Fractionation: Cracked hydrocarbon stream is separated into various products.

The type of catalytic cracking processes is fluid catalytic cracking (FCC). The catalytic cracking process is very flexible, and operating parameters can be adjusted to meet changing product demand. In addition to cracking, catalytic activities include dehydrogenation, hydrogenation, and isomerization.

Fluid Catalytic Cracking (FCC)

Fluid catalytic cracking or "cat cracking" is the basic gasoline-making process. Using intense heat (about 1000 degrees Fahrenheit), low pressure and a powdered catalyst (a substance that accelerates chemical reactions), the cat cracker can convert most relatively heavy fractions into smaller gasoline molecules. The fluid cracker consists of a catalyst section and a fractionating section that operate together as an integrated processing unit. The catalyst section contains the reactor and regenerator, which, with the standpipe and riser, forms the catalyst circulation unit. The fluid catalyst is continuously circulated between the reactor and the regenerator using air, oil vapors, and steam as the conveying media.

A typical FCC process involves mixing a preheated hydrocarbon charge with hot, regenerated catalyst as it enters the riser leading to the reactor. The charge is combined with a recycle stream within the riser, vaporized, and raised to reactor temperature (900～1000°F) by the hot catalyst. As the mixture travels up the riser, the charge is cracked at 10～30 psi. In the more modern FCC units, all cracking takes place in the riser. The "reactor" no longer functions as a reactor; it merely serves as a holding vessel for the cyclones. This cracking continues until the oil vapors are separated from the catalyst in the reactor cyclones. The resultant product stream (cracked product) is then charged to a fractionating column where it is separated into fractions, and some of the heavy oil is recycled to the riser.

Spent catalyst is regenerated to get rid of coke that collects on the catalyst during the process. Spent catalyst flows through the catalyst stripper to the regenerator, where most of the coke deposits burn off at the bottom where preheated air and spent catalyst are mixed. Fresh catalyst is added and worn-out catalyst removed to optimize the cracking process.

New Words and Expressions

petroleum [pi'trəuliəm, pə-] *n.* 石油

catalyst ['kætəlist] *n.* 催化剂；刺激因素

gasoline ['gæsəliːn] *n.* 汽油

thermal ['θəːməl] *a.* 热的，热量的

antiknock [ˌænti'nɔk] *n.* 抗爆剂；抗爆

　　　　　　　　　　　　a. 抗爆的；抗震的

kerosene ['kerəsiːn] *n.* 煤油，火油

facilitate [fə'siliteit] *vt.* 促进；帮助；使容易

severe [si'viə] *a.* 严峻的；严厉的；剧烈的；苛刻的

hydrosilicate ['haidrəu'silikit, -keit] *n.* 含水硅酸盐

bentonite ['bentənait] *n.* [土壤]膨润土

bauxite ['bɔːksait] *n.* 矾土，[矿物]铁铝氧石；[矿物]铝土矿

bead [biːd] *n.* 珠子；滴；念珠

pellet   ['pelit]   *n.* 小球；[军]小子弹（枪用）

regeneration   [ri,dʒenə'reiʃən, ri:-]   *n.* [生物][化][物]再生，重生；重建

fractionation   [,frækʃə'neiʃən]   *n.* 分馏

flexible   ['fleksibl]   *a.* 灵活的；柔韧的；易弯曲的

parameter   [pə'ræmitə]   *n.* 参数；系数；参量

dehydrogenation   [di:haidrədʒə'neiʃən]   *n.* [化学]脱氢作用

hydrogenation   [,haidrədʒi'neiʃən]   *n.* 加氢；[化学]氢化作用

isomerization   [ai,sɔmərai'zeiʃən, -ri'z-]   *n.* [化学]异构化；异构化作用

accelerate   [ək'seləreit]   *vt.* 使…加快；使…增速

integrated   ['intigreitid]   *a.* 综合的；完整的；互相协调的
                         v. 整合；使…成整体

standpipe   ['stændpaip]   *n.* 立管；储水管；管体式水塔

riser   ['raizə]   *n.* [化]提升管；气门

circulate   ['sə:kjuleit]   *vi.* 传播，流传；循环；流通

convey   [kən'vei]   *vt.* 传达；运输；让与

cyclone   ['saikləun]   *n.* 旋风；[气象]气旋；飓风

stripper   ['stripə]   [化]汽提塔；剥离器

worn-out   ['wɔ:n'aut]   *a.* 磨破的；穿旧的；不能再用的

optimize   ['ɔptimaiz]   *vt.* 使最优化，使完善

petroleum refining   [油气] 石油加工,石油炼制

a variety of   种种；各种各样的…

thermal cracking   [油气]热裂解

evolve into   发展成，进化成

catalytic cracking   [油气]催化裂化

fluid catalytic cracking   [化]流化床催化裂化

in addition to   除…之外

get rid of   摆脱，除去

the reactor cyclones   旋风分离器

spent catalyst   废催化剂；用过的催化剂

Notes

1. Cracking is a petroleum refining process in which heavy-molecular weight hydrocarbons are broken up into light hydrocarbon molecules by the application of heat and pressure, with or without the use of catalysts, to derive a variety of fuel products.裂化是一种石油炼制过程，指在有或无催化剂的作用下，通过加热和加压使大分子的重组分碳氢化合物分解成轻组分碳氢化合物分子，从而获得多种燃料油产品。本句是由一个主句和一个定语从句组成，采用了分译法。

2. Cracking is one of the principal ways in which crude oil is converted into useful fuels such as motor gasoline, jet fuel, and home heating oil. 裂化是把原油转化为像汽油、机油和家用燃料油之类的有用燃料的主要方法之一。本句是由一个主句和一个定语从句组成。采用了合译法。

3. Heavy oils were heated under pressure in large drums until they cracked into smaller

molecules with better antiknock characteristics.在容积很大的反应器中，重油在加压下被加热为具有较强抗爆性的小分子为止。根据上下文的内容，drums译为"反应器"较贴切。

4. This process rearranges the molecular structure of hydrocarbon compounds to convert heavy hydrocarbon feedstock into lighter fractions such as kerosene, gasoline, liquified petroleum gas (LPG), heating oil, and petrochemical feedstock.这个过程使碳氢化合物的分子结构重排，从而使重组分碳氢化合物原料转化为像煤油、汽油、液化石油气、燃油和石油化工原料这类轻组分产品。

5. A typical FCC process involves mixing a preheated hydrocarbon charge with hot, regenerated catalyst as it enters the riser leading to the reactor.当催化剂进入通往反应器的提升管时，典型的流化床催化裂化过程使已经预热的碳氢化合物原料与经再生的热催化剂混合。本句是由一个主句和一个时间状语从句组成。状语从句的主语it指代"催化剂"。根据上下文内容，名词charge译为"原料"较恰当。mix…. with…把…和…混合。

6. The charge is combined with a recycle stream within the riser, vaporized, and raised to reactor temperature (900~1000℉) by the hot catalyst.在提升管内，原料与循环的催化剂流相化合，原料被汽化并提升到反应器中，反应器由于热催化剂的作用温度达到900~1000℉。本句是简单句，主语the charge有3个谓语，分别是combined, vaporized, raised。采用的是分译法。

Exercises

1. Put the following into Chinese

petroleum refining process　　　　　　　crude oil

thermal cracking　　　　　　　　　　　better antiknock characteristics

catalytic cracking　　　　　　　　　　　petrochemical feedstock

2. Put the following into English

流化床催化裂化　　　　　　　　　　　用过的催化剂

汽油　　　　　　　　　　　　　　　　机油

柴油　　　　　　　　　　　　　　　　石油化工原料

3. Questions

What are the main differences between the catalytic cracking and the thermal cracking?

Lesson Thirteen　Catalytic Reforming

Catalytic reforming is a chemical process used to convert petroleum refinery naphthas, typically having low octane rating, into high-octane liquid products called reformates which are components of high-octane gasoline (also known as petrol). Basically, the process rearranges or re-structures the hydrocarbon molecules in the naphtha feedstocks as well as breaking some of the molecules into smaller molecules. The overall effect is that the product reformate contains hydrocarbons with more complex molecular shapes having higher octane values than the hydrocarbons in the naphtha feedstock. In so doing, the process separates hydrogen atoms from the hydrocarbon molecules and produces very significant amounts of byproduct hydrogen gas, which is used in a number of the other processes involved in a modern petroleum refinery. Other byproducts are small amounts of methane, ethane, propane and butanes.

The reaction chemistry

There are a good many chemical reactions that occur in the catalytic reforming process, all of which occur in the presence of a catalyst and a high partial pressure of hydrogen. Depending upon the type or version of catalytic reforming used as well as the desired reaction severity, the reaction conditions range from temperatures of about 495 to 525℃ and from pressures of about 5 to 45 atm.

The commonly used catalytic reforming catalysts contain noble metals such as platinum and/or rhenium, which are very susceptible to poisoning by sulfur and nitrogen compounds. Therefore, the naphtha feedstock to a catalytic reformer is always pre-processed in a hydrodesulfurization unit which removes both the sulfur and the nitrogen compounds.

The four major catalytic reforming reactions are:

1. The dehydrogenation of naphthenes to convert them into aromatics as exemplified in the conversion of methylcyclohexane to toluene, as shown below:

2. The isomerization of normal paraffins to isoparaffins as exemplified in the conversion of normal octane to 2, 5-Dimethylhexane, as shown below:

3. The dehydrogenation and aromatization of paraffins to aromatics (commonly called dehydrocyclization) as exemplified in the conversion of normal heptane to toluene, as shown below:

$$n\text{-Heptane} \longrightarrow \text{Toluene} + 4H_2$$

4. The hydrocracking of paraffins into smaller molecules as exemplified by the cracking of

normal heptane into isopentane and ethane, as shown below:

$$n\text{-Heptane} + H_2 \longrightarrow \text{Isopentane} + \text{Ethane}$$

The hydrocracking of paraffins is the only one of the above four major reforming reactions that consumes hydrogen. The isomerization of normal paraffins does not consume or produce hydrogen. However, both the dehydrogenation of naphthenes and the dehydrocyclization of paraffins produce hydrogen. The overall net production of hydrogen in the catalytic reforming of petroleum naphthas ranges from about 50 to 200 cubic meters of hydrogen gas (at 0℃ and 1 atm) per cubic meter of liquid naphtha feedstock. In many petroleum refineries, the net hydrogen produced in catalytic reforming supplies a significant part of the hydrogen used elsewhere in the refinery (for example, in hydrodesulfurization processes).

Process description

The most commonly used type of catalytic reforming unit has three reators, each with a fixed bed of catalyst, and all of the catalyst is regenerated in situ during routine catalyst regeneration shutdowns which occur approximately once each 6 to 24 months. Such a unit is referred to as a semi-regenerative catalytic reformer (SRR).

Some catalytic reforming units have an extra spare or swing reactor and each reactor can be individually isolated so that any one reactor can be undergoing in situ regeneration while the other reactors are in operation. When that reactor is regenerated, it replaces another reactor which, in turn, is isolated so that it can then be regenerated. Such units, referred to as cyclic catalytic reformers, are not very common.

The latest and most modern type of catalytic reformers are called continuous catalyst regeneration reformers (CCR). Such units are characterized by continuous in-situ regeneration of part of the catalyst in a special regenerator, and by continuous addition of the regenerated catalyst to the operating reactors.

Many of the earliest catalytic reforming units (in the 1950s and 1960's) were non-regenerative in that they did not perform in situ catalyst regeneration. Instead, when needed, the aged catalyst was replaced by fresh catalyst and the aged catalyst was shipped to catalyst manufacturer's to be either regenerated or to recover the platinum content of the aged catalyst. Very few, if any, catalytic reformers currently in operation are non-regenerative.

New Words and Expressions

octane　['ɔktein]　*n.* 辛烷
reformate　[ri'fɔːmeit]　*n.* [油气]重整油；重整产品
rearrange　[ˌriːə'reindʒ]　*vt.* [化] (分子)重排
restructure　[riː'strʌktʃə]　*vt.* 重构；重建；更改结构
ethane　['eθein]　*n.* [有机化学]乙烷[亦作 dimethyl]

propane   ['prəupein]   n. [化]丙烷

butane   ['bju:tein]   n. [化]丁烷

version   ['və:ʃən]   n. 版本；译文；倒转术

severity   [si'veriti]   n. 严重；严格；猛烈

rhenium   ['ri:niəm]   n. [化]铼（75号元素，符号为Re）

susceptible   [sə'septəbl]   a. 易受影响的；易感动的；容许…的
                                n. 易得病的人

sulfur   ['sʌlfə]   vt. 用硫黄处理
                        n. 硫黄；硫黄色

nitrogen   ['naitrədʒən]   n. [化]氮

hydrodesulfurization   ['haidrəudi,sʌlfjuərai'zeiʃən,-ri'z-]   n. 加氢脱硫

naphthene   ['næfθi:n, 'næp-]   n. [有化]萘，[有化]环烷属烃

aromatic   [,ærəu'mætik]   a. 芳香的，芬芳的；芳香族的
                                n. 芳香植物；芳香剂

exemplify   [ig'zemplifai]   vt. 例证；例示

methylcyclohexane   ['mi:θail,saikləu'heksein]   n. 甲基环己烷；甲基溶纤剂

paraffin   ['pærəfin]   n. 石蜡；[有化]链烷烃；硬石蜡

aromatization   [,ərəumətai'zeiʃən, -ti'z-]   n. [有化]芳构化；香花作用；香味

dehydrocyclization   [di:haidrəsaikli'zeiʃən]   n. 脱氢环化（作用）

heptane   ['heptein]   n. [有化]庚烷

hydrocracking   ['haidrəu,krækiŋ]   n. [油气]加氢裂化；氢化裂解

isopentane   [,aisəu'pentein]   n. [有化]异戊烷

cubic   ['kju:bik]   a. 立方体的，立方的

shutdown   ['ʃʌtdaun]   n. 关机；停工；关门；停播

individually   [,indi'vidjuəli, -dʒu-]   adv. 个别地，单独地

petroleum refinery naphthas   石油炼厂石脑油

octane rating   辛烷值

a good many   许多，很多

partial pressure   [物]分压；[物]分压力

be susceptible to   对…敏感；易患…；易受…影响

2,5-dimethylhexane   2,5-二甲基己烷

the aged catalyst   失活的催化剂

Notes

1. There are a good many chemical reactions that occur in the catalytic reforming process, all of which occur in the presence of a catalyst and a high partial pressure of hydrogen.在催化剂作用下和较高氢气分压下，催化重整过程中发生了多种化学反应。本句由一个主句和两个定语从句组成。主句是there be句型，采取了省译法，没有译出"有"。两个定语从句的先行词都是chemical reactions。all of which occur in the presence of a catalyst and a high partial pressure of

hydrogen定语从句译成了译文的条件状语。

2. The hydrocracking of paraffins is the only one of the above four major reforming reactions that consumes hydrogen.以上4种主要重整反应中，链烷烃加氢裂化是唯一一个耗氢反应。本句由一个主句、一个定语从句组成。定语从句that consumes hydrogen的先行词是the only one，故此关系代词必须使用that，从句的翻译简化为一个词组"耗氢"，这样言简意赅。

3. The most commonly used type of catalytic reforming unit has three reactors, each with a fixed bed of catalyst, and all of the catalyst is regenerated in situ during routine catalyst regeneration shutdowns which occur approximately once each 6 to 24 months. 最常用的催化重整系统有3个反应器，每个反应器均有催化剂固定床，在常规的催化剂再生停车期间，所有这些催化剂现场再生，大约每6～12个月停车一次。本句是一个复合句，由两个并列分句，一个定语从句组成。定语从句的先行词是shutdowns，其翻译采用了分译法。

4. When that reactor is regenerated, it replaces another reactor which, in turn, is isolated so that it can then be regenerated.在这一反应器被再生之后，反过来，它代替另一个独立的反应器，以便被代替的反应器去再生。本句是一个复合句，由一个主句、一个时间状语从句、一个定语从句和一个目的状语从句组成。时间状语从句的连接词when 译为在…之后。定语从句which, in turn, is isolated先行词是another reactor，in turn 是插入语，该定语从句的翻译简化为一个词组"独立的"。句中出现两个it，第一个it指代that reactor，第二个it指代another reactor。

5. Many of the earliest catalytic reforming units (in the 1950s and 1960's) were non-regenerative in that they did not perform in situ catalyst regeneration.一些早期的催化重整系统是非再生的，因为它们没有实行原位催化剂再生。in that they did not perform in situ catalyst regeneration.是原因状语从句，位于主句后，对主句补充说明，其翻译采用顺译法。In so doing, the process separates hydrogen atoms from the hydrocarbon molecules and produces very significant amounts of byproduct hydrogen gas, which is used in a number of the other processes involved in a modern petroleum refinery.

Exercises

1. Put the following into Chinese

catalytic reforming   low octane ratings

the naphtha feedstocks   the catalytic reforming process

the type or version of catalytic reforming   the desired reaction severity

catalytic reformer   the hydrocracking of paraffins

2. Put the following into English

环烷烃脱氢   正构链烷烃异构化为异构链烷烃

链烷烃脱氢并芳构化为芳香烃   链烷烃加氢裂化

原位催化剂再生   老化的催化剂

3. Questions

What is the latest and most modern type of catalytic reformers?

What are such units characterized by?

Reading Material: Crude Oil

Crude oil (petroleum) is a naturally occurring brown to black flammable liquid. Crude oils are principally found in oil reservoirs associated with sedimentary rocks beneath the earth's surface. Although exactly how crude oils originated is not established, it is generally agreed that crude oils derived from marine animal and plant debris subjected to high temperatures and pressures. It is also suspected that the transformation may have been catalyzed by rock constituents. Regardless of their origins, all crude oils are mainly constituted of hydrocarbons mixed with variable amounts of sulfur, nitrogen, and oxygen compounds.

Metals in the forms of inorganic salts or organometallic compounds are present in the crude mixture in trace amounts. The ratio of the different constituents in crude oils, however, vary appreciably from one reservoir to another.

Normally, crude oils are not used directly as fuels or as feed stocks for the production of chemicals. This is due to the complex nature of the crude oil mixture and the presence of some impurities that are corrosive or poisonous to processing catalysts.

Crude oils are refined to separate the mixture into simpler fractions that can be used as fuels, lubricants, or as intermediate feedstock to the petrochemical industries. A general knowledge of this composite mixture is essential for establishing a processing strategy.

Properties of Crude Oils

Crude oils differ appreciably in their properties according to origin and the ratio of the different components in the mixture. Lighter crudes generally yield more valuable light and middle distillates and are sold at higher prices. Crudes containing a high percent of impurities, such as sulfur compounds, are less desirable than low-sulfur crudes because of their corrosivity and the extra treating cost. Corrosivity of crude oils is a function of many parameters among which are the type of sulfur compounds and their decomposition temperatures, the total acid number, the type of carboxylic and naphthenic acids in the crude and their decomposition temperatures. It was found that naphthenic acids begin to decompose at 600℉. Refinery experience has shown that above 750°F there is no naphthenic acid corrosion. The subject has been reviewed by Kane and Cayard. For a refiner, it is necessary to establish certain criteria to relate one crude to another to be able to assess crude quality and choose the best processing scheme. The following are some of the important tests used to determine the properties of crude oils.

Density, Specific Gravity

Density is defined as the mass of unit volume of a material at a specific temperature. A more useful unit used by the petroleum industry is specific gravity, which is the ratio of the weight of a given volume of a material to the weight of the same volume of water measured at the same temperature.

Specific gravity is used to calculate the mass of crude oils and its products. Usually, crude oils and their liquid products are first measured on a volume basis, then changed to the corresponding masses using the specific gravity.

Salt Content

The salt content expressed in milligrams of sodium chloride per liter oil (or in pounds/barrel) indicates the amount of salt dissolved in water. Water in crudes is mainly present in an emulsified form. A high salt content in a crude oil presents serious corrosion problems during the refining process. In addition, high salt content is a major cause of plugging heat exchangers and heater pipes.

Sulfur Content

Determining the sulfur content in crudes is important because the amount of sulfur indicates the type of treatment required for the distillates. To determine sulfur content, a weighed crude sample (or fraction) is burned in an air stream. All sulfur compounds are oxidized to sulfur dioxide, which is further oxidized to sulfur trioxide and finally titrated with a standard alkali.

Identifying sulfur compounds in crude oils and their products is of little use to a refiner because all sulfur compounds can easily be hydrodesulfurized to hydrogen sulfide and the corresponding hydrocarbon. The sulfur content of crudes, however, is important and is usually considered when determining commercial values.

Pour Point

The pour point of a crude oil or product is the lowest temperature at which an oil is observed to flow under the conditions of the test. Pour point data indicates the amount of long-chain paraffins (petroleum wax) found in a crude oil. Paraffinic crudes usually have higher wax content than other crude types. Handling and transporting crude oils and heavy fuels is difficult at temperatures below their pour points Often, chemical additives known as pour point depressants are used to improve the flow properties of the fuel. Long-chain n-paraffins ranging from 16–60 carbon atoms in particular, are responsible for near-ambient temperature precipitation. In middle distillates, less than 1% wax can be sufficient to cause solidification of the fuel.

Ash Content

This test indicates the amount of metallic constituents in a crude oil. The ash left after completely burning an oil sample usually consists of stable metallic salts, metal oxides, and silicon oxide. The ash could be further analyzed for individual elements using spectroscopic techniques.

科技英语翻译六 名词性从句的翻译方法

英语中的名词性从句包括主语从句、表语从句、宾语从句和同位语从句4种，它们在句子中的功能相当于名词或名词短语。英语中引导名词性从句的连接词有以下3种。

连接代词：who, whoever, whom, whose, what, whatever, which, whichever

连接副词：when, where, why, how

从属连词：that, whether, if

一、主语从句的译法

在句中，凡是充当主语成分的句子就是主语从句。它主要有两种形式：一种是"主语从句+谓语+其他成分"，即从句位于主句主语的位置；另一种是"it+谓语+主语从句"，即以 it 为先行词作形式宾语，真正的主语从句在主句的谓语之后。

1."主语从句+谓语+其他成分"结构的译法

汉译时，通常采用顺译法。

➤ **What we call "petroleum"** is a mixture of several different materials.

我们称之为石油的东西是多种物质的混合物。

➤ **What spiders require to synthesis silk** are the products of the digestion of insects and enzymes.

蜘蛛用来合成丝的物质是昆虫和酶消化产物。

2."it+谓语+主语从句"结构的译法

（1）顺译法

所谓顺译法就是按照原文中句子的词序翻译，即先译主语，然后再译主语从句，如下。

➤ It is notable **that water is a good conductor**.

值得注意的是，**水是一种良导体**。

➤ It is not doubtable **that sulfuric acid is an important industrial chemical**.

毋庸置疑，**硫酸是一种重要的工业化学品**。

采用顺译法翻译的这类句型，汉语中也有固定的译法，常见的如下：

It is a fact that …事实是…

It is a wonder that…令人奇怪的是…

It is apparent that…很明显…

It is desirable that…最好是…

It is evident that…很明显…

It is likely that…可能…

It is noteable that…值得注意的是…

It is supposed that…假定…

It will be seen from this that…由此可见…

（2）倒译法

所谓倒译法就是把真正的主语从句先译出，为了强调，it 可以译出来，如果不需要强调，it 也可以不译出来。

> It is important **that the catalytic reforming reactor be regenerated in situ**.

催化裂解反应器原位再生，这一点很重要。

二、宾语从句的译法

在句中，凡是充当宾语成分的句子叫做宾语从句。英语的宾语从句有 3 种，一是动词后的宾语从句（包括不定式、分词、动名词的宾语从句）；二是介词后的宾语从句；三是 it 作形式宾语，真正的宾语是谓语动词后的从句。翻译宾语从句大都采用顺译法，即照原文顺序翻译，但是 it 作形式宾语的从句，it 概不译出。

1. 动词宾语从句

> We know **that phenol is produced from cumene by a two-step process**.

我们知道由异丙苯经过两步可以生产苯酚。

2. 介词宾语从句

Catalytic cracking is similar to thermal cracking except **that catalysts facilitate the conversion of the heavier molecules into lighter products**.

除了催化剂能促进大分子转变成小分子产品之外，催化裂化与热裂化相似。

> Green chemists gain clues as to **how processes may be changed to make them more benign**.

绿色化学家们在如何改变工艺过程，使反应更温和地发生方面得到启发。

3. it 作形式宾语的宾语从句

> We think it true **that the human body is also a good conductor**.

我们认为，人体也是电的良导体。

三、表语从句的译法

在句中，凡是充当表语成分的句子叫做表语从句。翻译表语从句一般都可以按原文顺序翻译，即先译主语后译从句，多采用"是"的句式，但也可以灵活处理，如下。

> One of the advantages of the catalytic cracking is **that it can increase the yield of products under milder operating conditions**.

催化裂化反应的优点之一是能在较温和的条件下提高产物的产率。

> The monomer ethene is **what the production of polyethylene needs**.

单体乙烯是生产聚乙烯所需要的东西。

四、同位语从句的译法

在句中，凡是充当同位语成分的句子叫做同位语从句。同位语是用来进一步解释名词或代词的。同位语从句一般由 that 引导。同位语从句常常解释和说明的名词主要有 fact, thought, theory, idea, hope, news, doubt, conclusion, question, problem, evidence, certainty, belief, rumor, mystery, suggestion, order, answer, decision, discovery, explanation, information, knowledge, law, opinion, principle, truth, promise, report, statement, message, saying, rule 等。同位语从句的译法主要有以下几种情况。

1. 译成独立句

有时可以把同位语从句译为一个独立的句子，这时其前可以增译"即"字，或采用冒号或破折号。这种方法适合于较长的同位语从句，如下。

➤ We come to the conclusion **that the climate is changing due to the emission of the greenhouse gas into the biosphere.**

我们得出的结论是：由于温室气体被释放到生物圈中，使气候发生改变。

有时为了修辞需要，也可以把同位语从句译成独立的句子，置于句首，如下。

➤ The principle **that gas can function while expanding has been applied to the steam engine.**

气体在膨胀时能做功，这一原理已应用于蒸汽机上。

2. 译成汉语的定语

尽管同位语从句不是定语从句，但有时其意义上和形式上接近定语从句，故汉译时也常把同位语从句转译为定语，如下。

➤ We all know the fact **that all elements are made up of atoms.**

我们都知道元素都是由原子组成的这一事实。

3. 转换译法

有时同位语说明的名词常常含有动作意义，如 suggestion, discovery, doubt, hope 等。一般可把这类名词转译为动词，故同位语从句往往随之被转译为汉语的主谓结构短语（类似宾语从句），如下。

➤ He made a suggestion **that the biosynthetic method can be used to reduce the amount of solvent used in a chemical industry.**

他建议采用生物合成法来降低溶剂在化学工业中的使用。

➤ There is now an increasing expectation **that not only their synthesis be considered, but also their use and disposal.**

人们越来越期望（化学家们）不仅要考虑化学品的合成，还要考虑它们的使用和处理。

Unit Seven   Macromolecular Material

Lesson Fourteen   Polymerizations by Chain Reactions

General properties of polymerizations

A chain polymerization consists of three stages:

- **Initiation**: an initiating reaction creates an active site on a monomer.
- **Propagation**: starting from the 'activated' monomer, the chain grows step by step by repetitive addition of a monomer and regeneration of the active site at each step of the growth process.
- **Termination**: a termination reaction destroys the active site; the macromolecule is definitely constituted.

A chain polymerization can be radicalar, anionic, or stereospecific according to the type of initiator used. The reaction may occur in bulk, in suspension, in emulsion and in solution. It is necessary to choose adequate temperatures for a good control of the processes.

(a) In bulk: the liquid monomer is placed in the presence of an initiator; the removal of heat may be difficult, especially when the monomer is a solvent of the polymer, because in this case the viscosity of the mixture increases in the course of the reaction.

(b) In suspension: the monomer is suspended in small droplets in a liquid (water, in general); the initiator is dissolved in the monomer and the reaction takes place in the droplets, the water being used for the removal of heat.

(c) In emulsion: the monomer is in aqueous emulsion and polymerization takes place in the micelles. However, the initiator is soluble in water (and not in the monomer). Each micelle can contain only one radical, and consequently very high molecular masses can be obtained.

(d) In solution: the monomer and the initiator are dissolved in a solvent; very often the polymer is also soluble in the solvent.

Free-radical polymerization

Radical polymerizations are very commonly used. In this case, the active site is an atom bearing a unpaired electron (free bond). The initiator is an organic material which can spontaneously split by hemolytic breaking and in this way can produce free radicals able to attack the monomer and thus to initiate the process. Actually, as initiators, one uses peroxides (R' —O—O—R''), hydroperoxides (R' —O—O—H) (for instance hydrogen peroxide; H_2O_2, or cumene hydroperoxide) and aliphatic azo (R—N=R'').

Generation of Free Radicals

One of the most common initiators is benzoic anhydride (benzoyl peroxide)with the formula

$$\varphi-\underset{\underset{O}{\|}}{C}-O-O-\underset{\underset{O}{\|}}{C}-\varphi$$

Where φ represents a benzene ring ($\varphi \rightarrow C_6H_5$).

This initiator is used for the preparation of polystyrene. One reaction commonly used to produce free radicals is the thermal or photochemical decomposition of benzoyl peroxide. For instance, around 70℃, benzoyl peroxide decomposes into 'primary' radicals.

$$\varphi-\underset{\underset{O}{\|}}{C}-O-O-\underset{\underset{O}{\|}}{C}-\varphi \longrightarrow 2\varphi-\underset{\underset{O}{\|}}{C}-O^{\bullet}$$

$$\varphi-\underset{\underset{O}{\|}}{C}-O^{\bullet} \longrightarrow \varphi^{\bullet} + CO_2$$

Initiation

The carbon-carbon double bond of styrene is, because of its relatively low stability, particulary susceptible to attack by a free radical. The free radical $\varphi^{\bullet}$ can react on a monomer (styrene), that is , the free radical $\varphi^{\bullet}$ adds to the double bond of styrene with the regeneration of another radical.

$$\varphi^{\bullet} + CH_2=\underset{\underset{\varphi}{|}}{CH} \longrightarrow \varphi-CH_2-\underset{\underset{\varphi}{|}}{CH}^{\bullet}$$

The regeneration of the radical is characteristic of chain reactions.

Propagation

The free radical molecule produced in this manner can now react on another monomer

$$\varphi-CH_2-\underset{\underset{\varphi}{|}}{CH}^{\bullet} + CH_2=\underset{\underset{\varphi}{|}}{CH} \longrightarrow \varphi-CH_2-\underset{\underset{\varphi}{|}}{CH}-CH_2-\underset{\underset{\varphi}{|}}{CH}^{\bullet}$$

and so on.

In a general way, the reaction can be written

$$R^{\bullet} + M \longrightarrow R - M^{\bullet}$$
$$R - M_N^{\bullet} + M \longrightarrow R - M_{N+1}^{\bullet}$$

where $R^{\bullet}$ is a primary radical and M is the monomer.

Termination

Propagation would continue until the supply of monomer was exhausted were it not for the strong tendency of radical to react in pairs to form a paired-electron covalent bond with loss of radical activity.

The deactivation occurs by recombination of radicals with one another

$$R - M_N^{\bullet} + {}^{\bullet}M_{N'}-R \longrightarrow R - M_{N+N'}-R$$

(and also $R^{\bullet} + {}^{\bullet}R \longrightarrow R-R$) or by dismutation, in which the migration of hydrogen from a radical to another radical results in the formation of two molecules with one saturated and one unsaturated end group .

$$-\underset{\underset{}{}}{\overset{H}{\underset{H_2}{C}}}-\underset{\underset{X}{|}}{\overset{|}{C}}^{\bullet} + -\underset{\underset{}{}}{\overset{H}{\underset{H_2}{C}}}-\underset{\underset{X}{|}}{\overset{|}{C}}^{\bullet} \longrightarrow -\underset{\underset{}{}}{\overset{H}{\underset{H_2}{C}}}-\underset{\underset{X}{|}}{\overset{|}{CH}} + -\underset{}{\overset{}{C}}=\underset{\underset{X}{|}}{\overset{H}{\underset{H}{C}}}$$

The chain length depends on the relative quantities of polymer and initiator that are used but also on the transfer frequency. The lifetime of a radical varies from 10^{-1} to 10 seconds. The polymerization reaction stops spontaneously by deactivation.

New Words and Expressions

polymerization [ˌpɔliməraiˈzeiʃən, -riˈz-] *n.* 聚合；[高分子] 聚合作用

initiate [iˈniʃieit, iˈniʃiət, -eit] *vt.* 开始，创始；发起；使初步了解，现在分词 initiating

monomer [ˈmɔnəmə] *n.* 单体；单元结构

repetitive [riˈpetətiv] *a.* 重复的

termination [ˌtəːmiˈneiʃən] *n.* 结束，终止

macromolecule [ˌmækrəuˈmɔlikjuːl] *n.* [高分子] 高分子；[化] 大分子

definitely [ˈdefinitli] *adv.* 清楚地，当然；明确地，肯定地

anionic [ˌænaiˈɔnik] *a.* 阴离子的，带负电荷的离子的

stereospecific [ˌsteriəuspiˈsifik, ˌstie-] *a.* [化] 立体有择的，立体定向的 [亦作 stereoregular]

adequate [ˈædikwit] *a.* 充足的；适当的；胜任的

viscosity [viˈskɔsəti] *n.* [物] 黏性，[物] 黏度

dissolve [diˈzɔlv] *vt.* 使溶解；使分解；使液化

aqueous [ˈeikwiəs] *a.* 水的，水般的

emulsion [iˈmʌlʃən] *n.* [物化] 乳状液；感光乳剂

micelle [miˈsel, mai-] *n.* [化，物，生] 胶粒；胶束，胶囊

soluble [ˈsɔljubl] *a.* 可溶的，可溶解的；可解决的

radical [ˈrædikəl] [化] 基的；[物化] 原子团

consequently [ˈkɔnsiˌkwəntli] *adv.* 因此；结果；所以

electron [iˈlektrɔn] *n.* 电子

spontaneously [spɔnˈteiniəsli] *adv.* 自发地；自然地；不由自主地

actually [ˈæktʃuəli] *adv.* 实际上；事实上

aliphatic [ˌæliˈfætik] *a.* 脂肪质的，[有化] 脂肪族的

azo [ˈæzəu] *a.* [化] 偶氮(基)的

hemolytic [hiːˈmɔlitik] *a.* [生理][免疫] 溶血的

anhydride [ænˈhaidraid] *n.* [化] 酸酐；脱水物

polystyrene [ˌpɔliˈstaiəriːn, -ˈstiərin] *n.* [高分子] 聚苯乙烯

photochemical [ˌfəutəuˈkemikəl] *a.* 光化学的

　　　　　　　　　　　　　　　n. 光催化学物

peroxide [pəˈrɔksaid] *n.* 过氧化物；过氧化氢

　　　　　　　　　　vt. 以过氧化氢漂白；以过氧化物处理

　　　　　　　　　　a. 以过氧化氢漂白的

propagation [ˌprɔpəˈgaeiʃən] *n.* 链增长；传播；繁殖；增殖

styrene [ˈstairiːn, ˈsti-] *n.* [有化] 苯乙烯

exhausted [igˈzɔːstid] *a.* 耗尽的；疲惫的

　　　　　　　　　　v. 用尽；耗尽；使…筋疲力尽

covalent [kəuˈveilənt]   a. [化]共价的；[化]共有原子价的

deactivation [di:ˌækti'veiʃən]   n. [物化] 减活化作用；钝化作用

recombination [ˌri:kɔmbi'neiʃən]   n. 复合，再结合；[遗] 重组

dismutation [ˌdismju'teiʃən]   n. 歧化作用

migration [mai'greiʃən]   n. [化学] [物] 移动，徙动

saturated ['sætʃəreitid]   a. 饱和的；深颜色的；渗透的

　　　　　　　　　　　　 v. 使渗透，使饱和

consist of   由…构成

step by step adv.   逐步地

according to   根据，按照；取决于；据…所说

in bulk   在本体中

in suspension   在悬浮液中

in emulsion   在乳液中

hemolytic breaking   平拆分解、均裂

hydrogen peroxide   [无化] 过氧化氢

benzoyl peroxide   [有化] 过氧化苯甲酰

Notes

1. Propagation: starting from the "activated" monomer, the chain grows step by step by repetitive addition of a monomer and regeneration of the active site at each step of the growth process.链增长：链从这个"被激活的"单体开始，通过重复地加入单体和活性位在每一步链成长过程中的再生，使得链逐步地长大。本句是一个简单句。现在分词短语 starting from the "activated" monomer 的逻辑主语是句子的主语 the chain。

2. The initiator is an organic material which can spontaneously split by hemolytic breaking and in this way can produce free radicals able to attack the monomer and thus to initiate the process.引发剂是一种有机物，通过均裂可以自发地分解，以这种方式引发剂能够产生易于进攻单体从而引发聚合反应的自由基。本句由一个主句和一个定语从句组成。able to attack the monomer and thus to initiate the process 是形容词短语做后置定语修饰 free radicals。

3. Propagation would continue until the supply of monomer was exhausted were it not for the strong tendency of radical to react in pairs to form a paired-electron covalent bond with loss of radical activity. 若不是自由基具有强烈地成对反应生成双电子的共价键的趋势,使自由基失活的话，链增长会一直进行下去，直到单体被耗尽。本句由一个主句、一个时间状语从句，一个条件状语从句组成。全句使用了虚拟语气,条件句 were it not for the strong tendency of radical to react in pairs to form a paired-electron covalent bond with loss of radical activity 由于包含了 were，省略了 if，把 were 放在了主语 it 前，这种结构在口语中很少使用。

Exercises

1. Put the following into Chinese

radical chain polymerization　　　　　the active site

in bulk   in suspension
in emulsion   in solution
free radicals   the thermal decomposition of benzoyl peroxide

2. Put the following into English

自由基的产生   链引发
链增长   链终止
初级自由基   自由基的寿命

3. Questions

How many stages does a chain polymerization consists of ?
What are they?

Lesson Fifteen   Polyethylene

Polyethylene or polyethene is a thermoplastic product heavily used in commodity (over 60M tons are produced worldwide every year). Its name originates from the monomer ethene. In the polymer industry the name is sometimes shortened to PE. Polyethylene is resistant to water, acids, alkalies, and most solvents. Its many applications include films or sheets for packaging, shower curtains, unbreakable bottles, pipes, pails, drinking glasses, and insulation for wire and cable.

It can be produced through radical polymerization, anionic polymerization, ion coordination polymerization or cationic polymerization. Each of these methods results in a different type of polyethylene.

Classification of Polyethylenes

Polyethylene is classified into several different categories based mostly on its density and branching. The mechanical properties of PE depend significantly on variables such as the extent and type of branching, the crystal structure, and the molecular weight.

- UHMWPE (ultra high molecular weight PE)
- HDPE (high density PE)
- PEX (cross-linked PE)
- MDPE (medium density PE)
- LDPE (low density PE)
- LLDPE (linear low density PE)

UHMWPE is polyethylene with a molecular weight numbering in the millions, usually between 3.1 and 5.67 million. The high molecular weight makes it a very tough material. UHMWPE can be made through any catalyst technology, although Ziegler catalysts are most common. Because of its outstanding toughness and its cut, wear and excellent chemical resistance, UHMWPE is used in a diverse range of applications. These include can and bottle handling machine parts, moving parts on weaving machines, bearings, gears, artificial joints, edge protection on ice rinks and butchers' chopping boards.

HDPE is defined by a density of 0.941 g/cm^3. HDPE has a low degree of branching and thus stronger intermolecular forces and tensile strength. HDPE can be produced by chromium/silica catalysts, Ziegler-Natta catalysts or metallocene catalysts. HDPE is used in products for packaging such as milk jugs, detergent bottles, margarine tubs, garbage containers and water pipes. One third of all toys are manufactured from HDPE. In 2007 the global HDPE consumption reached a volume of more than 30 million tons.

PEX is a medium-to high-density polyethylene containing cross-link bonds, which can chang the thermoplast into an elastomer. The high-temperature properties of the polymer are improved, its flow is reduced and its chemical resistance is enhanced. PEX is used in some potable water plumbing systems, because tubes made of the material can be expanded to fit over a metal nipple, and it will slowly return to its original shape, forming a permanent, water-tight connection.

MDPE is defined by a density range of 0.926~0.940 g/cm^3. MDPE can be produced by chromium/silica catalysts, Ziegler-Natta catalysts or metallocene catalysts. MDPE has good shock and drop resistance properties. MDPE is typically used in gas pipes and fittings, sacks, shrink film, packaging film, carrier bags and screw closures.

LDPE is defined by a density range of 0.910 ~ 0.940g/cm^3. LDPE has less strong intermolecular forces, which results in a lower tensile strength and increased ductility. LDPE is created by free radical polymerization. LDPE is used for both rigid containers and plastic film applications such as plastic bags and film wrap.

LLDPE is defined by a density range of 0.915~0.925 g/cm^3. LLDPE is a substantially linear polymer, with significant numbers of short branches, commonly made by copolymerization of ethylene with short-chain alpha-olefins (e.g. 1-butene, 1-hexene, and 1-octene). LLDPE is used predominantly in film applications due to its toughness, flexibility and relative transparency. Product examples range from agricultural films, saran wrap, and bubble wrap, to multilayer and composite films.

Recently much research activity has focused on the nature and distribution of long chain branches in polyethylene.

New Words and Expressions

polyethylene [ˌpɔliːˈeθəˌliːn] *n*. [高分子] 聚乙烯

thermoplastic [ˌθəːməuˈplæstik] *a*. 热塑性的

                                                    n. [塑料] 热塑性塑料

consumer [kənˈsjuːmə] *n*. 消费者；用户，顾客

ethene [ˈeθiːn] *n*. 乙烯（等于 ethylene）

insulation [ˌinsjuˈleiʃən, ˈinsə-] *n*. 绝缘；隔离，孤立

ion [ˈaiən] *n*. [化] 离子

category [ˈkætigəri] *n*. 种类，分类；[数] 范畴

branching [ˈbræntʃiŋ] *a*. 发枝的；分歧的

                                           n. 分支；分歧

toughness [ˈtʌfnis] *n*. [力] 韧性；有黏性

diverse [daiˈvəːs, di-] *a*. 不同的；多种多样的；变化多的

bearing [ˈbɛəriŋ] *n*. [机] 轴承

gear [giə] *n*. 齿轮；装置，工具；传动装置

artificial [ˌɑːtiˈfiʃəl] *a*. 人造的；仿造的

joint [dʒɔint] *n*. 关节

rink [ˈriŋk] *n*. 溜冰场，室内溜冰场；冰球场

butcher [ˈbutʃə] *n*. 屠夫

aramid [ˈærəmid] *n*. [材料学] 芳族聚酰胺纤维；芳族聚酰胺；芳纶

articular [ɑːˈtikjulə] *a*. [解剖学] 关节的

implant [imˈplɑːnt, -ˈplænt, ˈimplɑːnt, -plænt] *n*. [医] 植入物；植入管

                                           vi. 被移植

hip [hip] *n*. 髋关节

tensile ['tensail, -səl] *a.* [物] 张力的；拉力的；抗张力的

metallocene [mi'tæləusi:n] *n.* [化] 金属茂(合物)；茂(合)金属

jug [dʒʌg] *n.* [轻] 水壶；监牢

margarine [,mɑ:dʒə'ri:n] *n.* 人造黄油；人造奶油

tub [tʌb] *n.* 浴盆；桶

garbage ['gɑ:bidʒ] *n.* 垃圾；废物

cross-link ['krɔ:s,liŋk] *n.* [化] (聚合物的)交联；交联键

thermoplast ['θə:məuplæst] *n.* [化] 热塑性塑料

elastomer [i'læstəmə] *n.* [化] 弹性体，高弹体

nipple ['nipl] *n.* 螺纹接套；乳头，奶头；奶嘴

permanent ['pə:mənent] *a.* 永久的，永恒的；不变的

substantially [səb'stænʃəli] *adv.* 实质上；大体上；充分地

alpha ['ælfə] *n.* [化] α-位，子位；α-位(或子位)异构(化合)物

olefin ['əuləfin, 'ɔ-] *n.* 烯烃

flexibility [,fleksə'biliti] *n.* 弹性；适应性；灵活性

transparency [træns'pærənsi, -'pɛə-, trænz-, trɑ:n-] *n.* 透明，透明度

multilayer ['mʌlti,leiə] *a.* 有多层的
                              n. 多分子层

originate from   发源于

be resistant to   对…有抵抗作用

Ziegler-Natta   齐格勒催化剂

potable water plumbing systems   饮用水管道系统

water-tight connection.   防水连接

saran wrap   保鲜膜

Notes

1. Because of its outstanding toughness and its cut, wear and excellent chemical resistance, UHMWPE is used in a diverse range of applications.由于其突出的韧性和切割性、耐磨性以及优良的耐化学性，超高分子量聚乙烯用于不同的应用范围。

2. PEX is used in some potable water plumbing systems, because tubes made of the material can be expanded to fit over a metal nipple, and then it will slowly return to its original shape, forming a permanent, water-tight connection. PEX 用于某些饮用水管道系统,这种材料制成的管子能延展,以适应金属的螺纹接头，然后它将会慢慢地回到原来的形状,形成一个永久性防水连接。

3. LDPE has less strong intermolecular forces, which results in a lower tensile strength and increased ductility.低密度聚乙烯分子间作用力较弱，这使它拉伸强度降低、韧性提高。

Exercises

1. Put the following into Chinese

polyethylene (PE)   ultra high molecular weight PE high density PE   high density cross-linked PE

cross-linked PE   medium density PE

low density PE   linear low density PE

2. Questions

Please give the short form of the following substances.

Polyethylene   ultra high molecular weight polyethylene

high density polyethylene   high density cross-linked polyethylene

cross-linked polyethylene   medium density polyethylene

 low density polyethylene   linear low density polyethylene

Reading Material: History of Plastics

Historians frequently classify the early ages of man according to the materials that he used for making his implements and other basic necessities. The most well known of these periods are the Stone Age, the Iron Age and the Bronze Age. Such a system of classification cannot be used to describe subsequent periods for with the passage of time man learnt to use other materials and by the time of the ancient civilisations of Egypt and Babylonia he was employing a range of metals, stones, woods, ceramics, glasses, skins, horns and fibres. Until the 19th century man's inanimate possessions, his home, his tools, his furniture, were made from varieties of these eight classes of material.

During the last century and a half, two new closely related classes of material have been introduced which have not only challenged the older materials for their well-established uses but have also made possible new products which have helped to extend the range of activities of mankind. Without these two groups of materials, rubbers and plastics, it is difficult to conceive how such everyday features of modern life such as the motor car, the telephone and the television set could ever have been developed.

Whereas the use of natural rubber was well established by the start of the twentieth century, the major growth period of the plastics industry has been since 1930. This is not to say that some of the materials now classified as plastics were unknown before this time since the use of the natural plastics may be traced well into antiquity.

we read that the mother of Moses 'when she could no longer hide him, she took for him an ark of bull rushes and daubed it with slime and with pitch, and put the child therein and she laid it in the flags by the river's brink. Biblical commentaries indicate that slime is the same as bitumen but whether or not this is so we have here the precursor of our modem fibre-reinforced plastics boat.

In Ancient Egypt mummies were wrapped in cloth dipped in a solution of bitumen in oil of lavender which was known variously as Syrian Asphalt or Bitumen of Judea. On exposure to light the product hardened and became insoluble. It would appear that this process involved the action of chemical cross-linking, which in modem times became of great importance in the vulcanization of rubber and the production of thermosetting plastics. It was also the study of this process that led Niepce to produce the first permanent photograph and to the development of lithography.

In Ancient Rome, Pliny the Elder dedicated 37 volumes of *Natural History* to the emperor Titus. In the last of these books, dealing with gems and precious stones, he describes the properties of the fossil resin, amber. The ability of amber to attract dust was recognised and in fact the word electricity is derived from *elektron*, the Greek for amber.

Further east another natural resin, lac, had already been used for at least a thousand years before Pliny was born. Lac is mentioned in early Vedic writings and also in the *Kama Sutra* of Vatsyayona. In 1596 John Huyglen von Linschoeten undertook a scientific mission to India at the instance of the King of Portugal. In his report he describes the process of covering objects with shellac, now known as Indian turnery and still practiced.

Early records also indicate that cast mouldings were prepared from shellac by the ancient Indians. In Europe the use of sealing wax based on shellac can be traced back to the Middle Ages. The first patents for shellac mouldings were taken out in 1868.

The introduction to western civilisation of another natural resin from the east took place in the middle of the 17th century. To John Tradescant (1608-1662), the English traveller and gardener, is given the credit of introducing gutta percha. The material became of substantial importance as a cable insulation material and for general moulding purposes during the 19th century and it is only since 1940 that this material has been replaced by synthetic materials in undersea cable insulation.

Prior to the eastern adventures of Linschoeten and Tradescant, the sailors of Columbus had discovered the natives of Central America playing with lumps of natural rubber. These were obtained, like gutta percha, by coagulation from a latex; the first recorded reference to natural rubber was in Valdes *La historia natural y general de las Indias,* published in Seville (1535—1557). In 1731 la Condamine, leading an expedition on behalf of the French government to study the shape of the earth, sent back from the Amazon basin rubber-coated cloth prepared by native tribes and used in the manufacture of waterproof shoes and flexible bottles.

The coagulated rubber was a highly elastic material and could not be shaped by moulding or extrusion. In 1820 an Englishman, Thomas Hancock, discovered that if the rubber was highly sheared or masticated, it became plastic and hence capable of flow. This is now known to be due to severe reduction in molecular weight on mastication. In 1839 an American, Charles Goodyear, found that rubber heated with sulphur retained its elasticity over a wider range of temperature than the raw material and that it had greater resistance to solvents. Thomas Hancock also subsequently found that the plastic masticated rubber could be regenerated into an elastic material by heating with molten sulphur. The rubber-sulphur reaction was termed vulcanisation by William Brockendon, a friend of Hancock. Although the work of Hancock was subsequent to, and to some extent a consequence of, that of Goodyear, the former patented the discovery in 1843 in England whilst Goodyear's first (American) patent was taken out in 1844.

In extensions of this work on vulcanisation, which normally involved only a few per cent of sulphur, both Goodyear and Hancock found that if rubber was heated with larger quantities of sulphur (about 50 parts per 100 parts of rubber) a hard product was obtained. This subsequently became known variously as ebonite, vulcanite and hard rubber. A patent for producing hard rubber was taken out by Nelson Goodyear in 1851.

The discovery of ebonite is usually considered as a milestone in the history of the rubber industry. Its importance in the history of plastics materials, of which it obviously is one, is generally neglected. Its significance lies in the fact that ebonite was the first thermosetting plastics material to be prepared and also the first plastics material which involved a distinct chemical modification of a natural material. By 1860 there was a number of manufacturers in Britain, including Charles Macintosh who is said to have started making ebonite in 1851. There are reports of the material having been exhibited at the Great Exhibition of 1851.

科技英语翻译七　定语从句的翻译方法

在句中，用来修饰某一名词或代词，而起定语作用的句子叫做定语从句。定语从句通常位于它所修饰的词之后。定语从句主要分为限制性定语从句和非限制性定语从句，另外还有一些特殊结构的定语从句，如由 as 引导的定语从句的定语从句等。

引导定语从句的词称为关系词，分为关系代词，如 which、that、who、whom、whose、as 等和关系副词，如 when、where、why、how 等。

一、限制性定语从句的译法

限制性定语从句用来修饰、限制它所说明的先行词，互相之间关系紧密，通常定语从句与先行词之间没有逗号。

1. 合译法

合译法就是把英语原文的定语从句译成汉语带"的"字的定语词组，这样，原英语的主句和定语从句就被合译成了汉语的单句。从定语从句位置的变化角度讲，定语从句译在了先行词前，所以也叫倒译法。这种方法尤其适合于翻译不太复杂的定语从句，如下。

➤ The mixture of steam and gas enters the reformer **which is filled with a nickel-based reforming catalyst**.

水蒸气和天然气的混合气体进入**装满镍基催化剂的**重整反应器中。

➤ Cracking is a petroleum refining process **in which heavy-molecular weight hydrocarbons are broken up into light hydrocarbon molecules.**

催化裂化是**一种把大分子量的碳氢化合物分解为小分子碳氢化合物的**石油炼制过程。

2. 分译法

分译法主要用于两种情况：一是较长的限制性定语从句；一是定语从句虽然不长，但先行词的前置修饰语较多。在这两种情况下，多采用分译法，即将定语从句译为一个并列分句，并放在所修饰的词的后面。此类翻译方法就是在后置的并列分句的译文中增加了"它"、"这"、"这些"等代词以重复关系词所代表的含义。

（1）重复先行词

➤ Thermal cracking is a refining process **in which heat (～800℃) and pressure (～700 kPa) are used to break down, rearrange, or combine hydrocarbon molecules.**

热裂化是一种精制过程，**该过程在高温(～800℃)高压(～700kPa)下使碳氢化合物分子分解、重排和化合。**

➤ The cracked product is charged to a fractionating column **where it is separated into fractions.**

裂解产物被送到分馏塔，**在那里它被分离成各种馏分。**

（2）省译先行词

➤ The initiator is an organic material **which can spontaneously split by hemolytic breaking.**

引发剂是一种有机物，能自发地均裂而分解。

3. 译为词组

任何语言都要求在表达上尽可能地做到简练、明确，这叫做"经济原则"。英语中的定语从句是一个起定语作用的句子，结构往往比较复杂，但是我们有时可以把定语从句（一般为限制性定语从句）简化为汉语的一个词组。这样做，不仅与原义并行不悖，且更言简意赅，如下。

➤ The hydrocracking of paraffins is the only one reforming reaction **that consumes hydrogen**.

链烷烃加氢裂化是唯一一个耗氢重整反应。

➤ Diamond is the hardest natural substance **that is known**.

金刚石是已知最硬的天然物质。

二、非限制性定语从句的译法

英语非限制性定语从句与其修饰的先行词关系不很紧密，只起描写、叙述、解释或补充说明的作用。非限制性定语从句最明显的标志是与被它所修饰的词用逗号分开，that 作为关系代词不能引导非限制性定语从句。非限制性定语从句的译法主要有以下几种情况。

1. 合译法

英语中大多数非限制性定语从句汉译时，可译为并列分句或各种状语从句。但是，如果非限制性定语从句比较简短，且与主句关系密切时，也可以与主句合译，将非限制性定语从句译为汉语的 "的" 字结构定语，如下。

➤ The mixture, **which has a 3:1 mole ratio of hydrogen and nitrogen**, is cooled to 38℃.

氢气和氮气的摩尔比为3:1的混合物被冷却到38℃。

2. 分译法

如果非限制性定语从句补充说明某个词时，汉译时常常可以译为并列分句，分句主语可重复先行词，也可用"他（它）"、"他（它）们"、"该"、"这"等词来代替先行词，如下。

➤ The basis for both of these observations is the law of conservation of mass, **which states that mass can neither be created nor destroyed**.

观察这两种事物的依据是质量守恒定律，该定律阐述了物质既不能被创生也不能被消灭。

➤ The catalytic reforming catalysts contain the noble metals, **which are very susceptible to poisoning by sulfur and nitrogen compounds**.

催化重整催化剂中含有贵金属，它们易被含硫和氮的化合物毒化。

3. 译成独立句

有时 which 引导的非限制性定语从句不是修饰句子中的某个名词，而是指前面整个句子的意思，这种特殊的定语从句也可译为一个独立的单句，这个独立的主语常常用代词"这"来代替，如下。

➤ Liquid water changes to vapor, **which is called evaporation**.

液体水变成蒸汽，这就叫蒸发。

➤ **As is well known to us**, there are two different kinds of uranium: uranium-238, uranium-235.

如我们所知，有两种不同的铀：铀238和铀235。

上一例句中 as 作为关系代词，置于了句首，另外它也可以放在句中和句末。在大多数情况下，从句中的谓语动词可以省去一部分。As 可以与其他词搭配形成固定词组，且有固定的译法，常见的有：

as is well know to all	众所周知
as expected	正如所料
as mentioned above	如上所述
as shown in the figure	如图所示
as seen from the table	正如表中看出

三、状语化定语从句的翻译方法

所谓状语化定语从句，就是这种从句在形式上是定语，在功能上是状语。因此，不能把这类从句译成定语从句。翻译时，我们应视其全句的逻辑关系及内含语义，将这类状语化的定语从句译成表示原因、结果、时间或让步等的分句。

1. 译成时间状语从句

➤ Electrical energy **that is supplied to a lamp** can be turned into light energy.

把电供给电灯时，它就转变成光能。

2. 译成原因状语从句

➤ Transformers cannot operate by direct current, **which would burn out the wires in the transformers**.

变压器不能使用直流电，因为直流电会烧坏其中的导线。

3. 译成结果状语从句

➤ The reaction is catalyzed by Co or Rh, **which considerably enhances the rate of the reaction**.

由钴或铑催化这个反应，这样可以大大地提高该反应速率。

4. 译成条件状语从句

➤ The remainder of atom **from which one or more electrons are removed** must be positively charged.

如果从原子中移走一个或多个电子，则该原子的其余部分必定带正电荷。

5. 译成让步状语从句

➤ Atoms, **which are very, very small**, can be broken up into still smaller particles—electrons, protons and neutrons.

原子虽然很小很小，但仍能分解为更小的颗粒——电子、质子和中子。

Unit Eight   Fine Chemical Engineering

Lesson Sixteen   Surfactant

Surfactants Adsorb at Interfaces

Surfactant is an abbreviation for surface active agent, which literally means active at a surface. In other words, a surfactant is characterized by its tendency to absorb at surfaces and interfaces. The term interface denotes a boundary between any two immiscible phases; the term surface indicates that one of the phases is a gas, usually air. Altogether five different interfaces exist:

- Solid-vapour   surface
- Solid-liquid
- Solid-solid
- Liquid-vapour   surface
- Liquid-liquid

The driving force for a surfactant to adsorb at an interface is to lower the free energy of that phase boundary. The term interfacial tension is often used instead of interfacial free energy. When that boundary is covered by surfactant molecules, the surface tension is reduced.The denser the surfactant packing at the interface, then the larger the reduction in surface tension.

Surfactants may adsorb at all of the five types of interfaces listed above. Here, the discussion will be restricted to interfaces involving a liquid phase. The liquid is usually, but not always water. Examples of the different interfaces and products are given in Table 8.1.

Table 8.1   Examples of interfaces involving a liquid phase

Interface	Type of system	Product
solid-liquid	suspension	solvent-borne paint
liquid-liquid	emulsion	milk, cream
liquid-vapour	foam	shaving, cream

All of the interfaces are stabilized by surfactants. The total interfacial area of such a system is immense: the oil-water and solid-water interfaces of one litre of paint may cover several football fields.

As mentioned above, the tendency to accumulate at interfaces is a fundamental property of a surfactant. In principle, the stronger the tendency, then the better the surfactant. The degree of surfactant concentration at a boundary depends on the surfactant structure and also on the nature of the two phases that meet at the interface. Therefore, there is no universally good surfactant, suitable for all uses. The choice will depend on the application. A good surfactant should have low solubility in the bulk phases.

There is, of course, a limit to the surface and interfacial tension lowering effect by the surfactant. In the normal case that limit is reached when micelles start to form in bulk solution.

Surfactants Aggregate in Solution

As discussed above, one characteristic feature of surfactants is their tendency to adsorb at interfaces. Another fundamental property of surface active agents is that unimers in solution tend to form aggregates, so-called micelles. (The free or unassociated surfactant is referred to in the literature either as 'monomer' or 'unimer'.) Micelle formation, or micellization, can be viewed as an alternative mechanism to adsorption at the interfaces for removing hydrophobic groups from contact with water, thereby reducing the free energy of the system. The micelles may be seen as a reservoir for surfactant unimers.

Micelles are already generated at very low surfactant concentrations in water. The concentration at which micelles start to form is called the critical micelle concentration, or CMC, and is an important characteristic of a surfactant.

Surfactants are Amphiphilic

The name amphiphile is sometimes used synonymously with surfactant. The word is derived from the Greek word amphi, meaning both, and the term relates to the fact that all surfactant molecules consist of at least two parts, one which is soluble in a specific fluid (the lyophilic part) and one which is insoluble(the lyophobic part). When the fluid is water one usually talks about the hydrophilic and hydrophobic parts, respectively. The hydrophilic part is referred to as the head group and the hydrophobic part as the tail (see Figure 8.1).

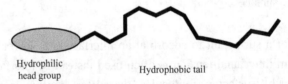

Hydrophilic
head group   Hydrophobic tail

Figure 8.1   Schematic illustration of a surfactant

Surfactants are Classified by the polar Head Group

The primary classification of surfactants is made on the basis of the charge of the polar head group. It is common practice to divide surfactants into the classes anionics, cationics, non-ionics and zwitterionics.

A non-ionic surfactant has no charge groups in its head. The head of an ionic surfactant carries a net charge. If the charge is negative, the surfactant is more specifically called anionic; if the charge is positive, it is called cationic. If a surfactant contains a head with two oppositely charged groups, it is termed zwitterionic (see Figure 8.2) .

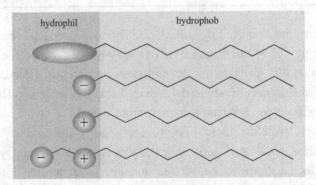

hydrophil   hydrophob

Figure 8.2   anionics, cationics, non-ionics and zwitterionics

New Words and Expressions

surfactant　[səˈfæktənt]　*n.* [化]表面活性剂
　　　　　　　　　　　　a. [化]表面活性剂的
literally　[ˈlitərəli]　*adv.* 照字面地；逐字地
denote　[diˈnəut]　*vt.* 表示，指示
immense　[iˈmens]　*a.* 巨大的，广大的；无边无际的；[口]非常好的
litre　[ˈliːtə]　*n.* 公升
application　[ˌæpliˈkeiʃən]　*n.* 应用；申请；应用程序；敷用
solubility　[ˌsɔljuˈbiləti]　*n.* 溶解性；可溶性；溶解度
bulk　[bʌlk]　*n.* 体积，容量；大块；大多数，大部分
　　　　　　vt. 使扩大，使形成大量；使显得重要
aggregate　[ˈæɡriɡət, ˈæɡriɡeit]　*vi., vt.* 聚集；集合；合计
tendency　[ˈtendənsi]　*n.* 倾向，趋势；癖好
unimers　[ˈjuːnimə(r)]　*n.* [化]单聚体
micellization　[miˌselaiˈzeiʃən, -liˈz-]　*n.* 胶束形成；胶束化
alternative　[ɔːlˈtəːnətiv]　*a.* 供选择的；选择性的；交替的
mechanism　[ˈmekənizəm]　*n.* 机制；原理，途径；进程；机械装置；技巧
reservoir　[ˈrezəvwɑː]　*n.* 储藏所；仓库；水库；蓄水池
amphiphile　[ˈæmfiˌfail]　*n.* [化]两亲物；亲水脂分子
synonymous　[siˈnɔniməs]　*a.* 同义的；同义词的；同义突变的
cationic　[ˌkætaiˈɔnik]　*n.* 阳离子
　　　　　　　　　　　a. 阳离子的
zwitterionics　[ˌzwitəraiˈɔnik]　*n.* 两性离子
　　　　　　　　　　　　　a. 两性离子的
be restricted to　仅限于…；局限于…
in principle　大体上，原则上
hydrophobic groups　疏水基
the critical micelle concentration　临界胶束浓度
the lyophilic part　亲水部分
is referred to as　被称为…
common practice　惯例、常见的做法

Notes

1. The degree of surfactant concentration at a boundary depends on the surfactant structure and also on the nature of the two phases that meet at the interface. 界面表面活性剂浓度的大小取决于表面活性剂的结构和构成界面的两相的性质。the surfactant structure 和 the nature of the two phases that meet at the interface 是并列成分，做 depends on 的宾语。the nature of the two phases that meet at the interface 中的 that meet at the interface 是定语从句修饰 two phases。

2. There is, of course, a limit to the surface and interfacial tension lowering effect by the surfactant. 当然，表面活性剂使表面或者界面张力降低的效果是有限度的。of course 是插入语。原句是 there be 句型。a limit to something 某事物的限度（限制）。the surface and interfacial tension lowering effect by the surfactant 中的 lowering effect by the surfactant 是现在分词短语做后置定语修饰 the surface and interfacial tension。

3. The concentration at which micelles start to form is called the critical micelle concentration, or CMC, and is an important characteristic of a surfactant. 胶束开始生成的浓度称为临界胶束浓度，或者是 CMC，临界胶束浓度也是表面活性剂的一个重要性质。The concentration at which micelles start to form 是主语部分，其中 which micelles start to form 是定语从句修饰 concentration。is called the critical micelle concentration, or CMC 和 is an important characteristic of a surfactant 是并列结构，主语同是 The concentration。

4. The word is derived from the Greek word amphi, meaning both, and the term relates to the fact that all surfactant molecules consist of at least two parts, one which is soluble in a specific fluid (the lyophilic part) and one which is insoluble(the lyophobic part). 这个词源于希腊语的 amphi，意思是两个，这个术语关系到这样一个事实，即所有表面活性剂分子至少由两部分组成，一部分溶于某一液体中（亲水部分），另一部分不能溶于该液体（疏水部分）。that all surfactant molecules consist of at least two parts, one which is soluble in a specific fluid (the lyophilic part) and one which is insoluble(the lyophobic part)是同位语从句，说明 the fact 的内容。

Exercises

1. Put the following into Chinese

surfactant	surface
interface	boundary
interfacial tension	interfacial free energy
aggregate	micelle formation

2. Put the following into English

临界胶束浓度	亲水的
疏水的	阴离子
阳离子	非离子
两性离子	液相

3. Questions

What is a surfactant?

What is a surfactant characterized by?

Lesson Seventeen   Detergent Formulation

A Detergent Formulation is Complex

Removal of soil from fabric, i.e. detergency, is a complex process involving interactions between surfactants, soil and the textile surface. The choice of surfactant is the key to success and surfactant-based cleaning compositions are one of the oldest forms of formulated products for technical use. The traditional surfactants are sodium and potassium salts of fatty acids, made by saponification of triglycerides. Soaps are still included in smaller amounts in many detergent formulations but the bulk surfactants in use today are synthetic non-ionics and anionics, with alcohol ethoxylates, alkylaryl sulfonates, alkyl sulfates and alkyl ether sulfates being the most prominent.

The term oily 'soil' refers to petroleum products, such as motor oil and vegetable oil, e.g. butter, but also skin sebum. Surfactants play the key role in removing oily soil but hydrolytic enzymes, which are present in most detergent formulations today, are important for hydrolysis of triglycerides, proteins and starch. In practice, oily soil is removed by the combined action of surfactants and enzymes.

Particulate soil, which may consist of clay and other minerals, is usually removed by a wetting and dispersing process in which the surfactant is assisted by highly charged anionic polyelectrolytes normally included in the formulation.

Some stains, such as those from tea and blood, may be difficult to remove even with optimized surfactant-enzyme combinations. Bleaching agents are often effective in eliminating such spots. These normally act by oxidizing the stain chromophores into non-coloured products which may, or may not, be removed by the action of surfactant.

A detergent formulation also contains a large amount of so-called 'builders', such as zeolite or phosphate, which function as sequestering agents for divalentions, thus preventing surfactant precipitation as Ca or Mg salts in areas of hard water. Other, less vital, additives are anti-redeposition agents, fluorescing agents, perfumes, etc.

In the following, the discussion will be limited to the action of surfactants on oily soil.

Various Mechanisms have been Proposed for Oily Soil Removal

The three most important mechanisms for the removal of oily soil are as follows:

(1) Roll-up (Figure 8.3).This mechanism is related to fabric wetting, i.e. the surfactant-fabric interaction is decisive. Good soil release is usually obtained when the contact angle is larger than 90°. This is typically the case for oily soil on polar textiles such as cotton. On polyester and other more non-polar fabrics, a contact angle of less than 90° is usually obtained.

(2) Emulsification (Figure 8.4).A low interfacial tension between oil and the surfactant solution is required. The mechanism involves surfactant-oil interaction and the process is independent of the nature of the fabric.

(3) Solubilization (Figure 8.5).The oily soil is solubilized into an in situ formed microemulsion. Similar to the emulsification mechanism, solubilization occurs independently of the underlying surface. The process requires ultra-low interfacial tension between oil and the surfactant solution.

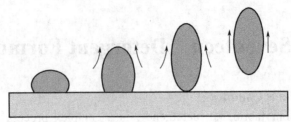

Figure 8.3   The roll-up mechanism of removal of oily soil from a solid surface

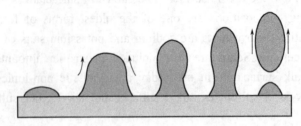

Figure 8.4   The emulsification mechanism of removal of oily soil from a solid surface

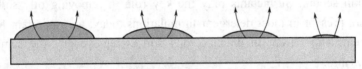

Figure 8.5   The solubilization mechanism of removal of oily soil from a solid surface

These three mechanisms for the removal of oily soil obviously do not operate independently. It is probably true to say, though, that whereas roll-up is the most important mechanism on polar textiles, emulsification and solubilization govern the results on non-polar materials. It is also true to say that whereas roll-up is relatively simple to achieve—most surfactants are good enough wetting agents — emulsification and, in particular, solubilization need finetuning of the surfactant composition. Effective solubilization is only obtained with surfactants that bring the interfacial tension of oil and water down to ultra-low values.

New Words and Expressions

detergent   [di'tə:dʒənt]   n. 清洁剂；去垢剂
detergency   [di'tə:dʒənsi,-dʒəns]   n. 洗净（作用）；去垢力，去垢性
formulation   [ˌfɔ:mju'leiʃən]   n. 配制；配方；制剂；配制成的材料；构想，规划；公式化
saponification   [səˌpɔnifi'keiʃən]   n. 皂化
triglycerides   [trai'glisəraid, -rid]   n. 甘油三酸酯
ethoxylate ['eθəksileit]   n. 乙氧基化物
sulfate   ['sʌlfeit]   n. 硫酸盐
                    vt. 使成硫酸盐；用硫酸处理；
alkyl ['ælkil]   a. 烷基的，烃基的
                    n. 烷基，烃基
ether ['i:θə]   n. 醚
prominent   ['prɔminənt]   a. 突出的，显著的；杰出的；卓越的

sebum ['siːbəm] n. 皮脂；牛羊脂

hydrolytic [ˌhaidrə'litik] a. 水解的，水解作用的

enzyme ['enzaim] n. 酶

starch [stɑːtʃ] n. [化]淀粉；刻板，生硬

wetting ['wetiŋ] n. 润湿

dispersing [di'spəːsiŋ] n. 分配，分散

polyelectrolyte [ˌpɔlii'lektrəˌlait] n. 聚合电解质

stain [stein] n. 污点；瑕疵；着色剂

　　　　　　　　 vi. 污染；被沾污

　　　　　　　　 vt. 沾污；败坏；给…着色

bleaching ['bliːtʃiŋ] a. 漂白的

　　　　　　　　 n. 漂白

chromophore ['krəuməfɔː] n. 发色团

phosphate ['fɔsfeit] n. [化]磷酸盐；[地]皮膜化成

precipitation [priˌsipi'teiʃən] n. 沉淀，沉淀物；冰雹；坠落；鲁莽

redeposition ['riːdipɔ'ziʃən] n. 再沉淀，再沉积；再沈积作用

fluoresce ['fluə'res] vi. 发荧光

decisive [di'saisiv] a. 决定性的；果断的，坚定的

emulsification [iˌmʌlsifi'keiʃən] n. [化] 乳化；[化] 乳化作用；乳剂化

solubilization [ˌsɔljubilai'zeiʃən, -li'z-] n. 溶解，增溶

microemulsion [ˌmaikrəui'mʌlʃən] n. 微乳液；微型乳剂

whereas [hwɛə'æz] conj. 然而；鉴于；反之

alcohol ethoxylates 醇聚氧乙烯醚

alkylaryl sulfonates 烷基苯磺酸盐

alkyl sulfates 烷基硫酸盐

alkyl ether sulfates 烷基醚硫酸盐

sequestering agents 螯合剂

anti-redeposition agents 抗沉积剂

roll-up 卷起作用

be independent of 不依赖…；不受…支配；独立于…之外

in situ 在原地，就地；在原来位置

the underlying surface 基质表面

Notes

1. Soaps are still included in smaller amounts in many detergent formulations but the bulk surfactants in use today are synthetic non-ionics and anionics, with alcohol ethoxylates, alkylaryl sulfonates, alkyl sulfates and alkyl ether sulfates being the most prominent. 许多洗涤剂的配制仍就使用少量的皂类，但是现在却大量使用非离子和阴离子表面活性剂，比较典型的产品有醇聚氧乙烯醚、烷基芳磺酸盐、烷基磺酸盐和烷基醚硫酸盐。本句由两个并列分句组成。with…being the most prominent 是独立主格结构，该结构做状语，说明 synthetic non-ionics and anionics 的情况。

2. Surfactants play the key role in removing oily soil but hydrolytic enzymes, which are present in most detergent formulations today, are important for hydrolysis of triglycerides, proteins and starch. 表面活性剂对油垢的去除起关键的作用，但是，现在很多洗涤剂配方中有水解酶，它对甘油三酯、蛋白质和淀粉的水解起着重要的作用。本句由两个并列分句和一个非限定性定语从句组成。

3. Particulate soil, which may consist of clay and other minerals, is usually removed by a wetting and dispersing process in which the surfactant is assisted by highly charged anionic polyelectrolytes normally included in the formulation. 由黏土和其他矿物质组成的污垢颗粒的去除，通常是表面活性剂的润湿和分散作用的结果，配方中的多电荷阴离子聚电解质促进了表面活性剂的这种作用。本句是由一个主句，两个定语从句组成。which may consist of clay and other minerals 是非限定性定语从句，先行词是 particulate soil. in which the surfactant is assisted by highly charged anionic polyelectrolytes normally included in the formulation 是限制性定语从句，先行词是 process。included in the formulation 过去分词短语做后置定语修饰 polyelectrolytes。

4. It is probably true to say, though, that whereas roll-up is the most important mechanism on polar textiles, emulsification and solubilization govern the results on non-polar materials. 尽管作用于极性织物上的机理主要是卷起作用，而作用于非极性材料上的机理的主要是乳化和增溶作用，这可能是真实的。it 是形式主语，真正的主语是不定式 to say。

Exercises

1. Put the following into Chinese

saponification of triglycerides   detergent formulations

alcohol ethoxylates   alkyl sulfates

alkylaryl sulfonates   alkyl ether sulfates

2. Put the following into English

水解酶   螯合剂

抗沉积剂   荧光增白剂

卷起作用   乳化作用

增溶作用   固体表面

3. Questions

What is a detergent formulation according to what you learned from the text?

Reading Material: Production of Anionic Surfactants

Anionics are used in greater volume than any other surfactant class. A rough estimate of the worldwide surfactant production is 10 million tons per year, out of which approximately 60% are anionics. One main reason for their popularity is the ease and low cost of manufacture. Anionics are used in most detergent formulations and the best detergency is obtained by alkyl and alkylate chains in the $C_{12}\sim C_{18}$ range. The counterions most commonly used are sodium, potassium, ammonium, calcium and various protonated alkyl amines.

Soap is still the largest single type of surfactant. It is produced by saponification of natural oils and fats. Soap is a generic name representing the alkali metal salt of a carboxylic acid derived from animal fats or vegetable oils. Soap bars are usually based on mixtures of fatty acids obtained from tallow, coconut and palm oil. Under the right conditions soaps are excellent surfactants. Their sensitivity to hard water is a major drawback.

$$
\begin{array}{l}
RCOOCH_2 \\
| \\
RCOOCH \quad + \quad 3NaOH \longrightarrow 3RCOONa \quad + \\
| \\
RCOOCH_2
\end{array}
\qquad
\begin{array}{l}
CH_2OH \\
| \\
CHOH \\
| \\
CH_2OH
\end{array}
$$

Alkylbenzene sulfonates are widely used in household detergents as well as in a variety of industrial applications. They are made by sulfonation of alkylbenzenes. In large-scale synthesis, sulfur trioxide is the sulfonating agent of choice but other reagents, such as sulfuric acid, oleum ($H_2SO_4 \cdot nSO_3$), chlorosulfonic acid($ClSO_3H$) or amido sulfonic acid(sulfamic acid,H_2NSO_3H), may also be used and may be preferred for specific purposes. Industrial synthesis is usually carried out in a continuous process, using a falling film reactor. The first step of the synthesis results in the formation of pyrosulfonic acid, which slowly and spontaneously reacts further to give the sulfonic acid.

$$
R\text{—}\langle\bigcirc\rangle \; + \; 2\,SO_3 \xrightarrow[\text{fast}]{} R\text{—}\langle\bigcirc\rangle\text{—}SO_2OSO_3H \xrightarrow[\text{slow}]{R\text{—}\langle\bigcirc\rangle} R\text{—}\langle\bigcirc\rangle\text{—}SO_3H
$$

The sulfonic acid is subsequently neutralized, usually by caustic soda, to give the surface active alkylbenzene sulfonate salt. Due to the bulkiness of the alkyl substituent, the process gives almost exclusively p-sulfonation. R in the scheme above is typically an alkyl group of 12 carbon atoms. Originally, alkylbenzenes as surfactant intermediates were based on branched alkyls, but these have now almost entirely been replaced by their linear counterparts, thus giving the name linear alkylbenzene sulfonate(LABS or LAS).Faster biodegradation has been the main driving force for the transition to chains without branching. Alkylbenzenes are made by alkylation of benzene with an n-alkene or with alkyl chloride using HF or $AlCl_3$ as catalyst.

Sulfated alcohols constitutes another important group of anionics, widely used in detergent formulations. Both linear or branched alcohols, typically with eight to sixteen carbon atoms, are used as raw materials. The linear 12-carbon alcohol leads to the dodecyl monoester of sulfuric acid and, after neutralization with caustic soda, to sodium dodecyl sulfate (SDS), which is by far the most important surfactant within this category.

The process is similar to the sulfonation discussed above. Sulfur trioxide is the reagent used for large-scale production and, in analogy to sulfonation, the reaction proceeds via an intermediate pyrosulfate:

$$R\text{—}OH + 2SO_3 \xrightarrow[\text{fast}]{} R\text{—}O\text{—}SO_2OSO_3H \xrightarrow[\text{slow}]{R\text{—}OH} R\text{—}O\text{—}SO_3H$$

Such surfactants are good at producing foams and have a low toxicity to the skin and eye. They are popular in hand dishwashing and shampoo formulations.

Phosphate-containing anionic surfactants, both alkyl phosphates are made by treating the fatty alcohol with a phosphorylating agent, usually phosphorus pentoxide, P_4O_{10}. The reaction yields a mixture of mono-and diesters of phosphoric acid, and the ratio between the esters is governed by the ratio of the reactants and the amount of water in the reaction mixture:

$$6R\text{—}OH + P_4O_{10} \longrightarrow 2R\text{—}O\overset{\overset{O}{\|}}{\underset{\underset{OH}{|}}{P}}\text{—}OH + 2R\text{—}O\overset{\overset{O}{\|}}{\underset{\underset{OH}{|}}{P}}\text{—}O\text{—}R$$

All commercial phosphate surfactants contain both mono-and diesters of phosphoric acid, but the relative amounts vary from one producer to another. Since the physico-chemical properties of the alkyl phosphate surfactants depend on the ratio of the esters, alkyl phosphates from different suppliers. Phosphorus oxychloride, $POCl_3$, can also be used as a phosphorylating agent to produce alkyl phosphate surfactants. Also with $POCl_3$ a mixture of mono-and diesters of phosphoric acid is obtained.

Phosphate surfactants are used in the metal working industry where advantage is taken of their anticorrosive properties. They are also used as emulsifiers in plant protection formulations.

科技英语翻译八 状语从句的翻译方法 (一)

在句中，通常用来修饰动词、形容词、副词而起状语作用的句子称作状语从句。英语中状语从句用得比较多，位置也比较灵活。状语从句可以视情况置于主语之前，也可以置于主语之后。英语的状语从句一般由从属连接词和起连词作用的词组来引导。状语从句可分为时间状语从句、条件状语从句、原因状语从句、目的状语从句、结果状语从句、比较状语从句、方式状语从句、让步状语从句和地点状语从句。其译法分述如下。

一、时间状语从句的译法

英语中能够引导时间状语从句的连接词和连接短语较多，如 when, whenever, as, before, after, until, till, since, while, once, each time, 以及表示"一…就（立即）"的 as soon as, the moment, the instant, instantly, immediately, directly 等。时间状语从句的译法主要有以下几种。

1. 直译

把时间状语从句译成汉语的时间状语从句,并译出连接词本身的意义。要注意的是英语的时间状语从句既可以置于主句前，也可以置于主句后，有时也可以放在句子的中间。但汉译时，为了使译文符合汉语习惯，不论原句子中时间状语从句是在句首还是在句尾，或者是在句子的中间，原则是应译在句首，如下。

➢ **As the concentrations of C$_2$H$_4$ and H$_2$O decrease**, the rate of the forward reaction decreases.
随着乙烯和水的浓度降低，正反应速度减小。

➢ Batch processing is commonly used when small quantities of a product are to be produced on any single occasion.
当一次生产的产品量很少时，通常采用间歇反应过程。

2. when 引导的状语从句的特殊译法

（1）when 引导的时间状语从句除了译为"当…时"，还可以译为"在…之后"，如下。

➢ **When one reactor is regenerated**, it replaces another reactor.
一个反应器被再生之后，它就代替另一个反应器。

（2）when 引导的状语从句除了表示时间外，还可以表示条件，可译为"若"、"如果"、"一旦"等，如下。

➢ **When the phase boundary is covered by surfactant molecules**, the surface tension is reduced.
一旦表面活性剂分子覆盖相边界，表面张力就降低。

3. until 和 till 引导的时间状语从句的译法

（1）顺译法

英语中的 until 和 till 引导的时间状语从句多位于句尾（偶尔位于句首），汉译时通常按照其原文的词序仍然译在主句之后，所以称为顺译法，译为"直到"、"一直…为止"、"在…以前…一直"等，如下。

➢ This cracking continues **until the oil vapors are separated from the catalyst in the reactor**.

裂解反应会持续下去直到反应器中的油蒸汽与催化剂分离。

（2）倒译法

如果主句是否定句，即 not...until/till（相当于 not...before）句型，汉译时一般将原来位于句尾的从句译在句首，译为"直到（后）…才"、"在…以前不"，如下。

➤ The path is **not** completed **till wires are connected**.

直到导线接上后此电路才接通。

4. once 引导的状语从句的译法

once 引导的状语从句可以表示时间或条件，可译为"一旦"、"一经"、"如果"等，如下。

➤ If you start with ethylene and water, the forward reaction occurs; then **once ethanol is present**, the reverse reaction begins to take place.（$C_2H_4+H_2O == C_2H_5OH$）

如果反应时从乙烯和水开始的，那么反应向正向进行；**一旦有乙醇生成**，逆反应就发生。

二、条件状语从句的译法

英语中引导条件状语从句的连词有 if, as (so) long as, as (so) far as, unless, in case, provided (providing) that, should, suppose (supposing) that, assuming (assume) that, on condition that, in the event that 等。

1. 前置法

英语中条件状语从句的位置很灵活，既可以位于句首，也可以位于句尾。所谓的前置法就是按照汉语的表达习惯，将条件状语从句译在句首，并视情况使用汉语的关联词语。如："如果"、"如果…就"、"倘若"、"只要…就"、"除非…才"等，如下。

➤ **So long as enough fule is put in the rocket**, it will carry the satellite up into space.

只要给火箭加上足够的原料，它就能把卫星送入太空。

2. 转译法

If 引导的条件状语从句汉译时常常可以转译为时间状语从句，译为"当…时"并放在句首，如下。

➤ **If the values of all the variables in a process do not change with time**, the process is said to be operating at steady state.

当反应过程中所有的参数不随时间改变时，我们称该过程是在稳定态下操作的。

3. 后置法

英语中也有个别的条件状语从句往往表示一种补充说明的含义，这样的条件状语从句汉译时可以后置，如下。

➤ Iron or steel parts will rust, **if they are unprotected**.

铁件和钢件事会生锈的，如果不加保护的话。

三、原因状语从句的译法

英语中引导原因状语的连接词有 because, since, as, now that, seeing that, considering that, for, for the reason that, inasmuch as, in that 等。英语中原因状语从句的位置比较灵活，可以置于句首，也可以置于句尾或句中，按照汉语的表达习惯，原因状语从句一般应以在主句之前，但在科技英语中如果原文的原因从句处于主句之后，也可采用顺译法将从句保留在后面。

1. 前置法

所谓前置法，就是无论原文中的原因状语从句位于句首还是句尾，译文中均将原因状语从句译在句首，如下。

> The number of atoms of each atomic species must be the same on both sides of the equation, **since atoms can neither be created nor destroyed in chemical reactions**.

因为化学反应中原子既不能被创生也不能被消灭，所以方程式两边每一种原子的原子个数必须相同。

2. 后置法

在英语原文中原因状语从句多位于句尾，其意义在于对结果的补充说明，汉译时采用后置法（或称为顺译法）将从句保留在后面，如下。

> Many of the earliest catalytic reforming units were non-regenerative **in that they did not perform in situ catalyst regeneration**.

大多早期的催化重整设备是非再生性的，在于它们不能进行原位催化剂再生。

四、目的状语从句的译法

英语中引导目的状语从句的连词有：that, so that, in order that, for fear that, lest, for the purpose that, to the end that, in case 等。应注意的是 that 和 so that 既可以引导结果状语从句，也可以引导目的状语从句。判断从句是结果还是目的状语应从下面几个方面加以考虑：一般来说结果状语从句表示一种事实，而目的状语从句往往表示一种愿望和可能性；结果状语从句结构上很少用情态动词，而目的的状语从句常用 can, could, may, might 等情态动词；结果状语从句一般置于主句之后，而目的状语从句放在句首或句尾均可。

1. 前置法

翻译目的状语从句应注意两个特点：如果译作汉语的"为了"、"要（使）"等，习惯上将目的状语从句译在句首，如下。

> The moving parts of a machine should be often oiled **for the purpose that friction may be reduced**.

为了减少摩擦，机器的运动零件应经常上油。

2. 后置法

如果将目的状语从句译作汉语的"以"、"以便"、"为了是"、"以免"、"免得"、"以防"等，那么习惯上将目的状语从句译在句末，如下。

翻译目的状语从句所采用的两种方法（前置法和后置法）很多情况下可以相互转换，如下。

> Each reactor can be individually isolated **so that any one reactor can be undergoing in situ regeneration**.

每一个反应器各自独立，以便每个反应器都能原位再生。

> Steel parts are usually covered with grease **for fear that they should rust**.

钢制零件通常涂上润滑脂，以防生锈。

Unit Nine　Coal Chemical Engineering

Lesson Eighteen　Coal Liquefaction

Coal liquefaction is the process of producing synthetic liquid fuels from coal. The liquefaction processes are classified as direct conversion to liquids processes and indirect conversion to liquids processes.

Direct conversion processes

Direct processes are carbonization and hydrogenation.

Pyrolysis and carbonization processes

There are a number of carbonization processes. The carbonization conversion occurs through pyrolysis or destructive distillation, and it produces condensable coal tar, oil and water vapor, non-condensable synthetic gas, and a solid residue-char. The condensed coal tar and oil are then further processed by hydrogenation to remove sulfur and nitrogen species, after which they are processed into fuels.

The typical example of carbonization is the Karrick process. The process was invented by Lewis Cass Karrick in the 1920s. The Karrick process is a low-temperature carbonization process, where coal is heated at 680℉ (360℃) to 1380℉ (750℃) in the absence of air. These temperatures optimize the production of coal tars richer in lighter hydrocarbons than normal coal tar. However, the produced liquids are mostly a by-product and the main product is semi-coke, a solid and smokeless fuel.

The COED Process, developed by FMC Corporation, uses a fluidized bed for processing, in combination with increasing temperature, through four stages of pyrolysis. Heat is transferred by hot gases produced by combustion of part of the produced char. A modification of this process, the COGAS Process, involves the addition of gasification of char. The TOSCOAL Process, an analogue to the TOSCO II oil shale retorting process and Lurgi-Ruhrgas process, which is also used for the shale oil extraction, uses hot recycled solids for the heat transfer.

Liquid yields of pyrolysis and Karrick processes are generally low for practical use for synthetic liquid fuel production. Furthermore, the resulting liquids are of low quality and require further treatment before they can be used as motor fuels. In summary, there is little possibility that this process will yield economically viable volumes of liquid fuel.

Hydrogenation processes

One of the main methods of direct conversion of coal to liquids by hydrogenation process is the Bergius process. The Bergius process was developed by Friedrich Bergius in 1913. In this process, dry coal is mixed with heavy oil recycled from the process. Catalyst is typically added to the mixture. The reaction occurs at between 400℃ (752℉) to 5000℃ (9030℉) and 20 to 70MPa hydrogen pressure. The reaction can be summarized as follows:

$$n\,C + (n+1)\,H_2 \longrightarrow C_nH_{2n+2}$$

After World War I several plants were built in Germany; these plants were extensively used during World War II to supply Germany with fuel and lubricants. The Kohleoel Process, developed in Germany by Ruhrkohle and VEBA, was used in the demonstration plant with the capacity of 200 ton of lignite per day, built in Bottrop, Germany. This plant operated from 1981 to 1987. In this process, coal is mixed with a recycle solvent and iron catalyst. After preheating and pressurizing, H_2 is added. The process takes place in a tubular reactor at the pressure of 300 bar and at the temperature of 470℃ (880℉). This process was also explored by SASOL in South Africa.

In 1970 ~ 1980s, Japanese companies Nippon Kokan, Sumitomo Metal Industries and Mitsubishi Heavy Industries developed the NEDOL process. In this process, coal is mixed with a recycled solvent and a synthetic iron-based catalyst; after preheating H_2 is added. The reaction takes place in a tubular reactor at temperature between 430℃ (810℉) and 465℃ (870℉) at the pressure 150~200bar. The produced oil has low quality and requires intensive upgrading. H-Coal process, developed by Hydrocarbon Research, Inc., in 1963, mixes pulverized coal with recycled liquids, hydrogen and catalyst in the ebullated bed reactor. Advantages of this process are that dissolution and oil upgrading are taking place in the single reactor, products have high H/C ratio, and a fast reaction time, while the main disadvantages are high gas yield (this is basically a thermal cracking process), high hydrogen consumption, and limitation of oil usage only as a boiler oil because of impurities.

The SRC-I and SRC-II (Solvent Refined Coal) processes developed by Gulf Oil and implemented as pilot plants in the United States in the 1960s and 1970s. The Nuclear Utility Services Corporation developed hydrogenation process which was patented by Wilburn C. Schroeder in 1976. The process involved dried, pulverized coal mixed with roughly 1wt% molybdenum catalysts. Hydrogenation occurred by use of high temperature and pressure synthesis gas produced in a separate gasifier. The process ultimately yielded a synthetic crude product, Naphtha, a limited amount of C_3/C_4 gas, light-medium weight liquids ($C_5 \sim C_{10}$) suitable for use as fuels, small amounts of NH_3 and significant amounts of CO_2. Other single-stage hydrogenation processes are the Exxon Donor Solvent Process, the Imhausen High-pressure Process, and the Conoco Zinc Chloride Process.

There is also a number of two-stage direct liquefaction processes; however, after 1980s only the Catalytic Two-stage Liquefaction Process, modified from the H-Coal Process; the Liquid Solvent Extraction Process by British Coal; and the Brown Coal Liquefaction Process of Japan have been developed.

Shenhua, the Chinese coal miner, decided in 2002 to build a direct liquefaction plant in Inner Mongolia, with barrel capacity of 20 thousand barrels per day ($3.2 \times 10^3\ m^3/d$). First tests were implemented at the end of 2008. A second and longer test campaign was started in October 2009.

Chevron Corporation developed a process invented by Joel W. Rosenthal called the Chevron Coal Liquefaction Process (CCLP). It is unique due the close-coupling of the non-catalytic dissolver and the catalytic hydroprocessing unit. The oil produced had properties that were unique when compared to other coal oils; it was lighter and had far fewer heteroatom impurities. The process was scaled-up to the 6 ton per day level, but not proven commercially.

Indirect conversion processes

The main indirect process is the Fischer-Tropsch process. In this process, coal is first gasified to make syngas (a balanced purified mixture of CO and H$_2$ gas). Next, Fischer-Tropsch catalysts are used to convert the syngas into light hydrocarbons (like ethane) which are further processed into gasoline and diesel. This method was used on a large technical scale in Germany between 1934 and 1945 and is currently being used by Sasol in South Africa. In addition to creating gasoline, syngas can also be converted into methanol, which can be used as a fuel, or into a fuel additive.

Syngas may be converted to liquids through conversion of the syngas to methanol which is subsequently polymerized into alkanes over a zeolite catalyst. This process, named as the Mobil MTG Process, was developed by Mobil in early 1970s.

New Words and Expressions

liquefaction [ˌlikwi'fækʃən] n. 液化；熔解；液化(作用)

carbonization [ˌkɑːbənai'zeiʃən;-ni'z-] n. [化] 碳化，碳化作用；干馏

hydrogenation [ˌhaidrədʒi'neiʃən] n. 加氢；[化] 氢化作用

pyrolysis [paiə'rɔlisis;ˌpi-] n. [化] 热解(作用)；高温分解

destructive [di'strʌktiv] a. 破坏的；毁灭性的；有害的，消极的

char [tʃɑː] n. 炭；木炭；煤渣

optimize ['ɔptimaiz] vt. 使最优化，使完善

modification [ˌmɔdifi'keiʃən] n. 修改，修正；改变

analogue ['ænəlɔg] n. 类似物；类似情况；对等的人

shale [ʃeil] n. [岩] 页岩；泥板岩

retorting [ri'tɔːtiŋ] n. 干馏；蒸馏法

extraction [ik'strækʃən] n. 取出；抽出；拔出；抽出物；出身

viable ['vaiəbl] a. 可行的

lubricant ['luːbrikənt] n. 润滑剂；润滑油

demonstration [ˌdemən'streiʃən] n.(用标本、实例等)说明，表明，示范

lignite ['lignait] n. [矿物] 褐煤

pulverize ['pʌlvəraiz] vt. 粉碎；使成粉末；研磨

dissolution [ˌdisə'ljuːʃən] n. 分解，溶解

implement ['implimənt, 'impliment] vt. 实施，执行；实现，使生效

molybdenum [mɔ'libdinəm] n. [化学] 钼（金属元素，符号 Mo，原子序号 42）

gasifier ['gæsifaiə] n. 气化炉，燃气发生炉

ultimately ['ʌltimətli] adv. 最后；根本；基本上

dissolver [di'zɔlvə] n. 溶解装置；溶解器

heteroatom ['hetərəuˌætəm] n. [化] 杂原子，杂环原子

alkanes ['ælkeinz] n. [化] 链烷，烷(属)烃

a number of 若干；很多，许多

the ebullated bed reactor 沸腾床反应器

Notes

1. These temperatures optimize the production of coal tars richer in lighter hydrocarbons than normal coal tar.　在这样的温度下，优化产生的煤焦油与正常煤焦油相比富含轻质烃。

2. The COED Process, developed by FMC Corporation, uses a fluidized bed for processing, in combination with increasing temperature, through four stages of pyrolysis.半焦-油-能开发项目，由（美国）FMC 公司开发的，用多级流化床，通过四个温度阶段对煤进行热解。COED：Coke-Oil-Energy Development 指半焦-油-能开发项目。

3. The Kohleoel Process, developed in Germany by Ruhrkohle and VEBA, was used in the demonstration plant with the capacity of 200 ton of lignite per day, built in Bottrop, Germany. Kohleoel 工艺，由德国的 Ruhrkohle 公司和 VEBA 公司开发，在德国的 Bottrop 修建的示范工厂就使用这种工艺，具有一天转化 200t 褐煤的规模。

4. The SRC-Ⅰ and SRC-Ⅱ (Solvent Refined Coal) processes developed by Gulf Oil and implemented as pilot plants in the United States in the 1960s and 1970s.SRC-Ⅰ 和 SRC-Ⅱ 法（溶剂精炼煤法，简称 SRC 法,是将煤用溶剂制成浆液送入反应器，在高温和氢压下，裂解或解聚成较小的分子。按加氢深度的不同，分为 SRC-Ⅰ 和 SRC-Ⅱ 两种。）由海湾石油公司开发并于 20 世纪 60 年代和 70 年代在美国进行研究试验。

Exercises

1. Put the following into Chinese

coal liquefaction　　　　　　direct conversion

indirect conversion　　　　　carbonization process

condensable coal tar　　　　a solid residue-char

2. Put the following into English

加氢过程　　　　　干煤

管状反应器　　　　煤粉

沸腾床反应器　　　煤液化

3. Questions

What is the coal liquefaction?

How many processes are classified the liquefaction processes? What are they?

Lesson Nineteen   Coal Gasification

Coal gasification is the process of producing coal gas, a type of syngas–a mixture of carbon monoxide (CO) and hydrogen (H_2) gas—from coal. Carbon monoxide, which is a combustible gas, was traditionally used as a source of energy for municipal lighting and heat before the advent of industrial-scale production of natural gas, while the hydrogen obtained from gasification can be used for various purposes such as making ammonia, powering a hydrogen economy, or upgrading fossil fuels. Alternatively, the coal gas (also known as "town gas") can be converted into transportation fuels such as gasoline and diesel through additional treatment via the Fischer-Tropsch process.

Process

During gasification, the coal is blown through with oxygen and steam (water vapor) while also being heated (and in some cases pressurized). If the coal is heated by external heat sources the process is called "allothermal", while "autothermal" process assumes heating of the coal via exothermal chemical reactions occurring inside the gasifier itself （see Figure 9.1）. It is essential that the oxidizer supplied is insufficient for complete oxidizing (combustion) of the fuel. During the reactions mentioned, oxygen and water molecules oxidize the coal and produce a gaseous mixture of carbon dioxide (CO_2), carbon monoxide (CO), water vapour (H_2O), and molecular hydrogen (H_2). (Some by-products like tar, phenols, etc. are also possible end products, depending on the specific gasification technology utilized.) This process has been conducted in-situ within natural coal seams

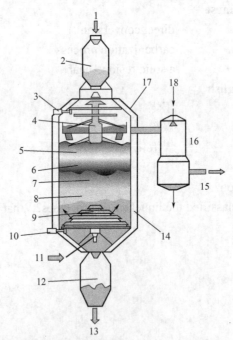

Figure 9.1   Scheme of a Lurgi gasifier

1—coal; 2—coal locking cabin; 3—coal distributor driver; 4—coal distributor; 5—dryer; 6—devolatilization device; 7—gasification zone; 8—combustion zone; 9—grate; 10—grate driver; 11—steam+oxygen; 12—ash locking cabin; 13—ash; 14—water jacket; 15—raw gas; 16—Scrubbing cooler; 17—steam jacket; 18—scrubbing water

(referred to as underground coal gasification) and in coal refineries. The desired end product is usually syngas (i.e., a combination of H_2 + CO), but the produced coal gas may also be further refined to produce additional quantities of H_2:

$$3C \text{ (i.e., coal)} + O_2 + H_2O \longrightarrow H_2 + 3CO$$

If the refiner wants to produce alkanes (i.e., hydrocarbons present in natural gas, gasoline, and diesel fuel), the coal gas is collected at this state and routed to a Fischer-Tropsch reactor. If, however, hydrogen is the desired end-product, the coal gas (primarily the CO product) undergoes the water gas shift reaction where more hydrogen is produced by additional reaction with water vapor:

$$CO + H_2O \longrightarrow CO_2 + H_2$$

Although other technologies for coal gasification currently exist, all employ, in general, the same chemical processes. For low-grade coals (i.e., "brown coals") which contain significant amounts of water, there are technologies in which no steam is required during the reaction, with coal (carbon) and oxygen being the only reactants. As well, some coal gasification technologies do not require high pressures. Some utilize pulverized coal as fuel while others work with relatively large fractions of coal. Gasification technologies also vary in the way the blowing is supplied.

"Direct blowing" assumes the coal and the oxidizer being supplied towards each other from the opposite sides of the reactor channel. In this case the oxidizer passes through coke and (more likely) ashes to the reaction zone where it interacts with coal. The hot gas produced then passes fresh fuel and heats it while absorbing some products of thermal destruction of the fuel, such as tars and phenols. Thus, the gas requires significant refining before being used in the Fischer-Tropsch reaction. Products of the refinement are highly toxic and require special facilities for their utilization. As a result, the plant utilizing the described technologies has to be very large to be economically efficient.

"Reversed blowing" (as compared to the previous type described which was invented first) assumes the coal and the oxidizer being supplied from the same side of the reactor. In this case there is no chemical interaction between coal and oxidizer before the reaction zone. The gas produced in the reaction zone passes solid products of gasification (coke and ashes), and CO_2 and H_2O contained in the gas are additionally chemically restored to CO and H_2. As compared to the "direct blowing" technology, no toxic by-products are present in the gas: those are disabled in the reaction zone.

Underground coal gasification

Underground coal gasification is an industrial *in-situ* gasification process, which is carried out in non-mined coal seams using injection of oxidants, and bringing the product gas to surface through production wells drilled from the surface. The product gas could to be used as a chemical feedstock or as fuel for power generation. The technique can be applied to resources that are otherwise not economical to extract and also offers an alternative to conventional coal mining methods for some resources. Compare to the traditional coal mining and gasification, the UCG has less environmental and social impact.

By-products

The by-products of coal gas manufacture included coke, coal tar, sulfur and ammonia; all useful products. Dyes, medicines, including sulfa drugs, saccharin and many organic compounds are therefore derived from coal gas.

Coke is used as a smokeless fuel and for the manufacture of water gas and producer gas. Coal tar was subjected to fractional distillation to recover various products, including

- tar, for roads
- benzole, a motor fuel
- creosote, a wood preservative
- phenol, used in the manufacture of plastics
- cresols, disinfectants

Sulfur is used in the manufacture of sulfuric acid and ammonia is used in the manufacture of fertilisers.

New Words and Expressions

combustible   [kəm'bʌstəbl]   *a.* 易燃的

municipal   [mjuː'nisipəl]   *a.* 市政的，市的；地方自治的

alternatively   [ɔːl'tə:nətivli]   *adv.* 非此即彼；二者择一地；作为一种选择

exothermal   [ˌeksəu'θə:mik,-'θə:məl]   *a.* 放热的；放能的

currently   ['kʌrəntli]   *adv.* 现在，现时，目前，当前

employ   [im'plɔi]   *n.* 使用；雇用

relatively   ['relətivli]   *adv.* 相当地；相对地，比较地

assume   [ə'sju:m; ə'su:m]   *vt.* 假定；采取；呈现

facility   [ʃə'siliti]   *n.* 设施；设备；容易；灵巧

economically   [ˌi:kə'nɔmikəli]   *adv.* 经济地；在经济上；节俭地

additionally   [ə'diʃənli]   *adv.* 此外；又，加之

injection   [in'dʒekʃən]   *n.* 注射；注射剂；充血；射入轨道

technique   [tek'ni:k]   *n.*(工艺或技术)技巧；技术

conventional   [kən'venʃənəl]   *a.* 符合习俗的，传统的；常见的；惯例的

sulfa   ['sʌlfə]   *a.* 磺胺的；磺胺药剂的

saccharin   ['sækərin]   *n.*[有化] 糖精；邻磺酰苯甲酰亚胺

benzole   ['benzɔl,-zəul]   *n.* 粗苯

creosote   ['kri:ə,səut]   *n.*[林] 木馏油；碳酸；杂芬油

cresol   ['kri:səul]   *n.*[化] 甲酚

vary in   在…方面变化；在…方面有差异

be derived from   来自，源自于；从…而产生出来的；由…得到

be subjected to   受到…；经受…

Notes

1. Carbon monoxide, which is a combustible gas, was traditionally used as a source of energy for municipal lighting and heat before the advent of industrial-scale production of natural gas, while the hydrogen obtained from gasification can be used for various purposes such as making ammonia, powering a hydrogen economy, or upgrading fossil fuels. 一氧化碳是一种可燃气体，在天然气工业规模生产以前，传统上被用做一种能源来供给市政照明及取暖；同时，从气化得到的氢气

也可用于各种用途，如合成氨、氢经济供给、或升级化石燃料。氢经济（Hydrogen Economy）一词，为美国通用汽车公司（General Motors）于 1970 年发生第一次能源危机时所创，主要为描绘未来氢气取代石油成为支撑全球经济的主要能源后，整个氢能源生产、配送、贮存及使用的市场运作体系。但随后二十年间中东形势趋缓、原油价格下跌，石油依旧成为交通运输业的首要选择，因此对于氢经济发展的相关研究渐少。直到 1990 年代末期气候变化（全球变暖等）问题引起重视以后，氢能与氢经济又再度成为世界各国研究的热点。

2. If the coal is heated by external heat sources the process is called "allothermal", while "autothermal" process assumes heating of the coal via exothermal chemical reactions occurring inside the gasifier itself. 如果煤炭是由外部热源加热的过程被称为"外热式"，而"自热式"形式煤所消耗的热量是由气化炉内部发生的放热化学反应供给的。

3. If, however, hydrogen is the desired end-product, the coal gas (primarily the CO product) undergoes the water gas shift reaction where more hydrogen is produced by additional reaction with water vapor. 然而，如果氢是理想的终端产品，经过水煤气的变换反应，煤气（主要是煤气中的一氧化碳）会与过量的水蒸气发生反应产生更多的氢气。However 是插入语。

4. Although other technologies for coal gasification currently exist, all employ, in general, the same chemical processes. 虽然目前煤的气化还有其他的工艺，但是总体上都采用的是相同的化学过程。all employ, in general, the same chemical processes 中 in general 是插入语。

Exercises

1. Put the following into Chinese

coal gasification   a combustible gas
natural gas   exothermal chemical reactions
low-grade coals   the reaction zone

2. Put the following into English

直吹法   地下煤气化
煤焦油   煤气
燃烧区   煤分配器

3. Questions

What is the coal gasification?

Reading Material: Coal

Coal is a combustible black or brownish-black sedimentary rock, normally occurring in rock strata in layers or veins called coal beds or coal seams. The harder forms, such as anthracite coal, can be regarded as metamorphic because of later exposure to elevated temperature and pressure. Coal is composed primarily of carbon along with variable quantities of other elements, chiefly sulfur, hydrogen, oxygen and nitrogen.

Coal begins as layers of plant matter accumulating at the bottom of a body of water. For the process to continue, the plant matter must be protected from biodegradation and oxidization, usually by mud or acidic water. The wide shallow seas of the Carboniferous period provided such conditions. This trapped atmospheric carbon in the ground in immense peat bogs that eventually were covered over and deeply buried by sediments under which they metamorphosed into coal.

Coal, a fossil fuel, is the largest source of energy for the generation of electricity worldwide, as well as one of the largest worldwide anthropogenic sources of carbon dioxide emissions. Gross carbon dioxide emissions from coal usage are slightly more than those from petroleum and about double the amount from natural gas. Coal is extracted from the ground by mining, either underground by shaft mining through the seams or in open pits.

Types

As geological processes apply pressure to dead biotic material over time, under suitable conditions it is transformed successively into:

- Peat, considered to be a precursor of coal, has industrial importance as a fuel in some regions, for example, Ireland and Finland. In its dehydrated form, peat is a highly effective absorbent for fuel and oil spills on land and in water.
- Lignite, also referred to as brown coal, is the lowest rank of coal and is used almost exclusively as fuel for electric power generation. Jet is a compact form of lignite that is sometimes polished and has been used as an ornamental stone since the Iron Age.
- Sub-bituminous coal, whose properties range from those of lignite to those of bituminous coal，is used primarily as fuel for steam-electric power generation. Additionally, it is an important source of light aromatic hydrocarbons for the chemical synthesis industry.
- Bituminous coal, dense sedimentary rock, black but sometimes dark brown, often with well-defined bands of bright and dull material, used primarily as fuel in steam-electric power generation, with substantial quantities also used for heat and power applications in manufacturing and to make coke. In China, it may be divided further into more than ten kinds of types according to the coal rank such as flame coal, steam coal, coking coal.
- Anthracite coal, the highest rank, a harder, glossy, black coal, is used primarily for residential and commercial space heating. It got its name because of smoke-free combustion. Good quality anthracite coal is a source of coal gasification, blast furnace injection, calcium carbide, electrodes and so on.
- Graphite, technically the highest rank, but difficult to ignite and is not so commonly used as fuel: it is mostly used in pencils and, when powdered, as a lubricant.

Uses today

Coal as fuel

Coal is primarily used as a solid fuel to produce electricity and heat through combustion. World coal consumption was about 6743786000 short tons in 2006 and is expected to increase 48% to 9.98 billion short tons by 2030. China produced 2.38 billion tons in 2006. India produced about 447.3 million tons in 2006. 68.7% of China's electricity comes from coal. The USA consumes about 14% of the world total, using 90% of it for generation of electricity.

When coal is used for electricity generation, it is usually pulverized and then combusted (burned) in a furnace with a boiler. The furnace heat converts boiler water to steam, which is then used to spin turbines which turn generators and create electricity.

Coking and use of coke

Coke is a solid carbonaceous residue derived from low-ash, low-sulfur bituminous coal from which the volatile constituents are driven off by baking in an oven without oxygen at temperatures as high as $1000\,℃$ ($1832\,℉$) so that the fixed carbon and residual ash are fused together. Metallurgical coke is used as a fuel and as a reducing agent in smelting iron ore in a blast furnace. The product is cast iron and is too rich in dissolved carbon, so must be treated further to make steel.

The coke must be strong enough to resist the weight of overburden in the blast furnace, which is why coking coal is so important in making steel by the conventional route.

Gasification

Coal gasification can be used to produce syngas ,a mixture of carbon monoxide (CO) and hydrogen (H_2) gas. This syngas can then be converted into transportation fuels like gasoline and diesel through the Fischer-Tropsch process.

Liquefaction

Coal can also be converted into liquid fuels such as gasoline or diesel by several different processes. In the direct liquefaction processes, the coal is either hydrogenated or carbonized. In the process of low-temperature carbonization, coal is coked at temperatures between $360\,℃$ ($680\,℉$) and $750\,℃$ ($1380\,℉$). These temperatures optimize the production of coal tars richer in lighter hydrocarbons than normal coal tar. The coal tar is then further processed into fuels. Alternatively, coal can be converted into a gas first, and then into a liquid, by using the Fischer-Tropsch process.

Refined coal

Refined coal is the product of a coal-upgrading technology that removes moisture and certain pollutants from lower-rank coals such as sub-bituminous and lignite (brown) coals. It is one form of several pre-combustion treatments and processes for coal that alter coal's characteristics before it is burned. The goals of pre-combustion coal technologies are to increase efficiency and reduce emissions when the coal is burned.

Industrial processes

Finely ground bituminous coal, known in this application as *sea coal*, is a constituent of foundry sand. While the molten metal is in the mould the coal burns slowly, releasing reducing gases at pressure and so preventing the metal from penetrating the pores of the sand. It is also contained in *mould wash*, a paste or liquid with the same function applied to the mould before casting. Sea coal can be mixed with the clay lining (the "bod") used for the bottom of a cupola furnace. When the heated coal decomposes and the bod becomes slightly friable, easing the process of breaking opens holes for tapping the molten metal.

科技英语翻译九 状语从句的翻译方法 (二)

五、地点状语从句

地点状语从句用来表示主句中的某一动作或状态发生的地点。英语中引导地点状语从句的连接词较少，仅有 where、wherever 等。

1. 直译

翻译地点状语从句大都词语直译，即译为地点状语从句，而且在英语原文中，如果从句位于句首，则译文也应位于句首；反之，若英语从句位于句尾，则需根据情况，也可将位于主句后的地点状语从句译于汉语句子的句首，如下。

> **Where there is sound**, there must be sound waves.

哪里有声音，哪里必有声波。

2. 转译

有时 where 和 wherever 引导的地点状语从句，在逻辑意义上相当于一个条件状语从句或让步状语从句，汉译时可以把这样的地点状语从句视情况转译为条件状语从句或让步状语从句，如下。

> **Wherever there is motion**, we see the process of conversion of mechanical energy into heat.

凡是有运动的地方，我们都能看到机械能转变为热能的过程。

> **Where the volt is too large a unit**, we use the milli-volt or microvolt.

如果伏特这个单位过大，我们就应该用豪伏或微伏。

六、结果状语从句

结果状语从句用来表示主句中某一动作或状态所产生的结果。引导这类从句的连词有：

（so）that, so…that, such that ,such…that, to the extent that, in so much as, in such a way that, with the result that 等。这类状语从句无论是英语还是汉语，都习惯放在主句之后，因此多数采用顺译法，汉译时要灵活译出汉语表示结果的状语，如下。

> A much higher temperature is required **so that we could change iron from a solid state into liquid**.

需要高得多的温度，以便我们能把铁从固体变成液体。

> The total number of the charge of the nucleus and that of electrons are equal **that the atom is electrically neutral**.

原子核的电荷总数和电子的电荷总数相等，因而原子是中性的。

> Atoms are so small **that we can not see them with the most powerful microscope**.

原子非常小，我们用功率最大的显微镜也看不到它们。

七、方式状语从句

方式状语从句用来表示主句中某一动作或状态发生的方式。引导方式状语从句的连词有：

as ,as if, as though, just as, in a manner that, in this way that, in such a way that, to the extent that, in degree as, according as, in the same as 等。

按照汉语的表达习惯，方式状语从句有如下 3 种译法。

1. 分译法

把方式状语从句译成汉语的一个方式分句，一般按照原文的顺序翻译，也称顺译法。

➤ Electric charges have the opposite polarities **just as magnets have north and south poles**.

电荷有相反的极性，就像磁铁有南北极一样。

➤ **Just as sound waves do**, light waves differ in frequency.

同声波一样，光波也有不同的频率。

Electricity flows through a wire **just as water flows through a pipe**.

电流通过导线，正像水流过管线一样。

2. 译成词组

如果方式状语从句比较短，便把它译成词组，充当句子的状语，同样能表达原文的语义。

➤ Gases have no definite shape **as liquids**.

气体像液体一样没有形状。

➤ Solids expand and contract **as liquids and gases do**.

固体像气体和液体一样地膨胀和收缩。

3. 译成定语

有时，as 引导的从句在结构上是方式状语从句，但汉译时，将它译成定语才能使语义清楚。

➤ Petroleum **as it is found in the earth** is a combination of several fractions.

从地下发现的石油是几种馏分组成的混合物。

➤ Light **as it comes from a laser** is essentially of one color.

来自激光器的光实质只有一种颜色。

八、让步状语从句

让步状语从句时用来表示主句中的某一动作或状态与从句的某一动作或状态在逻辑上有一定的矛盾，但并不影响主句的事实。引导此类从句的连词有：although, though ,even if, even though as, while if, whether, notwithstanding, no matter how (however), no matter whether , no matter what (whatever), no matter which(whichever), no matter when(whenever), no matter who(whoever), no matter where(wherever)等。

翻译时，大都将从句所表达的让步意义译在句首。只有在个别情况下，为照应上下文的需要才将其译在句中或句末。英语的让步状语从句，在汉译时分为以下两种情况。

1. 译为让步分句

➤ **Although energy can be changed from one form into another**, it can neither be created nor destroyed.

能虽然可以由一种形式转变为另一种形式，但它既不能创造也不能消灭。

➤ **Even though it is not so strong as the earth's**, the moon's gravity does something to the earth.

尽管月球引力不如地球引力那么大，但对地球仍有影响。

➤ **Light as air is**, it has weight.

空气虽轻，但有重量。

> **Although these particles are very light,** their energies are considerable because of their high speeds.

虽然这些粒子很轻，但由于速度很快，因而能量很大。

2. 译为汉语的无条件句

> **No matter what the shape of a magnet may be**, it can attract iron and steel.

不论磁体形状如何，它都能吸引钢铁。

> The salt is still salt **whatever form it is**.

不论盐是什么形式，它还是盐。

> **Whatever the state of the molecules may be**, they move as a group.

无论分子以何种状态存在，它们都以群的方式运动。

九、比较状语从句

比较状语从句用来表示主句中的某一动作或状态与从句中的某一动作或状态在数量、性质或程度上的比较。引导比较状语从句的连词有：as…as（像…一样），not so (as) … as（不像…那样），more…than（比），not more…than（不如，比不上），the more…the more（越…越）等。

比较状语从句一般都是省略句，省去与主句中相同的部分。翻译时一般采用顺译法。

> The speed of radio waves is as great as that of light.

无线电波的速度与光速一样快。

> Sound can not travel so fast as light can.

声音传播的速度不如光速快。

> Diamond is even harder than steel.

金刚石甚至比钢还硬。

> **The warmer** water is, **the faster** it evaporates.

水越热，蒸发得越快。

Unit Ten   Green Chemical Engineering

Lesson Twenty   Green Chemistry

When polyethene was first synthesised, the chemists involved almost certainly thought of a number of potential uses for their new chemical, but they would not have been able to foresee the multitude of uses to which it would eventually be put. As a result, they would also not have been able to predict the environmental problems generated by just one of its uses, as plastic shopping bags. While the wider community wishes to benefit from the development of new chemicals, there is now an increasing expectation that not only their synthesis be considered, but also their use and disposal. Fortunately, chemists possess the skills necessary to meet such challenges. This approach forms the basis of what has become known as "green chemistry".

Green chemistry targets pollution prevention at the source, stopping and/or reducing waste before it starts. Green chemistry is design of chemical products and processes that reduce or eliminate the use and/or the generation of hazardous substances.

The twelve principles of green chemistry are as follows:
- Prevent wastes
- Renewable materials
- Omit derivatization steps
- Degradable chemical products
- Use safe synthetic methods
- Catalytic reagents
- Temperature, pressure ambient
- In-process monitoring
- Very few auxiliary substances
- E-factor, maximize feed in product
- Low toxicity of chemical products
- Yes, it is safe

Green chemical processes adhere to 12 principles, shown here in a simplified version to form a mnemonic. Catalytic reagents reduce the amount of chemicals needed in a reaction; in-process monitoring allows harmful substances to be detected and eliminated; auxiliary substances are those that don't take part in the chemical reaction, such as solvents or separating agents; and the E-factor is the mass of waste generated in a process divided by the mass of product.

These twelve principles essentially fall into four groups:
- Efficient use of energy.

● Hazard reduction.

● Waster minimisation.

● Use of renewable resources.

Chemistry in the natural world most often occurs at ambient temperature and pressure, while chemistry in the industrial world frequently employs extremes of both temperature and pressure. Spider silk has an equivalent strength to Kevlar, yet all that spiders require to synthesis silk are the products of the digestion of insects and enzymes. In contrast, much less benign reagents and conditions are required for the synthesis of Kevlar. By looking at how nature solves chemical problems, green chemists gain clues as to how processes may be changed to make them more benign.

While there is often a temptation to think of green chemistry as a branch of environmental science, there are significant differences between the two. This may be best illustrated using the example of coal-fired power stations. The by-products of the process of generating electricity from coal have significant environmental implications. The environmental scientist's focus would be on the monitoring of the production of these by-products and the means by which they could be cleaned or treated so as to minimise their environmental damage. An idea currently being considered is that the carbon dioxide produced by the combustion of coal could be stored underground, so-called geosequestration. The green chemist's approach would be to think of an alternative way of generating the electricity without producing carbon dioxide. If there was not an alternative, they would then find a way of using the carbon dioxide in some other process.

New Words and Expressions

potential [pəu'tenʃəl] *a.* 潜在的；可能的；势的

foresee [fɔː'siː] *vt.* 预知；预见

multitude ['mʌltiˌtjuːd, -ˌtuːd] *n.* 许多；大量；多数

predict [pri'dikt] *vt.* 预报，预言；预知

　　　　　　　　　　vi. 作出预言；作预料，作预报

community [kə'mjuːniti] *n.* 社区；群落；共同体；团体

expectation [ˌekspek'teiʃən] *n.* 期待；预期；指望

disposal [dis'pəuzəl] *n.* 处理；支配；清理；安排

derivatization [dəˈrivəˌtizeiʃən] *n.* 衍生；衍生化；衍生化作用

degradable [di'greidəbi] *a.* [化](废料)可降解的，(复合化合物)可分解的，易受化学分解影响的

ambient ['æmbiənt] *a.* 周围的；外界的；环绕的

auxiliary [ɔːg'ziljəri] *a.* 辅助的；副的；附加的

maximize ['mæksimaiz] *vt.* 取…最大值；对…极为重视

　　　　　　　　　　vi. 尽可能广义地解释；达到最大值

toxicity [tɔk'sisəti] *n.* [毒理学] 毒性，毒力

version ['vəːʃən] *n.* 版本；译文；倒转术

mnemonic [niː'mɔnik] *a.* 记忆的；助记的；记忆术的

monitor ['mɔnitə] *vt.* 检测，监测；监控

renewable　　[ri'nju:əbl]　*a.* 可再生的；可更新的；可继续的
　　　　　　　　　　　　　n. 再生性能源
Kevlar　　['kevlɑ:]　　*n.* 芳纶；凯夫拉尔，纤维 B（一种合成纤维），是一种合成纤维，高硬度高抗张强度，重量轻，很好的抗磨损能力；用以代替汽车轮胎等中的钢丝
digestion　　[di:dʒestʃən, dai-]　*n.* 消化；领悟
benign　　[bi'nain]　*a.* 温和的；良性的；和蔼的，亲切的；吉利的
temptation　　[temp'teiʃən]　*n.* 引诱；诱惑物
implication　　[ˌimpli'keiʃən]　*n.* 含义；暗示；牵连，卷入 ；涉及，密切关系
as a result　　结果
the wider community　　广大市民
at ambient temperatures and pressure　　在室温和常压下
adhere to　　坚持
E-factor　　环境因子
geosequestration　　地质封存

Notes

1.　When polyethene was first synthesised, the chemists involved almost certainly thought of a number of potential uses for their new chemical, but they would not have been able to foresee the multitude of uses to which it would eventually be put. 当首次合成了聚乙烯时，几乎可以肯定的是相关化学家想到了这种新化学品的若干潜在用途，但是他们没能预见到它最终被投入使用后的多种用途。本句由一个主句，一个时间状语从句，一个并列分句和一个定语从句组成。the chemists involved 是并列分句的主语部分，involved 过去分词短语做后置定语修饰 the chemists，译为相关化学家。定语从句 to which it would eventually be put 的先行词是 uses，固定搭配 be put to uses 被投入使用。

2.　While the wider community wishes to benefit from the development of new chemicals, there is now an increasing expectation that not only their synthesis be considered, but also their use and disposal. 广大市民希望从新型化学品的使用中受益时，也越来越期望化学家们不仅要考虑化学品的合成，还要考虑它们的使用和处理。名词 development 的含义很多，这里译为"使用"。that not only their synthesis be considered, but also their use and disposal 是同位语从句，用来说明 expectation 的内容。

3.　Green chemistry is design of chemical products and processes that reduce or eliminate the use and/or the generation of hazardous substances. 绿色化学是基于对化工产品和其生产工艺过程的设计，以减少或消除有害物质的使用和产生。本句由一个主句和一个定语从句组成。定语从句的先行词是 processes。

4.　Spider silk has an equivalent strength to Kevlar, yet all that spiders require to synthesis silk are the products of the digestion of insects and enzymes. 蜘蛛丝和芳纶具有等效的强度，但是蜘蛛用来合成丝的物质是昆虫的消化产物和酶。that spiders require to synthesis silk 是定语从句，先行词是 all，关系代词在从句中做 require 的宾语。

5.　By looking at how nature solves chemical problems, green chemists gain clues as to how processes may be changed to make them more benign. 绿色化学家们通过观察大自然是如何解

决化学问题的，从而在如何改变工艺过程，使反应更温和地发生方面得到启发。介词词组 as to 的意思是"在…方面"，宾语从句 how processes may be changed to make them more benign 是介词词组 as to 的宾语。gain clues 获得启发。

6. The environmental scientist's focus would be on the monitoring of the production of these by-products and the means by which they could be cleaned or treated so as to minimise their environmental damage. 环境科学家关注的焦点是监测副产物的产生，净化和处理这些副产物的手段，以减少对环境的破坏。本句的主体结构是 The environmental scientist's focus would be on the monitoring…and the means…so as to minimise…; the monitoring 和 the means 同做介词 on 的宾语; so as to 表目的。

7. An idea currently being considered is that the carbon dioxide produced by the combustion of coal could be stored underground, so-called geosequestration. 目前正在考虑的一个想法是把煤燃烧产生的二氧化碳储存在地下，这种方法被称为地质封存法。

Exercises

1. Put the following into Chinese

plastic shopping bags	green chemistry
hazardous substances	renewable materials
safe synthetic methods	at ambient temperature and pressure

2. Put the following into English

绿色化学的 12 条原则如下：

防止废物的产生	是的，反应是安全的
减少生成衍生物的中间步骤	使用再生性物质
使用安全的合成方法	应用可降解的化学产物
使用催化剂	使用常温和常压
实时监测	尽量不使用辅助物质
环境因子，把原料最大化地转为产品	化工产品低毒

3. Questions

What are the twelve principles of green chemistry?

Lesson Twenty-one   Waste Minimization and Solvent Recovery

Minimizing Solvent Use

As solvents continue to play a large role in pharmaceutical processes, the minimization of solvent use and waste generation has become a key focal point for reducing the overall environmental footprint of the industry. Good solvent selection, elimination of hazardous solvents, and recycling have all been used as means to reduce solvent use and waste generation. The following sections will highlight four methods and how they can be used to reduce or eliminate the amount of solvent used in a pharmaceutical process.

1. Batch versus Continuous Reactors

Generally speaking, the amount of waste generated by batch processing is higher than it is in the case of continuous processing. By comparison, larger amounts of solvents are used in batch processes, as can be seen from the usual size of batch reactors, which can range from 1000 to more than 10000 liters.

2. Biosynthetic Processes

Biocatalysis has now become an area of great interest to many pharmaceutical companies because it can lead to reductions in the number of processing steps and the amount of solvent waste. There have been an increasing number of investigations of novel enzymatic biocatalysts to aid or replace organic synthetic reaction steps. Enzymes generally provide greater chemical selectivity for desired products while operating under mild conditions. Usually, biosynthetic reactions are carried out in water or without organic solvents. This offers the possibility of reducing or eliminating the use of hazardous solvents. Enzymes may also remove the need for toxic heavy/rare metal catalysts used in some reaction steps.

3. Solid-State Chemistry

The use of solid-state chemistry has become a major research area for the green production of many pharmaceutical compounds. Recently, many solid-state reactions have proven to be highly efficient, environmentally benign processes. There have been multiple reports of solid-state reactions used to produce APIs at 100% yield in a solventless system that produces no waste or by-products. The products are made in a state of very high purity and therefore do not require any additional workup, which also reduces solvent use and waste generation.

4. Telescoping

One of the most widely used methods to improve overall process efficiency is to reduce the number of steps and unit operations in a synthetic route. This is more commonly known as telescoping. This can lead to more efficient processes because of the smaller number of steps.

Recycling Solvents

Although several methods are used to reduce or eliminate solvent consumption within a pharmaceutical process, solvents are often used in excess.As solvents still have a great influence on the quality of the final products, it can be very difficult to find suitable replacements . It is therefore desirable to find solvents for a process that can be easily recovered, separated, and purified for reuse. Spent solvents that are not recovered must be disposed of as wastes, which can be quite costly and add to the environmental burden.

Currently, distillation is used for approximately 95% of all solvent separation processes. However, it leads to waste generation, such as the release of GHGs, high energy requirements, the inadequate condensing of overhead (distillate) products. In addition to these, some solvent mixtures can be very difficult to separate because of the closeness of boiling points and the formation of azeotropic mixtures.

Pervaporation (PV) is a membrane-based process used to separate aqueous, azeotropic solvent mixtures. This is done using a hydrophilic, non-porous membrane that is highly selective to water. PV can be used to overcome the separation barriers created by many azeotropic mixtures.

There are several alternatives for dealing with solvent mixtures that are difficult to separate. For example, they can be resold to other companies where the solvent purity requirements are much lower. Solvents containing small amounts of impurities may be used as substitute fuels for internal power stations. Solvents can also be incinerated both on-and off-site. The incineration of solvent wastes can be used for producing steam and electricity for direct use in a plant.

New Words and Expressions

pharmaceutical [ˌfɑːməˈsjuːtikəl] a. 制药（学）的
                                    n. 药物

minimization [ˌminimaiˈzeiʃən, -miˈz-] n. 减到最小限度；估到最低额；轻视

generation [ˌdʒenəˈreiʃən] n. 产生；一代人；生殖

footprint [ˈfutprint] n. 足迹；轮迹；（力等的）影响区；（噪声、电子束等的）影响范围

elimination [iˌlimiˈneiʃən] n. [化] 消除，消去

hazardous [ˌhæzədəs] a. 冒险的；碰运气的；有危险的

highlight [ˈhailait] vt. 突出；强调；使显著；加亮

biosynthetic [ˌbaiəusinˈθetik] a. 生物合成的

biocatalysis n. 生物催化；生物催化酶；生物催化作用

reduction [riˈdʌkʃən] n. 减少；下降；缩小

investigation [inˌvestiˈgeiʃən] n. 调查；调查研究

enzymatic [ˌenzaiˈmætik] a. [生化] 酶的

selectivity [silekˈtiviti] n. 选择性；分离性；选择度

benign [biˈnain] a. 良性的；和蔼的

multiple [ˈmʌltipl] a. 多样的；许多的；多重的

　　　　　　　　　　　　n. 并联；倍数

pervaporation　[pəˌveipəˈreiʃən]　*n.* 渗透蒸发；全蒸发

membrane　[ˈmembrein]　*n.* 膜；薄膜；羊皮纸

resell　[ˌriːˈsel]　*vt.* 再卖；转售

substitute　[ˈsʌbstitjuːt, -tuːt]　*n.* 代用品；代替者

　　　　　　　　　　　　　　vi. 替代

　　　　　　　　　　　　　　vt. 代替

incinerate　[inˈsinəreit]　*vi.* 把…烧成灰；烧弃

　　　　　　　　　　　　vt. 焚化；烧成灰

play a large role　发挥很大作用

solid-state reactions　固相反应

APIs　原料药

in excess　过量

have a great influence on　对…影响巨大

spent solvent　废溶剂

Notes

　　1. As solvents continue to play a large role in pharmaceutical processes, the minimization of solvent use and waste generation has become a key focal point for reducing the overall environmental footprint of the industry. 因为溶剂在制药工业中一直发挥着重要作用，因此减少溶剂的使用和降低废物的产生已成为整个环境工业领域减量化的一个焦点。本句由一个主句和一个从句组成。主句的主语部分是 the minimization of solvent use and waste generation 减少溶剂的使用和降低废物的产生。reducing 减量化，the overall environmental footprint of the industry 整个环境工业领域。

　　2.　There have been an increasing number of investigations of novel enzymatic biocatalysts to aid or replace organic synthetic reaction steps. 对新型酶生物催化剂的研究越来越多，以促进或者取代有机合成反应步骤。

　　3. There have been multiple reports of solid-state reactions used to produce APIs at 100% yield in a solventless system that produces no waste or by-products. 大量固相反应报告表明，在无溶剂系统中，固相反应能以100%的产率生产原料药，这个系统不产生废物和副产物。本句的主体结构是 There have been multiple reports of solid-state reactions。过去分词结构 used to produce APIs at 100% yield in a solventless system 修饰其前面的 reactions；定语从句 that produces no waste or by-products 修饰 system。

　　4.　Spent solvents that are not recovered must be disposed of as wastes, which can be quite costly and add to the environmental burden. 没有回收的废溶剂必须做废物处理，这使得处理成本相当高，同时增加了环境的负担。定语从句 that are not recovered 先行词是 spent solvents。定语从句 which can be quite costly and add to the environmental burden 中的关系代词 which 指代前面整个句子。

Exercises

1. Put the following into Chinese

hazardous solvents   a pharmaceutical process.

batch processes   continuous processes

Biosynthetic Processes   Solid-State Chemistry

2. Questions

How many methods can be used to reduce or elimination the amount of solvent used in a pharmaceutical process. What are they?

Lesson Twenty-two   Low-Carbon Economy and Cleaner Energy

Low-Carbon Economy

A low-carbon economy (LCE) is a concept that refers to an economy which has a minimal output of greenhouse gas (GHG) emissions into the biosphere, but specifically refers to the greenhouse gas carbon dioxide. Recently, most of scientific and public opinion has come to the conclusion there is such an accumulation of GHGs (especially CO_2) in the atmosphere that the climate is changing. The over-concentrations of the GHG are producing global warming with negative impacts on humanity.

Renewable energy and energy efficiency

Recent advances in technology will allow renewable energy and energy efficiency to play major roles in displacing fossil fuels, meeting global energy demand while reducing carbon dioxide emissions.

Renewable energy is energy which comes from natural resources such as sunlight, wind, rain, tides, and geothermal heat, which are renewable. In 2008, about 19% of global final energy consumption came from renewables. During the five-years from the end of 2004 through 2009, worldwide renewable energy capacity grew at rates of $10 \sim 60$ percent annually for many technologies.

Energy efficiency gains in recent decades have been significant, but there is still much more that can be achieved. With a concerted effort and strong policies in place, future energy efficiency improvements are likely to be very large. Heat is one of many forms of "energy wastage" that could be captured to significantly increase useful energy without burning more fossil fuels.

Solutions for Producing Cleaner Energy

Hydro power, currently supplying only six percent of the world's energy, is a renewable energy source. Energy is produced by hydraulic turbines that rotate with the force of rushing water (higher to lower elevation). It is one of the most clean and cheapest way of producing energy, but it can also change the flow of rivers and increase sediment which kills fish.

Wind power. Denmark is currently the world leader in wind power. By 2030, fifty percent of Denmark's energy could be produced by wind power. Wind power emits no greenhouse gases, but it takes up large amounts of land. In order for it to be a reliable source, scientists must develop better power storage techniques. Another concern of people is noise pollution that the large windmills produce along with the reliability of wind.

Solar power uses photovoltaic cells (PV's) to gather thermal energy directly from the sun and use it to produce electricity. Passive solar cells could also be used to heat water, replacing the need for today's hot water heaters. PV's do not emit any greenhouse gases, but they are very expensive.

Nuclear power is strong in Europe with about forty-two percent of their energy produced by fission. Nuclear generation provides about 17% of world electricity, avoiding the emission of up to 2.3 billion tonnes of carbon dioxide annually. France produces 76% and Lithuania produces 85.6% of its energy by nuclear fission. In the United States, people are antinuclear because of 3 Mile Island in 1979 and Chernobyl in 1986. However, many experts say that it is a safe, clean, and reliable source of energy. Nuclear Fission produces no greenhouse gases, but does produce highly toxic radioactive wastes.

New Words and Expressions

biosphere ['baiəsfiə] *n.* 生物圈

accumulation [ə,kju:mju'leiʃən] *n.* 积聚，累积；堆积物

negative ['negətiv] *a.* 负的；消极的；否定的；阴性的

fossil ['fɔsəl] *n.* 化石

　　　　　　a. 化石的

efficiency [i'fiʃənsi] *n.* 效率；效能；功效

capacity [kə'pæsəti] *n.* 能力；容量；资格，地位；生产力

significant [sig'nifikənt] *a.* 重大的；有效的；有意义的；值得注意的；意味深长的

concerted [kən'sə:tid] *a.* 一致的；协调的；协定的；商议定的

wastage ['weistidʒ] *n.* 损耗；消瘦；衰老

hydraulic [hai'drɔ:lik] *a.* 液压的；水力的；水力学的

turbine ['tə:bain, -bin] *n.* [动力] 涡轮；[动力] 涡轮机

elevation [,eli'veiʃən] *n.* 高地；高处；海拔；提高；崇高；正面图

sediment ['sedimənt] *n.* 沉积；沉淀物

reliable [ri'laiəbl] *a.* 可靠的；可信赖的

concern [kən'sə:n] *n.* 关系；关心；关心的事

windmill ['windmil] *n.* 风车；风车房；旋转玩具

photovoltaic [,fəutəuvɔl'teiik] *a.* 光电伏打的，光电的

passive ['pæsiv] *a.* 被动的，消极的；被动语态的

fission ['fiʃən] *n.* [物]裂变；分裂；分体

Lithuania [,liθju:'einiə] *n.* 立陶宛（国家名）

low-carbon economy (LCE) 低碳经济

greenhouse gas (GHG) 温室效应气体

come to the conclusion 得出结论

attribute…to 把…归因于

be likely to 有可能

hydro power 水力发电

along with 连同…一起；与…一道；随同…一起；（除…之外）又

3 Mile Island 三里岛，这里特指的是三里岛核电站事故

Chernobyl 切尔诺贝利（乌克兰的一座城市），这里特指切尔诺贝利核电站事故

Notes

1. Recent advances in technology will allow renewable energy and energy efficiency to play major roles in displacing fossil fuels, meeting global energy demand while reducing carbon dioxide emissions. 技术进步使得可再生能量和能源的有效利用在代替矿物燃料方面起了重要作用, 在满足全球能源需求的同时, 减低了二氧化碳的排放。

2. Heat is one of many forms of "energy wastage" that could be captured to significantly increase useful energy without burning more fossil fuels. 热是"耗能"方式之一, 如果把所耗能量回收, 那么无须燃烧矿物燃料, 就可以极大地提高有用能源 (产量)。定语从句 that could be captured, 根据上下文的含义, 把该定语从句译为条件状语从句。

3. Another concern of people is noise pollution that the large windmills produce along with the reliability of wind. 人们另一个担心是噪声污染, 巨大的风车在产生可靠的风的同时, 也产生了噪声。定语从句 that the large windmills produce along with the reliability of wind, 翻译时采用了分译法。

Exercises

1. Put the following into Chinese

low-carbon economy   greenhouse gas
come to the conclusion   reducing carbon dioxide emissions
fossil fuels   global energy demand

2. Put the following into English

氢能   风能
太阳能   核能
再生能源   能源消耗

3. Questions

How many solutions are there for producing cleaner energy? What are they?

Reading Material: Greenhouse Gases

Greenhouse gases naturally blanket the earth and keep it about 33 degrees Celsius warmer than it would be without these gases in the atmosphere. This is called the "Greenhouse Effect". Over the past century, the earth has increased in temperature by about 0.5 degrees Celsius and many scientists believe this is because of an increase in concentration of the main greenhouse gases: carbon dioxide, methane, nitrous oxide, and fluorocarbons. People are now calling this climate change over the past century the beginning of "Global Warming". Fears are that if people keep producing such gases at increasing rates, the results will be negative in nature, such as more severe floods and droughts, increasing prevalence of insects, sea levels rising, and earth's precipitation may be redistributed. These changes to the environment will most likely cause negative effects on society, such as lower health and decreasing economic development. The world has been emitting greenhouse gases at extremely high rates and has shown only small signs of reducing emissions until the last few years. After the 1997 Kyoto Protocol, the world has finally taken the first step in reducing emissions.

The "greenhouse effect" is the heating of the earth due to the presence of greenhouse gases. Shorter-wavelength solar radiation from the sun passes through earth's atmosphere, then is absorbed by the surface of the earth, causing it to warm. Part of the absorbed energy is then reradiated back to the atmosphere as long wave infared radiation. Little of this long wave radiation escapes back into space; the radiation cannot pass through the greenhouse gases in the atmosphere.

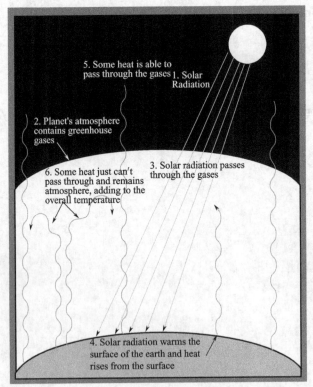

The greenhouse gases selectively transmit the infared waves, trapping some and allowing some to pass through into space. The greenhouse gases absorb these waves and reemit the waves downward, causing the lower atmosphere to warm.

Carbon Dioxide (CO_2) is a colorless, odorless non-flammable gas and is the most prominent greenhouse gas in earth's atmosphere. It is recycled through the atmosphere by the process photosynthesis, which makes human life possible. Photosynthesis is the process of green plants and other organisms transforming light energy into chemical energy. Light Energy is trapped and used to convert carbon dioxide, water, and other minerals into oxygen and energy rich organic compounds. Carbon dioxide is emitted into the air as humans exhale, burn fossil fuels for energy, and deforest the planet. Every year humans add over 30 billion tons of carbon dioxide in the atmosphere by these processes, and it is up thirty percent since 1750.

Methane is a colorless, odorless, flammable gas. It is formed when plants decay and where there is very little air. It is often called swamp gas because it is abundant around water and swamps. Bacteria that breakdown organic matter in wetlands and bacteria that are found in cows, sheep, goats, buffalo, termites, and camels produce methane naturally. Since 1750, methane has doubled, and could double again by 2050. Each year we add 350~500 million tons of methane to the air by raising livestock, coal mining, drilling for oil and natural gas, rice cultivation, and garbage sitting in landfills. It stays in the atmosphere for only 10 years, but traps 20 times more heat than carbon dioxide.

Nitrous oxide is another colorless greenhouse gas, however, it has a sweet odor. It is primarily used as an anesthetic because it deadens pain and for this characteristic is called "laughing gas". This gas is released naturally from oceans and by bacteria in soils. Nitrous oxide gas has risen by more than 15% since 1750. Each year we add 7~13 million tons into the atmosphere by using nitrogen based fertilizers, disposing of human and animal waste in sewage treatment plants, automobile exhaust, and other sources not yet identified. It is important to reduce emissions because the nitrous oxide we release today will still be trapped in the atmosphere 100 years from now.

Fluorocarbons is a general term for any group of synthetic organic compounds that contain fluorine and carbon. Many of these compounds, such as chlorofluorocarbons(CFCs), can be easily converted from gas to liquid or liquid to gas. Because of these properties, CFCs can be used in aerosol cans, refrigerators, and air conditioners. Studies in the 1970's showed that when CFCs are emitted into the atmosphere, they break down molecules in the earth's ozone layer. Since then, the use of CFCs has significantly decreased and they are banned from production in the United States. The substitute for CFCs is hydrofluorocarbons (HFCs). HFCs do not harm or breakdown the ozone molecule, but they do trap heat in the atmosphere, making it a greenhouse gas, aiding in global warming. HFCs are used in air conditioners and refrigerators. The way to reduce emissions of this gas is to be sure that in both devices the coolant is recycled and all leaks are properly fixed. Also, before throwing the appliances away, be sure to recover the coolant in each.

科技英语翻译十　被动语态的翻译方法

英语的被动语态是通过助动词 be 和及物动词的过去分词组合而成的。被动语态在英语中的使用比汉语要多得多。尤其是在科技英语中，大量使用被动语态可以说是科技英语的一大特征，所以英语被动语态的句子，译成汉语时，很多情况下都译成主动句或无主句，但有时仍然需要译成被动语态，必要时还可以译成其他的句子形式。所有这些都要求译者遵循翻译的基本标准，以译文能够准确表达原文意思，符合汉语表达方式为宗旨，灵活采用各种翻译方法和技巧。

一、译为主动句

英语的被动语态结构的句子译为汉语的主动语态结构的句子有下列几种译法。

1. 原句子中的主语在译文中仍作主语

英语中的被动句在汉译过程中，将原文句子中的主语仍译为译文中的主语一般有以下 3 种情况。

（1）当英语被动句子中的主语是无生命的名词，句子中也没有 by 引出的动作发出者，汉译时可以不改变原句子主语及句子的结构，直接译成汉语的主动语态，如下。

> The new reforming reactor **has been put into use**.

　　新型重整反应器已投入使用。

> The surface tension **is reduced.**

　　表面张力降低。

（2）英语中有些被动句，汉译时可以不改变原句子主语及句子的结构，译为带表语的主动句，实际上就是汉语的"是"字结构的句型，如下。

> Ammonia **is synthesized by reacting hydrogen with nitrogen at a molar ratio of 3 to 1**.

　　氨气是摩尔比为3:1的氢气和氮气合成的。

（3）科技英语在汉译时，为了使译文符合汉语的表达习惯，常常可以把英语被动语态的动词译为主语，而原英语被动句的主语被转换成汉语句子的定语，如下。

> A surfactant **is characterized by its tendency to absorb at surfaces and interfaces.**

　　表面活性剂的特征是在表面和界面有吸附的能力。

2. 原句子中的主语在汉译文中作宾语

将原英语句子中的主语译为译文中的宾语常用的方法一般有以下四种。

（1）如果被动句中由 by 引出动作的发出者，有时为了突出动作的发出者，可以把它转译成汉语句子的主语（有时可以是动宾结构的短语作主语），同时将原文中的主语转译为宾语，从而将英语被动句译成汉语的主动句，如下。

> When the phase boundary is covered **by surfactant molecules**, the surface tension is reduced.

　　一旦表面活性剂分子覆盖相边界，表面张力就降低。

（2）在译文中增译"人们"、"有人"、"大家"等泛指人称代词，在译文中作主语，同时将原文的主语译成宾语，从而将整个句子译为汉语的主动句，如下。

> Air **is known** to possess weight.

　　大家知道空气具有重量。

（3）英语被动句中一些地点状语、方式状语等的介词短语，其介词后的名词常常可译为汉语句子的主语（其中引导名词的介词常常省略不译），而原句子中的主语译为汉语句子的宾语，从而将整个句子译为汉语的主动句，如下。

> Larger amounts of solvents **are used in batch processes**.

　　间歇生产过程使用大量溶剂。

（4）当英语的被动句中含有动词不定式时，一般可将原文句子的主语和谓语合译为汉语的动宾结构短语（这时原句的主语转译为动宾结构短语中的宾语），在译文中作主语，并将动词不定式转译为译文的谓语，从而将整个句子译为汉语的主动句，如下。

> **Biosynthetic method is used** to reduce or eliminate the amount of solvent used in a pharmaceutical process.

　　利用生物合成法来减低和消除制药工艺中所用的溶剂量。

二、译为无主句

科技英语中大量使用被动语态来描述科学事实、科学过程和科学理论，汉译时，为了更好地反映科技英语的这一特点，并使译文符合汉语的表达习惯，故经常将被动语态的句子译为汉语的无主句，同时，原被动句的主语转译成汉译的宾语，如下。

> The feed **is charged (fed)** into a vessel at the beginning of the process and the vessel contents **are removed** sometime later.

　　在化学过程开始时向容器中加入原料，一段时间后把容器内容物移除。

三、译为被动句

在翻译被动句时，如果要着重强调被动的动作，英语的被动句也可直译为汉语的被动句。在翻译时可通过增加汉语中一些表达被动语态的词语来体现译文的被动意义。

1. 增译"被"

> LDPE **is used** to make rigid containers.

　　低密度聚乙烯**被用来**制作刚性容器。

2. 增译"受"

> Without the ozone layer, plants and animals would also **be affected**.

　　如果没有臭氧层，动植物也将**受到**影响。

3. 增译"由"

> By 2030, fifty percent of Denmark's energy could **be produced by wind power**.

　　到 2030 年，丹麦 50%的能量能**由风能产生**。

4. 增译"用"

> LDPE **is defined by a density range of 0.910～0.940 g/cm^3**.

　　用 0.910～0.940 g/cm^3 的密度范围来定义低密度聚乙烯。

5. 增译"靠"、"通过"、"以"

➢ Rapid condensation **is complished by means of condenser.**

迅速冷凝是靠冷凝器来完成的。

6. 增译"加以"、"予以"、"得到"

➢ The leakage of steam should **be paid attenion to.**

蒸气泄漏问题应予以重视。

7. 增译"（为）…所"、"之所以"

➢ **Effective solubilization is obtained** with surfactants that bring the interfacial tension of oil and water down to ultra-low values.

增溶效果之所以好，是因为表面活性剂使油和水的界面张力降到极低。

四、译为"把"字句

所谓的"把"字句，是汉语中独有的一种句型，在翻译有些英语的被动句（无论有无 by 引导的短语）时，可将汉语的"把"字放在原文句子之前，即将原英语被动句的主语转译成"把"字的宾语，并将整个句子译为汉语的"把"字句。"把"字句有两种译法。

1. 译为无主语的"把"字句

在翻译原文不含有 by 引导的被动句时，只要将汉语的"把"字放在原文句子的主语之前，整个译文句子没有主语，如下。

➢ **The synthesis gas is cooled to** $0{}^\circ\!\text{C}$.

把合成气冷却到零摄氏度。

2. 译为带主语的"把"字句

如原文是含有 by 引导的被动句时，通常将 by 后面的名词译为句子主语，并同时省译介词 by，并将整个句子译成汉语的带主语的"把"字句。

➢ **CO_2 removal can be done** by using 2 methods.

两种方法能把 **CO_2** 除去。

五、it 作形式主语的被动句译法

英语中有些被动句时 it 作形式主语的，在翻译此类结构的被动句时，通常要译成主动形式，其方法有两种：

1. 译为无主句

将 it 作形式主语的被动句译成无主句，通常汉语中有约定俗成的表达方法，如下。

➢ It should be noted that the hydrocracking of paraffins is the only one reforming reaction that consumes hydrogen.

应该注意到链烷烃的催化裂解是唯一一个耗氢反应。

2. 增译主语

就是在译文中增加泛指的主语，如"人们"、"有人"、"大家"、"我们"等，如下。

➢ **It is pointed** that the over-concentrations of the GHG are producing global warming.

有人指出温室气体浓度过高导致全球变暖。

➢ **It is desired** that some solvents can be easily recovered, separated, and purified for reuse.

人们希望某些溶剂能被很容易地回收、分离和纯化，以再利用。

Vocabulary (词汇表)

A

a small fraction of 一小部分【10】

a variety of 种种；各种各样的…【12】

absorption column 吸收塔【4】

absorption [əb'sɔ:pʃən] n. 吸收，吸收过程；吸收作用【4】

accelerate [ək'seləreit] vt. 使…加快；使…增速【12】

accomplished [ə'kʌmpliʃt] a. 熟练的，有技巧的；完成的；有修养的；有学问的【8】

accordance [ə'kɔ:dəns] n. 一致；和谐【6】

accumulate [ə'kju:mjuleit] vi. 累积，积聚
vt. 积攒【3】

accumulation [ə,kju:mju'leiʃən] n. 积聚，累积；堆积物【22】

acetic [ə'si:tik] a. 醋的，乙酸的【10】

acetone ['æsitəun] n. [化]丙酮【11】

acetylsalicylic [ə'si:til,sæli'silik] a. 乙酰水杨酸的【11】

activated ['æktiveitid] a. 活性化的；活泼的
v. 使活动起来；使激活；有生气【8】

additionally [ə'diʃənli] adv. 此外；又，加之【19】

adequate ['ædikwit] a. 充足的；适当的；胜任的【14】

adhere to 坚持【20】

adhere [əd'hiə] vi. 黏附，附着【4】

adipic [ə'dipik] a. 脂肪的，油质的【11】

adsorption [æd'sɔ:pʃən] n. 吸附(作用)【4】

aggregate ['ægrigət, 'ægrigeit] vi., vt. 集；集合；合计【16】

agitator ['ædʒi,teitə] n. 搅拌器【7】

alcohol ethoxylates 醇聚氧乙烯醚【17】

aliphatic [,æli'fætik] a. 脂肪质的, [有化] 脂肪族的【14】

alkali ['ælkəlai] n. 碱；可溶性无机盐
a. 碱性的【11】

alkanes ['ælkeinz] n. [化] 链烷，烷(属)烃 【18】

alkyl ['ælkil] a. 烷基的，烃基的
n. 烷基，烃基【17】

alkyl ether sulfates 烷基醚硫酸盐【17】

alkyl sulfates 烷基硫酸盐【17】

alkylaryl sulfonates 烷基磺酸盐【17】

alkylate ['ælkileit, 'ælkileit] vt. 使烷基化【11】

along with 连同…一起；与…一道；随同…一起；（除…之外）又【22】

alpha ['ælfə] n. [化]α-位，子位；α-位(或子位)异构(化合)物【15】

alpha-olefins α-烯烃【15】

alternative [ɔ:l'tə:nətiv] a. 供选择的；选择性的；交替的【16】

alternatively [ɔ:l'tə:nətivli] adv. 非此即彼；二者择一地；作为一种选择【19】

alumina [ə'lju:minə] n. [无化] 氧化铝；矾土【10】

ambient ['æmbiənt] a. 周围的；外界的；环绕的【20】

amine [ə'mi:n, 'æmin] n. 胺【8】

ammonia [ə'məunjə] n. [化]氨【1】

amphiphile ['æmfi,fail] n. [化]两亲物；亲水脂分子【16】

anaerobic [,ænɛə'rəubik] a. 厌氧的，厌气的；没有气而能生活的【10】

analogous [ə'næləgəs] a. 类似的【1】

analogue ['ænəlɔg] n. 类似物；类似情况；对等的人【18】

analyze ['ænəlaiz] vt. 对…进行分析，分解【3】

anhydride [æn'haidraid] n. [化] 酸酐；脱水物【14】

anhydrous [æn'haidrəs] a. [化]无水的【8】

anionic [,ænai'ɔnik] a. 阴离子的，带负电荷的离子的【14】

anthropogenic [,ænθrəupəu'dʒenik] a. 人为的；人类起源的【22】

注：【 】内教学表示介绍该词汇的课文序号。

antifreeze ['æntifri:z] *n.* 防冻剂【10】

antiknock [,ænti'nɔk] *n.* 抗爆剂；抗爆
　　　　　　　　　　a. 抗爆的；抗震的【12】

antioxidant [,ænti'ɔksidənt] *n.* 抗氧化剂；硬化
　　防止剂；防老化剂【11】

anti-redeposition agents　抗沉积剂【17】

a number of　若干；很多，许多【18】

APIs　原料药【21】

application [,æpli'keiʃən] *n.* 应用；申请；应用
　　程序；敷用【16】

approach [ə'prəutʃ] *vt.* 接近；着手处理
　　　　　　　　　　vi. 靠近
　　　　　　　　　　n. 方法；途径；接近【2】

appropriate [ə'prəuprieit, ə'prəupriət] *a.* 适当的
　　【10】

approximately [ə'prɔksimitli] *adv.* 大约，近似
　　地；近于【1】

aqueous ['eikwiəs] *a.* 水的，水般的【14】

aramid ['ærəmid] *n.* [材料学] 芳族聚酰胺纤维；芳
　　族聚酰胺；芳纶【15】

argon ['ɑ:gɔn] *n.* [化]氩（18号元素）【8】

aromatic [,ærəu'mætik] *a.* 芳香的，芬芳的；芳
　　香族的
　　　　　　　　　　n. 芳香植物；芳香剂【13】

aromatization [,ərəumətai'zeiʃən, -ti'z-] *n.* [有化]
　　芳构化；香花作用；香味【13】

articular [ɑ:'tikjulə] *a.* [解剖学] 关节的【15】

artificial [,ɑ:ti'fiʃəl] *a.* 人造的；仿造的【15】

asbestos [æz'bestɔs] *n.* [矿]石棉【9】

assemble [ə'sembl] *vt.* 集合，聚集；装配；收集
　　　　　　　　　　vi. 集合，聚集【6】

assume [ə'sju:m,ə'su:m] *vt.* 假定；采取；呈现
　　【19】

at ambient temperatures and pressure　在室温和常压
　　下【20】

atmosphere ['ætməˌsfiə] *n.* 气氛；大气；空气【3】

atmospheric [,ætmə'sferik] *a.* 大气的；大气层
　　的；大气引起的【7】

atomic [ə'tɔmik] *a.* 原子的，原子能的；微粒子
　　的【1】

atomic weight　原子量【1】

atom [ætəm] *n.* 原子【1】

attach [ə'tætʃ] *vt. & vi.* 贴上；系；附上【6】

attribute...to　把…归因于【22】

autothermal reforming　自热转化【10】

auxiliary [ɔ:g'ziljəri] *a.* 辅助的；副的；附加的
　　【20】

available [ə'veiləbl] *a.* 有效的，可得的；可利用
　　的；空闲的【10】

average molecular weight　平均分子量【1】

azeotrope [ə'zi:ətrəup] *n.* 共沸混合物, 恒沸物【5】

azo ['æzəu] *a.* 【化学】偶氮(基)的【14】

B

bacteria [bæk'tiəriə] *n.* 细菌【10】

bactericide [bæk'tiəriˌsaid] *n.* [药] 杀菌剂【11】

baffle spacing　挡板间距【6】

baffle ['bæfl] *n.* 挡板；困惑【6】

barrier ['bæriə] *n.* 栅栏，关卡，障碍，隔阂【4】

based on　以…为基础，基于【3】

batch [bætʃ] *n.* 一批；一炉；一次所制之量【3】

batch process　间歇过程；分批工艺，分批法；批流
　　程【3】

bauxite ['bɔ:ksait] *n.* 矾土, [矿物] 铁铝氧石；
　　[矿物] 铝土矿【12】

be converted to　被转化成【1】

be derived from　来自，源自于；从…而产生出来的；
　　由…得到【19】

be discharged into　被排入【9】

be equal to　相等；胜任；合适【1】

be equivalent to　等（同）于；相等（当）于…；与…
　　等效【13】

be independent of　不依赖…；不受…支配；独立
　　于…之外【17】

be likely to　有可能【22】

be purged to　清除【8】

be referred to as　被称为…【10】

be replaced with　被替换成【7】

be resistant to　对…有抵抗作用【15】

be restricted to　仅限于…；局限于…【16】

be subdivided into　被再分成【5】

be subjected to　受到…；经受…【19】

be susceptible to　对…敏感；易患…；易受…影响
　　【13】

bead [bi:d] *n.* 珠子；滴；念珠【12】

bearing [,bɛəriŋ] *n.* [机] 轴承【15】

benign [bi'nain] *a.* 温和的；良性的；和蔼的，亲
　　切的；吉利的【20】

bentonite ['bentənait] *n.* [土壤] 膨润土【12】

benzene ['benzi:n] *n.* [化]苯【11】

benzoic [ben'zəuik] *a.* 安息香的【11】

benzole ['benzɔl,-zəul] *n.* 粗苯【19】

benzoyl peroxide [有化] 过氧化苯甲酰【14】

biocatalysis *n.* 生物催化；生物催化酶；生物催化作用【21】

biomass ['baiəumæs] *n.* 生物质【10】

biosphere ['baiəsfiə] *n.* 生物圈【22】

biosynthetic [,baiəusin'θetik] *a.* 生物合成的【21】

blast ['baiəu,blæst] *n.* 一阵；爆炸；冲击波【10】

blast furnacen. 鼓风炉，高炉【10】

bleaching ['blitʃiŋ] *a.* 漂白的
　　　　　　　　　　　　n. 漂白【17】

blend [blend] *vt.* 混合【3】

boil up 上升蒸汽【4】

boiler ['bɔilə] *n.* 锅炉；烧水壶，热水器；盛热水器【8】

boiling point 沸点【4】

boundary ['baundəri] *n.* 边界；范围；分界线【3】

boxlike ['bɔkslaik] *a.* 像箱子一样的【9】

branching ['bræntʃiŋ] *a.* 发枝的；分歧的
　　　　　　　　　　　　n. 分支；分歧【15】

braze [breiz] *vt.* 铜焊，用黄铜镀或制造【6】

brine [brain] *n.* 盐水；卤水；海水【8】

bubble ['bʌbl] *n.* 气泡，泡沫，泡状物；透明圆形罩，圆形顶
　　　　　　　vi. 沸腾，冒泡；发出气泡声
　　　　　　　vt. 使冒泡；滔滔不绝地说【4】

bubble point 泡点【4】

buildup ['bildʌp] *n.* 积累；增强；发展；形成；组合【8】

bulk [bʌlk] *n.* 体积，容量；大块；大多数，大部分
　　　　　　　vt. 使扩大，使形成大量；使显得重要【16】

butane ['bju:tein] *n.* [化] 丁烷【13】

butcher ['butʃə] *n.* 屠夫【15】

C

calculate ['kælkjuleit] *vi.* 计算；以为；作打算
　　　　　　　　　vt. 计算；预测；认为；打算【1】

calculation [,kælkju:leiʃən] *n.* 计算；估计；深思熟虑；计算的结果【7】

caprolactam [,kæprəu'læktəm] *n.* [有化] 己内酰胺【11】

carbonization [,kɑ:bənai'zeiʃən;-ni'z-] *n.* [化] 碳化，碳化作用；干馏【18】

carrier ['kæriə] *n.* 载体【9】

carry out 执行，实行；贯彻；实现；完成【2】

cascade [kæs'keid] *n.* 小瀑布；喷流；层叠
　　　　　　　vi. 像瀑布般冲下或倾泻
　　　　　　　v. 使瀑布似地落下【5】

catalyst ['kætəlist] *n.* 催化剂；刺激因素【12】

catalytic [kætə'litik] *a.* 接触反应的；起催化作用的【8】

catalytic cracking [油气] 催化裂化【12】

catalytic steam reforming 催化蒸汽转化【8】

catalyze ['kætəlaiz] *vt.* [化]催化；刺激，促进【10】

category ['kætigəri] *n.* 种类，分类；范畴【3】

cation ['kætaiən] *n.* [化] 阳离子；[化] 正离子【11】

cationic [,kætai'ɔnik] *n.* 阳离子；
　　　　　　　　　　a. 阳离子的【16】

caustic ['kɔ:stik] *a.* [化] 腐蚀性的；[化] 苛性的；刻薄的；焦散的【11】

centrifuge ['sentrifju:dʒ] *n.* 离心机【4】

chamber ['tʃeimbə] *n.* (身体或器官内的) 室，腔；房间；会所【9】

char [tʃɑ:] *n.* 炭；木炭；煤渣【18】

characteristic [,kæriktə'ristik] *a.* 特有的，典型的【7】

chemical equilibrium [化]化学平衡【2】

chernobyl 切尔诺贝利（乌克兰的一座城市），这里特指切尔诺贝利核电站事故【22】

chiller ['tʃilə] *n.* 冷却装置【8】

chlorine ['klɔ:ri:n] *n.* 氯（17 号化学元素）【8】

chlorobenzene [,klɔ:rəu'benzi:n] *n.* [有化] 氯苯【11】

chromium ['krəumjəm] *n.* [化]铬（24 号元素，符号 Cr）【8】

chromophore ['krəuməfɔ:] *n.* 发色团【17】

circular ['sə:kjulə] *a.* 圆形的，环形的；循环的【6】

circulate ['sə:kjuleit] *vi.* 传播，流传；循环；流通【12】

circumferential [sə,kʌmfə'renʃəl] *a.* 圆周的【6】

classification [,klæsifi'keiʃən] *n.* 分类；类别，等级【3】

cleavage ['kli:vidʒ] *n.* [化] 裂解；劈开，分裂【11】

coefficient [,kəui'fiʃənt] *n.* [数]系数；[物]率；协

同因素【2】

coil [kɔil] *n.* 蛇管式换热器，(一)卷，(一)圈；盘卷之物【7】

colorless ['kʌləlis] *a.* 无趣味的；苍白的；无色的【9】

column ['kɔləm] *n.* 圆柱，柱形物；纵队，列；专栏【3】

combustible [kəm'bʌstəbl] *a.* 易燃的【19】

combustion [kəm'bʌstʃən] *n.* 燃烧，氧化；骚动【8】

combustion furnace　燃烧炉【4】

come to the conclusion　得出结论【22】

commercially [kə'məːʃəli] *adv.* 商业上；通商上【9】

commodity [kə'mɔditi] *n.* 产品【7】

common practice　惯例、常见的做法【16】

community [kə'mjuːniti] *n.* 社区；群落；共同体；团体【20】

comparable ['kɔmpərəbl] *a.* 类似的，同类的，相当的，可比较的，比得上的【6】

component [kəm'pəunənt] *a.* 组成的，构成的 *n.* 成分；组件；元件【1】

compress [kəm'pres, 'kɔmpres] *vt.* 1. 压紧，压缩 2. 精简【4】

concentration [,kɔnsən'treiʃən] *n.* 浓度；集中；浓缩；专心【1】

concern [kən'səːn] *n.* 关系；关心；关心的事【22】

concerted [kən'səːtid] *a.* 一致的；协调的；协定的；商议定的【22】

condensation [,kɔnden'seiʃən] *n.* 冷凝，凝聚，冷凝液【4】

cone [kəun] *n.* 圆锥体，圆锥形；球果【9】

consequence ['kɔnsi,kwəns] *n.* 结果；重要性；推论【4】

conservation [,kɔnsə'veiʃən] *n.* 保存，保持；保护【3】

conserve [kən'səːv, 'kɔnsəːv] *vt.* 保存；使守恒；（物理、化学变化或进化过程中）使（能量等）守恒【3】

constant ['kɔnstənt] *a.* 不变的；恒定的；经常的 *n.* 常数；恒量【3】

constitute ['kɔnstitjuːt] *vt.* 组成，构成；建立；任命【1】

constraint [kən'streint] *n.* 约束；局促，态度不自然；强制【2】

construction [kən'strʌkʃən] *n.* 建造，建设；建

筑业【6】

consumption [kən'sʌmpʃən] *n.* 消费；消耗【2】

contact process　[化] 接触过程；接触法【9】

container [kən'teinə] *n.* 集装箱；容器【3】

continuous distillation　连续蒸馏【5】

continuous process　连续过程；连续法；连续加工【3】

continuous-flow　[流] 连续流；持续气流【7】

convenient [kən'viːnjənt] *a.* 方便的【1】

conventional [kən'venʃənəl] *a.* 符合习俗的，传统的；常见的；惯例的【19】

conversion [kən'vəːʃən] *n.* 转换；变换；兑换【1】

conversion factor　换算因数；转换因子；变换因数【1】

converter [kən'vəːtə] *n.* 转化器；变流器，整流器【8】

convey [kən'vei] *vt.* 传达；运输；让与【12】

coordination [kəu,ɔːdi'neiʃən]　【15】

coproduct ['kəu,prɔdəkt] *n.* 副产物【11】

correspond [,kɔːri'spɔnd] *vi.* 符合，一致；相应；通信【7】

corresponding [,kɔːri'spɔndiŋ] *a.* 相符的；相当的，相应的；一致的【2】

corresponding to　与…相一致【2】

corrosive [kə'rəusiv] *a.* 腐蚀的；侵蚀性的 *n.* 腐蚀物【9】

countercurrent ['kauntə,kʌrənt] *n.* 逆流,反向电流 *adv.* 相反地【5】

covalent [kəu'veilənt] *a.* [化] 共价的；[化]共有原子价的【14】

creosote ['kriːə,səut] *n.* [林] 木馏油；碳酸；杂芬油【19】

cresol ['kriːsəul] *n.* [化] 甲酚【19】

crossflow ['krɔsfləu] *n.* 横流式的，横向气流【6】

cross-link ['krɔːs,liŋk] *n.* [化] (聚合物的)交联；交联键【15】

crystal ['kristəl] *n.* 水晶；结晶，晶体；水晶饰品 *a.* 水晶的；透明的，清澈的【4】

crystalline ['kristəlain] *a.* 透明的；水晶般的；水晶制的【11】

crystallization [,kristəlai'zeiʃən] *n.* 结晶化【4】

cubic ['kjuːbik] *a.* 立方体的，立方的【13】

cumene ['kjuːmin] *n.* 异丙基苯，枯烯【11】

currently ['kʌrəntli] *adv.* 现在，现时，目前，当前【19】

customary unit　常用的单位【13】

cyclone ['saikləun] *n.* 旋风；[气象] 气旋；飓风【12】

D

deactivation [di:,ækti'veiʃən] n. [物化] 减活化作用；钝化作用【14】

deal with 处理；涉及；做生意【10】

decanter [di'kæntə] n. 玻璃水瓶【4】

decisive [di'saisiv] a. 决定性的；果断的，坚定的【17】

decomposition [,di:kɔmpə'ziʃən] n. 分解【11】

definitely ['definitli] adv. 清楚地，当然；明确地，肯定地【14】

degradable [di'greidəbi] a. [化] (废料)可降解的，(复合化合物)可分解的，易受化学【18】

dehydrocyclization [di:haidrəsaikli'zeiʃən] n. 脱氢环化（作用）【13】

dehydrogenation [di:haidrədʒə'neiʃən] n. [化] 脱氢作用【12】

demonstration [,demən'streiʃən] n. (用标本、实例等)说明，表明，示范【18】

denaturant [di:'neitʃərənt] n. 变性剂【10】

denominator [di'nɔmineitə] n. 分母；命名者【1】

denote [di'nəut] vt. 表示，指示【16】

density ['densiti] n. 密集，稠密，[物，化] 密度【7】

derivatization n. 衍生；衍生化；衍生化作用【20】

derive [di'raiv] vt. 得到，取得，获得【12】

descend [di'send] vt. & vi. 下来，下去【5】

destructive [di'strʌktiv] a. 破坏的；毁灭性的；有害的，消极的【18】

desulfurization [di:sʌlfjurai'zeiʃən, -ri'z-] n. 脱硫作用；直接脱硫【8】

detergency [di'tə:dʒənsi,-dʒəns] n. 洗净（作用）；去垢力，去垢性【17】

detergent [di'tə:dʒent] n. 清洁剂；去垢剂【17】

dew point 露点【4】

diameter [dai'æmitə] n. 直径【5】

diffuse from into 从扩散到【5】

diffusion [di'fju:ʒən] n. [物，化] 扩散；漫射【5】

digestion [di:dʒestʃən, dai-] n.消化；领悟【20】

dilute [dai'lju:t, di-] a. 稀释的；淡的【9】

dilute acid 稀酸【9】

dimension [di'menʃən] n. 尺寸，度量【6】

dioxide [dai'ɔksaid] n. [化]二氧化物【8】

dismutation [,dismju'teiʃən] n. 歧化作用【14】

dispersing [di'spə:siŋ] n. 分配，分散【17】

disposal [dis'pəuzəl] n. 处理；支配；清理；安排【20】

dissolution [,disə'lju:ʃən] n. 分解，溶解【18】

dissolve [di'zɔlv] vt. 使溶解；使分解；使液化【14】

dissolver [di'zɔlvə] n. 溶解装置；溶解器【18】

distill [dis'til] vt. 蒸馏；提取；使滴下
　　　　　　　vi. 滴下；蒸馏；作为精华产生【11】

distillation [,disti'leiʃən] n. 蒸馏，净化；蒸馏法；精华，蒸馏物【3】

distillation column 蒸馏塔【4】

distillation [,distə'leiʃən] n. (各种释义的)蒸馏(过程) 2.蒸馏物【4】

distinctive [dis'tiŋktiv] a. 有特色的，与众不同的【10】

diverse [dai'və:s, di-] a. 不同的；多种多样的；变化多的【15】

dominant ['dɔminənt] a. 显性的；占优势的；支配的，统治的【9】

double-pipe exchanger 套管式换热器【6】

downcomer['daun,kʌmə] n. 降液管【5】

droplet ['drɔplit] n. 小滴，微滴【4】

duration [djuə'reiʃən] n. 持续；持续期间，存在期间【3】

E

economical [,ikə'nɔmikəl] a.节约的, 节俭的, 经济【6】

economically [,i:kə'nɔmikəli] adv. 经济地；在经济上；节俭地【19】

E-factor 环境因子【20】

effluent ['efluənt] n. 污水；流出物；废气
　　　　　　　a. 流出的，发出的【8】

elastic [i'læstik] a. 有弹力的, 有弹性的, 可伸缩的, 灵活的【6】

elastomer [i'læstəmə] n. [化] 弹性体，高弹体【15】

electric heating mantle 电加热【7】

electrolysis [,ilek'trɔlisis] n. 电解，电解作用；以电针除痣【8】

electron [i'lektrɔn] n. 电子【14】

elevation [,eli'veiʃən] n. 高地；高处；海拔；提

高；崇高；正面图【22】

eliminate [i'limineit] *vt.* 消除；排除【17】

elimination [i,limi'neiʃən] *n.* [化] 消除，消去【21】

emerge [i'məːdʒ] *vi.* 出现；显出；暴露【4】

emission [i'miʃən] *n.*（光、热等的）发射，散发；喷射；发行【8】

employ [im'plɔi] *n.* 使用；雇用【19】

emulsification [i,mʌlsifi'keiʃən] *n.* [化] 乳化；[化] 乳化作用；乳化剂【17】

emulsion [i'mʌlʃən] *n.* [物，化] 乳状液；感光乳剂【14】

enclosure [in'kləuʒə] *n.* 附件；围墙；围场【9】

encounter [in'kauntə] *vt.* 遭遇，邂逅；遇到【1】

endothermic [,endəu'θəːmik,-məl] *a.* [化] 吸热的【10】

enrichment [in'ritʃmənt] *n.* 丰富,肥沃,浓缩,富集【5】

entrain [in'trein] *vt.* 导致；产生；携带；带走【5】

enzymatic [,enzai'mætik] *a.* [生化] 酶的【21】

enzyme ['enzaim] *n.* 酶【17】

epoxy [ep'ɔksi] *a.* 环氧的

　　　　　　　　n. 环氧基树脂【11】

equation [i'kweiʒən, -ʃən] *n.* 方程式，等式；相等；反应式【2】

equilibrium [,iːkwi'libriəm] *n.* 均衡；平静；保持平衡的能力【2】

equivalent [i'kwivələnt] *a.* 等价的，相等的；同意义的

　　　　　　　　n. 等价物，相等物【1】

essentially [i'senʃəli] *adv.* 本质上；本来【2】

ethane ['eθein] *n.* [有化] 乙烷[亦作 dimethyl]【13】

ethanol ['eθə,nɔl] *n.* [化] 乙醇，酒精【2】

ethene ['eθiːn] *n.* 乙烯（等于 ethylene）【15】

ether ['iːθə] *n.* 乙醚；以太；苍天；天空醚【10】

ethoxylate ['eθəksileit] *n.* 乙氧基化物【17】

ethylene ['eθiliːn] *n.* [化] 乙烯【2】

evaporate [i'væpəreit] *vt. & vi.*(使某物)蒸发掉【4】

eventually [i'ventʃuəli] *adv.* 最后，终于【2】

evolve into　发展成，进化成【12】

exchange [iks'tʃeindʒ] *n.* 交换，互换【6】

exchanger [iks'tʃeindʒə] *n.* 交换器；交易所；交换程序【8】

exemplify [ig'zemplifai] *vt.* 例证；例示【13】

exhausted [ig'zɔːstid] *a.* 耗尽的；疲惫的

　　　　　　　　v. 用尽；耗尽；使…筋疲力尽【14】

exotherm ['eksəu,θəːm] *n.* [化] 放热曲线；（因释放化学能而引起的）升温【7】

exothermal [,eksəu'θəːmik,-'θəːməl] *a.* 放热的；放能的【19】

exothermic [,eksəu'θəːmik,-'θəːməl] *a.* 发热的；放出热量的【10】

expectation [,ekspek'teiʃən] *n.* 期待；预期；指望【22】

extraction [ik'strækʃən] *n.* 取出；抽出；拔出；抽出物；出身【18】

extrudate [iks'truːdeit] *n.* 挤出物；压出型材【12】

<h1 align="center">F</h1>

facilitate [fə'siliteit] *vt.* 促进；帮助；使容易【12】

facility [fə'siliti] *n.* 设施；设备；容易；灵巧【19】

fall into　分成【3】

fasten ['fɑːsən] *vt.* 系紧，拴牢【6】

feedstock ['fiːdstɔk] *n.* 原料；给料（指供送入机器或加工厂的原料）【8】

ferrous ['ferəs] *a.* [化] 亚铁的；铁的，含铁的【9】

fertilizer ['fəːtilaizə] *n.* 肥料【9】

filter cake　滤饼【4】

filter ['filtə] *n.* 过滤，过滤器

　　　　　　vt. & vi. 透过，过滤【4】

fission ['fiʃən] *n.* [物] 裂变；分裂；分体【22】

flammable ['flæməbl] *a.* 易燃的；可燃的；可燃性的

　　　　　　　　n. 易燃物【10】

flexibility [,fleksə'biliti] *n.* 弹性；适应性；灵活性【15】

flow down　向下流【4】

flow rate　流速【5】

flow up　向上流【4】

fluctuation [,flʌktju'eiʃən] *n.* 起伏，波动【3】

fluid catalytic cracking　[化工] 流化床催化裂化【12】

fluoresce ['fluə'res] *vi.* 发荧光【17】

footprint ['futprint] *n.* 足迹；轮迹；(力等的)影响区；(噪声、电子束等的)影响范围【21】

foresee [fɔː'siː] *vt.* 预知；预见【20】

formaldehyde [fɔː'mældihaid] *n.* [化] 蚁醛，甲醛

【10】

formula ['fɔ:mjulə] n. 公式, 准则；配方【2】

formulation [,fɔ:mju'leiʃən] n. 配制；制剂；配制成的材料；构想，规划；公式化【17】

hydrolytic [,haidrə'litik] a. 水解的，水解作用的【17】

fortify ['fɔ:tifai] vt. 加强；增强 vi. 筑防御工事【8】

fossil ['fɔsəl] n. 化石；a. 化石的【22】

foul [faul] vt. 弄脏；犯规；淤塞；缠住，妨害
a. 邪恶的；污秽的；犯规的；淤塞的
vi. 犯规；缠结；腐烂
n. 犯规；缠绕
adv. 违反规则地，不正当地【6】

G

garbage ['gɑ:bidʒ] n. 垃圾；废物【15】

gasifier ['gæsifaiə] n. 气化炉，燃气发生炉【18】

gasoline ['gæsəli:n] n. 汽油【12】

Gay-Lussac tower [化]盖-吕萨克塔【9】

Gear [giə] n. 齿轮；装置，工具；传动装置【15】

geosequestration 地质封存【20】

geothermal [,dʒi:əu'θə:məl] a. 地热的；地温的【22】

get rid of 摆脱，除去【12】

give off 发出（光等）；长出（枝、杈等）【10】

H

have a great influence on 对…影响巨大【21】

hazardous ['hæzədəs] a. 冒险的；碰运气的；有危险的【21】

heat exchanger 换热器【6】

heat-transfer coefficient 传热系数【6】

hemolytic [hi:'mɔlitik] a. [生理][免疫] 溶血的【14】

hemolytic breaking 平拆分解、均裂【14】

heptane ['heptein] n. [有化] 庚烷【13】

herbicide ['hə:bisaid, 'ə:-] n.[农药] 除草剂【11】

heteroatom ['hetərəu,ætəm] n. [化] 杂原子，杂环原子【18】

highlight ['hailait] vt. 突出；强调；使显著；加亮【21】

hip [hip] n.髋关节【15】

horizontal [,hɔri'zɔntəl] a. 水平的，与地平线平行的【4】

hydraulic [hai'drɔ:lik] a. 液压的；水力的；水力

fraction ['frækʃən] n. [数] 分数；部分；小部分；稍微【1】

fractionation [,frækʃə'neiʃən] n. 分馏【12】

frothy ['frɔθi] a. 多泡的；起泡的；空洞的，浅薄的【5】

fuller's earth 漂白土【12】

fuming [fjumiŋ] a. 熏的；冒烟的【9】

fundamental [,fʌndə'mentəl] a. 基本的，根本的 n. 基本原理；基本原则【2】

furnace ['fə:nis] n. 熔炉，火炉【4】

fusion ['fju:ʒən] n. 融合；熔化；熔接；融合物【11】

glassware ['glɑ:swɛə, 'glæs-] n. 玻璃器具类【7】

Glover tower 格洛弗塔；喷淋式气体洗涤塔【9】

good practice 良好的做法；良好的习惯做法【2】

gradient ['greidiənt] n. 梯度；倾斜度；坡度 a. 倾斜的；步行的【7】

gravity ['græviti] n. 万有引力；地心引力；重力【4】

greenhouse gas (GHG) 温室效应气体【22】

groove [gru:v] n.槽【6】

学的【22】

hydro power 水力发电【22】

hydrocarbon [,haidrəu'kɑ:bən] n. 碳氢化合物【12】

hydrocracking ['haidrəu,krækiŋ] n. [油气] 加氢裂化；氢化裂解【13】

hydrodesulfurization ['haidrəudi,sʌlfjuərai!zeiʃən,-ri'z-] n. 加氢脱烃【13】

hydrogen ['haidrədʒən] n. 氢【8】

hydrogen peroxide [无化] 过氧化氢【14】

hydrogenation [,haidrədʒi'neiʃən] n. 加氢；[化] 氢化作用【12】

hydrolyze ['haidrəlaiz] vt. 使水解 vi. 水解【2】

hydroperoxide [,haidrəupə'rɔksaid] n. 氢过氧化物【11】

hydrophobic groups 疏水基【16】

hydrosilicate ['haidrəu'silikit, -keit] *n.* 含水硅酸盐【12】

hydroxybenzene [hai,drɔksi'benziːn] *n.* [化]酚;

[化] 羟基苯【11】

hydroxylation [haidrɔksi'leiʃən] *n.* [有化] 羟基化【11】

I

ICI abbr.   英国化学工业公司（Imperial Chemical Industries Ltd.）【10】

immaterial [,imə'tiəriːəl] *a.* 不重要的, 不相干的 [,imə'tiəriəl]【5】

immense [i'mens] *a.* 巨大的, 广大的; 无边无际的; [口] 非常好的【16】

immiscible [i'misəbl] *a.*不能混合的,不融和的【4】

implant [im'plɑːnt, -'plænt, 'implɑːnt, -plænt] *n.* [医] 植入物; 植入管
vi. 被移植【15】

implement ['implimənt, 'impliment] *vt.* 实施,执行; 实现, 使生效【18】

implication [,impli'keiʃən] *n.* 含义; 暗示; 牵连, 卷入 ; 涉及, 密切关系【20】

impose constraints on   施加约束【2】

impurities [im'pjuəritis] *n.* 杂质（impurity 的复数）【8】

in accordance with   与···一致;【6】

in an effort to   企图（努力想）; 试图要【3】

in bulk   在本体中【14】

in emulsion   在乳液中【14】

in excess   过量【21】

injection [in'dʒekʃən] *n.* 注射; 注射剂; 充血; 射入轨道【19】

In principle   大体上, 原则上【16】

in situ   在原地, 就地; 在原来位置【17】

in succession   接连地, 连续地【9】

in suspension   在悬浮液中【14】

inadequate [in'ædikwit] *a.*不充足的,不适当的【6】

incinerate [in'sinəreit] *vi.* 把···烧成灰; 烧弃
vt. 焚化; 烧成灰【21】

indicate ['indikeit] *vt.* 表明; 指出; 预示; 象征【2】

individual [,indi'vidjuəl] *a.*个别的, 单独的, 个人的【7】

individually [,indi'vidjuəli, -dʒu-] *adv.* 个别地, 单独地【13】

inhibitor [in'hibitə] *n.* [化]抑制剂, 抗化剂; 抑制者【8】

initiate [i'niʃieit, i'niʃiət, -eit] *vt.* 开始, 创始; 发起; 使初步了解; 现在分词 initiating 【14】

initiator [i'niʃieitə] *n.* [化] 引发剂; 发起人, 创始者; 启动程序; 引爆器【8】

inject [in'dʒekt] *vt.* 注入; 注射【10】

inject into   把···注入【10】

injection [in'dʒekʃən] *n.* 注射; 注射剂; 充血; 射入轨道【11】

in-situ [in'saituː] *n.* 原位; 现场【10】

install [in'stɔːl] *vt.* 安装【6】

insulation [,insju'leiʃən, 'insə-] *n.* 绝缘; 隔离, 孤立【15】

integrated ['intigreitid] *a.* 综合的; 完整的; 互相协调的
v. 整合; 使···成整体【12】

intensively [in'tensivli] *adv.* 深入地; 强烈地; 集中地【10】

intentional [in'tenʃənəl] *a.* 故意的; 蓄意的; 策划的【3】

intermediate [,intə'miːdjət, -dieit] *n.*[化] 中间物; 媒介【11】

interphase ['intə(ː)feiz] *n.* 界面
a. 界间的,相间的【4】

intimate ['intimət] *a.* 亲密的; 私人的; 精通的
n. 至交; 知己
vt. 暗示; 通知; 宣布【5】

investigation [in,vesti'geiʃən] *n.* 调查; 调查研究【21】

ion ['aiən] *n.* [化] 离子【15】

iridium [ai'ridiəm, i'ri-] *n.* [化] 铱（Ir）【11】

irreversible [,iri'vəːsəbl] *a.* 不可逆的; 不能取消的; 不能翻转的【2】

is referred to as   被称为···【16】

isomerization [ai,sɔmərai'zeiʃən, -ri'z-] *n.* [化] 异构化; 异构化作用【12】

isopentane [,aisəu'pentein] *n.* [有化] 异戊烷【13】

isotope ['aisəutəup] *n.* [化]同位素【1】

J

jacket ['dʒækit] *n.* 保温套，绝热罩【7】

joint [dʒɔint] *n.* 关节【15】

jug [dʒʌg] *n.* [轻] 水壶；监牢【15】

K

kerosene ['kerəsi:n] *n.* 煤油，火油【12】

Kevlar ['kevlɑ:] *n.* 芳纶；凯夫拉尔，纤维 B（一种合成纤维），是一种合成纤维，高硬度高抗张强度，重量轻，很好的抗磨损能力，用以代替汽车

轮胎等中的钢丝【18】

kilopascal ['kiləu'pæskəl] *n.* 千帕【8】

kinetic [ki'netik, kai-] *a.* 动力学的；运动的；活跃的【2】

L

lane [lein] *n.* 小路，小巷【6】

law of conservation of mass 物质守恒定律【3】

lead chamber process 铅室法【9】

lead-lined chamber 衬铅室【9】

leak [li:k] *vi.* 漏，渗；泄漏出去
　　　　　vt. 使渗漏，泄露【3】

leakage ['li:kidʒ] *n.* 泄漏；渗漏物；漏出量【5】

let-down separator 让式冷水机组【8】

lignite ['lignait] *n.* [矿物] 褐煤【18】

liquefaction [,likwi'fækʃən] *n.* 液化；熔解；液化(作用)【18】

liquefy ['likwə,fai] *vt. & vi.* 液化，溶解，液化【4】

literally ['litərəli] *adv.* 照字面地；逐字地【16】

lithuania [,liθju:'einiə] *n.* 立陶宛（国家名）【22】

litre ['li:tə] *n.* 公升【16】

low-carbon economy (LCE) 低碳经济【22】

lubricant ['lu:brikənt] *n.* 润滑剂；润滑油【18】

M

macromolecule [,mækrəu'mɔlikju:l] *n.* [高分子] 高分子；[化] 大分子【14】

magnetic [mæg'netik] *a.* 有吸引力的；有磁性的；地磁的【7】

magnetic stirrer 磁力搅拌器【7】

mandrel ['mændril] *n.* 心轴【6】

mantle ['mæntl] *n.* 覆盖物;幕;披风;斗篷【7】

manufacture [,mænju'fæktʃə] *vt.* 制造；加工；捏造【8】

margarine [,mɑ:dʒə'ri:n] *n.* 人造黄油；人造奶油【15】

mass transfer 传质【7】

mature [mə'tjuə] *a.* 成熟的；充分考虑的；到期的；成年人的【10】

maximize ['mæksimaiz] *vt.* 取…最大值；对…极为重视
　　　　　　　　vi. 尽可能广义地解释；达到最大值【20】

measurement ['meʒəmənt] *n.* 测量；度量；尺寸；

量度制【3】

mechanical [mi'kænikəl] *a.* 机械的；呆板的；力学的；无意识的；手工操作的【7】

mechanical agitator 机械搅拌器【7】

mechanism ['mekənizəm] *n.* 机制；原理，途径；进程；机械装置；技巧【16】

medium ['mi:djəm] *n.* 媒介，手段，方法，工具【4】

membrane ['membrein] *n.* 膜;薄膜;羊皮纸【21】

merchant ['mə:tʃənt] *n.* 商人，批发商；店主【9】

metabolism [mi'tæbəlizəm, me-] *n.* 新陈代谢【10】

metallocene [mi'tæləusi:n] *n.* [化] 金属茂(合物);茂(合)金属【15】

methanation [,meθə'neiʃən] *n.* [化]甲烷化；甲烷化作用【8】

methane ['mi:θein] *n.* [化]甲烷；沼气【3】

methanol ['meθənɔl] *n.* 甲醇【10】

methyl ['mi:θail, 'miθil] *n.* 甲基；木精【10】

methylcyclohexane ['mi:θail,saiklə'heksein] *n.* 甲基环己烷；甲基溶纤剂【13】

methylene diphenyl diisocyanate 甲基二苯二异氰酸酯【11】

micelle [mi'sel, mai-] *n.* [化][物][生物] 胶粒；胶束，胶囊【14】

micellization [mi,selai'zei∫ən, -li'z-] *n.* 胶束形成；胶束化【16】

microemulsion [,maikrəui'mʌl∫ən] *n.* 微乳液；微型乳剂【17】

microgram ['maikrəugræm] *n.* 微克；微观图，显微照片【8】

migration [mai'grei∫ən] *n.* [化][物] 移动，徙动【14】

milliliter ['mili,li:tə] *n.* 毫升【7】

minimization [,minimai'zei∫ən, -mi'z-] *n.* 减到最小限度；估到最低额；轻视【21】

minor ['mainə] *a.* 较小的；次要的；未成年的；[音]小调的；二流的
n. 未成年人；副修科目；小调
vi. 副修【3】

mist [mist] *n.* 薄雾；视线模糊不清；模糊不清之物【5】

miticide ['mitisaid] *n.* [农药] 杀螨药【11】

mixer ['miksə] *n.* 搅拌器,混合器【4】

mnemonic [ni:'mɔnik] *a.* 记忆的；助记的；记忆术的【20】

moderate ['mɔdərət, 'mɔdəreit] *a.* 温和的；适度的，中等的；有节制的【10】

modification [,mɔdifi'kei∫ən] *n.* 修改，修正；改变【18】

mole [məul] *n.* [化] 摩尔，克分子(量)[亦作 mol]【1】

mole fraction 摩尔分数；克分子分数【1】

mole mass 摩尔质量【1】

molecular [mə'lekjulə] *a.* 分子的；由分子组成的【1】

molecular weight [化]分子量【1】

molecule ['mɔlikjul] *n.* 分子；微小颗粒，微粒【1】

molybdenum [mɔ'libdinəm] *n.* [化] 钼（金属元素，符号 Mo，原子序号 42）【18】

momentum [məu'mentəm] *n.* 动量；动力；冲力；势头【3】

monitor ['mɔnitə] *vt.* 检测，监测；监控【20】

monoethanolamine ['mɔnəu,eθənə'læmi:n] *n.* [化]单乙醇胺【8】

monomer ['mɔnəmə] *n.* 单体；单元结构【14】

monoxide [mɔ'nɔksaid, mə-] *n.* [化]一氧化物【1】

multilayer ['mʌlti,leiə] *a.* 有多层的
n. 多分子层【15】

multiple ['mʌltipl] *a.* 多样的；许多的；多重的
n. 并联；倍数【21】

multitude ['mʌlti,tju:d, -,tu:d] *n.* 许多；大量；多数【20】

municipal [mju:'nisipəl] *a.* 市政的，市的；地方自治的【19】

N

naphtha ['næfθə, 'næp-] *n.* 石脑油；挥发油；粗汽油【8】

naphthene ['næfθi:n, 'næp-] *n.* [有化] 环烷，[有化] 环烷属烃【13】

negative ['negətiv] *a.* 负的；消极的；否定的；阴性的【22】

neutralize ['nju:trəlaiz] *vt.* 使…中和；使…无效；使…中立【11】

neutron ['nju:trɔn] *n.* 中子【1】

nickel ['nikəl] *n.* 镍；镍币；五分镍币
vt. 镀镍于【8】

nipple ['nipl] *n.* 螺纹接套；乳头，奶头；奶嘴【15】

nitric ['naitrik] *a.* 氮的；硝石的；含氮的【11】

nitrogen ['naitrədʒən] *n.* [化]氮【8】

nitrogen ['naitrədʒən] *n.* [化]氮【13】

nitrous ['naitrəs] *a.* 氮的；硝石的；含氮的【9】

nonferrous [nɔn'ferəs] *a.* 非铁的；不含铁的【9】

nonionic [,nɔnai'ɔnik] *a.* 在溶液中不分解成离子的
n. 非离子物质【11】

numerator ['nju:məreitə] *n.* 分子；计算者；计算器【1】

numerically [nju:'merikəli] *adv.*数字上；用数字表示【1】

nylon ['nailɔn] *n.* 尼龙，[纺] 聚酰胺纤维；尼龙袜【11】

O

occasion [ə'keiʒən, əu-] *n.* 时机，机会；场合；理由【3】

occasionally [ə'keiʒənəli, əu-] *adv.* 偶尔，间或【1】

octane ['ɔktein] *n.* 辛烷【13】

octane rating 辛烷值【13】

odor ['əudə] *n.* 气味；名声【11】

odorless ['əudəlis] *a.* 没有气味的【9】

oil bath 油浴；油浴锅；【7】

olefin ['əuləfin, 'ɔ-] *n.* 烯烃【15】

oleum ['əuliəm] *n.* 发烟硫酸【9】

onwards ['ɔnwədz] *adv.* 向前；在前面【9】

optimize ['ɔptimaiz] *vt.* 使最优化，使完善【12】

ore [ɔː] *n.* 矿；矿石【9】

organic [ɔː'gænik] *a.* 有机的；器官的；组织的；根本的【7】

originate [ə'ridʒəneit] *vt.* 引起；创作
vi. 发源；发生；起航【5】

originate from 发源于【15】

outline ['autlain] *n.* 轮廓；大纲；概要；略图【2】

overhead ['əuvəhed, ,əuvə'hed] *adv.* 在头顶上；在空中；在高处
a. 高架的；在头上的；在头顶上的
n. 天花板；经常费用【4】

oxidise ['ɔksidaiz] *vt.* 使氧化；使生锈【9】

oxidize ['ɔksidaiz] *vt.* 使生锈；使氧化
vi. 氧化【11】

oxygen ['ɔksidʒən] *n.* 氧气，氧【2】

P

palladium [pə'leidiəm] *n.* [化] 钯【11】

paraffin ['pærəfin] *n.* 石蜡；[有化] 链烷烃；硬石蜡【13】

parallel ['pærəlel] *a.* (指至少两条线)平行【6】

parameter [pə'ræmitə] *n.* 参数；系数；参量【12】

partial ['pɑːʃəl] *a.* 局部的；部分的【10】

partial pressure [物] 分压；[物] 分压力【13】

participate [pɑː'tisipeit] *vi.* 参与，参加；分享【2】

participate in 参加；分享【2】

passive ['pæsiv] *a.* 被动的，消极的；被动语态的【22】

patent ['peitənt] *vt.* 授予专利；取得…的专利权【9】

pellet ['pelit] *n.* 小球；[军] 小子弹（枪用）【12】

pentachlorophenol [,pentə,klɔːrə'fiːnəul] *n.*[有化][农药] 五氯苯酚【11】

pentoxide [pen'tɔksaid,-sid] *n.* [化]五氧化物【9】

perforate ['pəːfəreit] *vt.*穿孔于，在…上打眼【6】

perforated ['pəːfəreitid] *a.* 穿孔的；有排孔的
v. 穿孔（perforate 的过去分词）【5】

perforated plate 筛板【5】

perforation [,pəːfə'reiʃən] *n.* 穿孔；贯穿【5】

permanent ['pəːmənənt] *a.* 永久的，永恒的；不变的【15】

peroxide [pə'rɔksaid] *n.* 过氧化物；过氧化氢
vt. 以过氧化氢漂白；以过氧化物处理
a. 以过氧化氢漂白的【14】

pervaporation [pə,veipə'reiʃən] *n.* 渗透蒸发；全蒸发【21】

petroleum [pi'trəuliəm, pə-] *n.* 石油【12】

petroleum refinery naphthas 石油炼厂石脑油【13】

petroleum refining [油气] 石油加工,石油炼制【12】

pharmaceutical [,fɑːmə'sjuːtikəl] *a.* 制药（学）的
n. 药物【21】

phenate ['fiːneit, 'fe-] *n.* 石炭酸盐；苯酚盐【11】

phenol ['fiːnɔl, fi'n-] *n.* [化] 苯酚，石炭酸【11】

phenolic [fi'nɔlik] *a.* [有化] 酚的；[胶黏] 酚醛树脂的；石炭酸的
n. [胶黏] 酚醛树脂【11】

phosphate ['fɔsfeit] *n.* [化]磷酸盐；[地]皮膜化成【17】

photochemical [,fəutəu'kemikəl] *a.* 光化学的
n. 光催化学物【14】

photovoltaic [,fəutəuvɔl'teiik] *a.* 光电伏打的,光电的【22】

pickling ['pikliŋ] *n.* 酸洗；浸酸【9】

pitch [pitʃ] *vt.* 投；定位于；掷；用沥青涂；扎

营；向前倾跌

　　　　　　n. 沥青；程度；音高；投掷；树脂；倾斜

　　　　　　vi. 投掷；倾斜；坠落；搭帐篷【6】

plate columns　　板式塔【5】

platformer　['plæt,fɔ:mə]　*n.* 铂重整装置【13】

platinum　['plætinəm]　*n.* 铂；白金【9】

play a large role　　发挥很大作用【21】

poison　['pɔizən]　*vt.* 污染；使中毒，放毒于；败坏【8】

polar　['pəulə]　*a.* 极地的；两极的；正好相反的　*n.* [数]极面；极线【10】

polycarbonate　[,pɔli'ka:bə,neit, -nit]　*n.* [高分子]聚碳酸酯【11】

polyelectrolyte　[,pɔlii'lektrə,lait]　*n.* 聚合电解质【17】

polyethylene　[,pɔli:'eθə,li:n]　*n.* [高分子] 聚乙烯【15】

polymerization　[,pɔlimərai'zeiʃən, -ri'z-]　*n.* 聚合；[高分子] 聚合作用【14】

polypropylene　[,pɔli'prəupə,li:n]　*n.* [高分子] 聚丙烯【15】

polystyrene　[,pɔli'staiəri:n, -'stiərin]　*n.* [高分子]聚苯乙烯【14】

porous medium　　多孔介质【4】

porous　['pɔ:rəs]　*a.* 能穿透的，能渗透的，有毛孔或气孔的【4】

potable water plumbing systems　　饮用水管道系统【15】

potassium　[pə'tæsjəm]　*n.* 钾【8】

potential　[pəu'tenfəl]　*a.* 潜在的；可能的；势的【20】

precede　[pri:'si:d, pri-]　*vt.* 领先，在…之前；优于，高于【2】

precipitation　[pri,sipi'teiʃən]　*n.* 沉淀，沉淀物；冰雹；坠落；鲁莽【17】

preheat　[pri:'hi:t]　*vt.* 预先加热【7】

preliminary　[pri'liminəri]　*a.* 初步的，预备的，开端的【7】

preparatory　[pri'pærətəri, 'prepə-]　*a.* 预备的【9】

preservative　[pri'zə:vətiv]　*n.* 防腐剂；预防法；防护层　*a.* 防腐的；有保存力的；有保护性的【11】

primary　['praiməri]　*a.* 主要的；初级的；基本的【8】

procedure　[prə'si:dʒə]　*n.* 程序，手续；步骤【2】

proceed　[prəu'si:d]　*vi.* 开始；继续进行；发生；行进【2】

prominent　['prɔminənt]　*a.* 突出的，显著的；杰出的；卓越的【17】

promote　[prə'məut]　*vt.* 提升，提拔【6】

propagation　[,prɔpə'geiʃən]　*n.* 传播；繁殖；增殖【14】

propane　['prəupein]　*n.* [化] 丙烷【13】

propel　[prəu'pel]　*vt.* 推进；推动【4】

proportion　[prəu'pɔ:ʃən]　*n.* 比例；部分；面积；均衡【2】

proton　['prəutɔn]　*n.* [物]质子【1】

pulverize　['pʌlvəraiz]　*vt.* 粉碎；使成粉末；研磨【18】

purify　['pjuərifai]　*vt.* 净化；使纯净 vi. 变纯净；净化【11】

purity　['pjuəriti]　*n.* 纯净；纯洁；纯粹；纯度【5】

pyrite　['pairait]　*n.* [矿]黄铁矿【9】

pyrolysis　[paiə'rɔlisis,pi-]　*n.* [化] 热解(作用)；高温分解【18】

R

radical　['rædikəl]　[化] 基的；[物, 化] 原子团【14】

rate　[reit]　*n.* 比率，率, (运动、变化等的)速度；进度【5】

rather than　　而不是【10】

ratio　['reiʃiəu, -ʃəu]　*n.* 比率，比例【1】

reactant　[ri'æktənt, ri:-]　*n.* [化]反应物;反应剂【2】

rearrange　[,ri:ə'reindʒ]　*vt.* [化] (分子)重排【13】

reboiler　[ri:'bɔilə]　*n.* 再沸器;重沸器;再煮器[锅];再蒸锅;加热再生器【5】

recombination　[,ri:kɔmbi'neiʃən]　*n.*复合，再结合；[遗] 重组【14】

rectification　[,rektifi'keiʃən]　*n.*[化] 精馏【5】

recycle　[,ri:'saikl]　*vt.*回收利用【4】

reddish　['rediʃ]　*a.* 微红的；略带红色的【11】

redeposition　[ri:,dipɔ'ziʃən]　*n.* 再沉淀，再沉积再沈积作用【17】

refinery　[ri'fainəri]　*n.* 精炼厂；提炼厂；冶炼厂【9】

reflux　['ri:flʌks]　*n.* 逆流,退潮【4】

reformate　[ri'fə:meit]　*n.* [油气] 重整油；重整产品【13】

reformer　[ri'fɔːmə]　*n.* 改革运动者；改革家；改良者【8】

reforming　[ri'fɔːmiŋ]　*n.* 变换；重整；改进【10】

regenerate　[ri,dʒenəreit, riː-]　*vt.* 使再生；革新
　　　　　　　　　　　　　　　vi. 再生；革新
　　　　　　　　　　　　　　　a. 再生的；革新的
　　　【8】

regeneration　[ri,dʒenə'reiʃən, riː-]　*n.* [生物][化][物]
　　再生，重生；重建【12】

relatively　['relətivli]　*adv.* 相当地；相对地，比较地【19】

reliable　[ri'laiəbl]　*a.* 可靠的；可信赖的【22】

remainder　[ri'meində]　*n.* 剩余物；残余部分【5】

removal　[ri'muːvəl]　*n.* 免职；移动；排除；搬迁【8】

renewable　[ri'njuːəbl]　*a.* 可再生的；可更新的；可继续的
　　　　　　　　　　　　　　n. 再生性能源【20】

repetitive　[ri'petətiv]　*a.* 重复的【14】

resell　[,riː'sel]　*vt.* 再卖；转售【21】

reservoir　['rezəvwɑː]　*n.* 储藏所；仓库；水库；蓄水池【16】

residual　[ri'zidʒuːəl]　*a.* 存留下来的;剩余的;残余的【4】

resin　['rezin]　*n.* 树脂；松香【11】

respectively　[ris'pektivli]　*adv.* 各自地，各个地，分别地【5】

restriction　[ri'strikʃən]　*n.* 限制；约束；束缚【3】

restructure　[riː'strʌktʃə]　*vt.* 重构；重建；更改结构【13】

resultant　[ri'zʌltənt]　*n.* 合力；结果；生成物
　　　　　　　　　　　　　a. 结果的；合成的【12】

retorting　[ri'tɔːtiŋ]　*n.* 干馏；蒸馏法【18】

reversible　[ri'vəːsəbl]　*a.* 可逆的；可撤销的；可反转的【2】

rhenium　['riːniəm]　*n.* [化] 铼（75 号元素，符号为 Re）【13】

rhodium　['rəudiəm]　*n.* [化] 铑（一种元素）【11】

rink　['riŋk]　*n.* 溜冰场，室内溜冰场；冰球场【15】

riser　['raizə]　*n.* [化工] 气门【12】

roast　[rəust]　*vt.* 烤，焙；烘，烘烤；暴露于某种热力下以得温暖【9】

rod　[rɔd]　*n.* 竿，杆，棒【6】

roll-up　卷起作用【17】

rotate　[rəu'teit]　*vt. & vi.* (使某物)旋转[转动]，(使某人或某物) 轮流[按顺序循环]【6】

S

saccharin　['sækərin]　*n.* [有化] 糖精；邻磺酰苯甲酰亚胺【19】

salicylic　[,sæli'silik]　*a.* 水杨酸的；得自水杨酸的【11】

salicylic acid　水杨酸；柳酸【11】

saponification　[sə,pɔnifi'keiʃən]　*n.* 皂化【17】

saran wrap　保鲜膜【15】

saturated　['sætʃəreitid]　*a.* 饱和的；深颜色的；渗透的
　　　　　　　　　　　　　　v. 使渗透，使饱和【14】

scrubbing　[skrʌbliŋ]　*n.* 洗涤【8】

sebum　['siːbəm]　*n.* 皮脂；牛羊脂【17】

sediment　['sedimənt]　*n.* 沉积；沉淀物【22】

segment　['segmənt, seg'ment, 'segment]　*vi.* 分割
　　　　　　　　　　　　　　　　　　　　n. 段；部分
　　　　　　　　　　　　　　　　　　　　vt. 分割【6】

selectivity　[silek'tiviti]　*n.* 选择性；分离性；选择度【21】

semibatch process　半间歇过程【3】

sequestering agents　螯合剂【17】

setscrew　['setskruː]　*n.* 固定螺丝钉【6】

severe　[si'viə]　*a.* 严峻的；严厉的；剧烈的；苛刻的【12】

severity　[si'veriti]　*n.* 严重；严格；猛烈【13】

shale　[ʃeil]　*n.* [岩] 页岩；泥板岩【18】

shell　[ʃel]　*n* (贝、卵、坚果等的)壳，外壳，框架【6】

shutdown　['ʃʌtdaun]　*n.* 关机；停工；关门；停播【13】

sieve-plate column　筛板塔【5】

silica　['silikə]　*n.* 二氧化硅；硅土【9】

silica-alumina　硅铝比【12】

simplify　['simplifai]　*vt.* 简化;使单纯;使简易【3】

situ　*n* 原地【13】

sludge　[slʌdʒ]　*n.* 烂泥；泥泞；泥状雪；沉淀物【9】

slurry　['sləːri, 'slʌ-]　*n.* 泥浆；悬浮液【4】

solid-state reactions　固相反应【21】

solubility　[,sɔlju'biləti]　*n.* 溶解性；可溶性；溶解度【16】

solubilization　[,sɔljubilai'zeiʃən, -li'z-]　*n.* 溶解，增溶【17】

soluble ['sɔljubl] *a.* 可溶的，可溶解的；可解决的【14】

solute ['sɔljuːt, sɔ'ljuːt] *n.* 溶质；溶解物【1】

solution [sə'luːʃən] *n.* 溶液；溶解；解答【1】

solvent ['sɔlvənt, 'sɔːl-] *a.* 有溶解力的；有偿付能力的 *n.* 溶剂；解决方法【1】

spacer ['speisə] *n.* 分程隔板【6】

species ['spiːʃiːz] *n.* 物种，种，种类；类型【4】

specified ['spesifaid] *a.* 规定的；详细说明的【2】

specify ['spesifai, -sə-] *vt.* 指定；详细说明；列举；把…列入说明书【3】

spent catalyst 废催化剂；用过的催化剂【12】

spent solvent 废溶剂【21】

split [split] *vt.* 分离；使分离；劈开；离开【11】

spontaneously [spɔn'teiniəsli] *a.* 自发地；自然地；不由自主地【14】

square [skwɛə] *n.* 正方形【6】

stack [stæk] *n.* 堆；堆叠；大量，许多【3】

stain [stein] *n.* 污点；瑕疵；着色剂
　　　　vi. 污染；被沾污
　　　　vt. 沾污；败坏；给…着色【17】

standard method 标准方法；标准措施【10】

standpipe ['stændpaip] *n.* 立管；储水管；管体式水塔【12】

starch [stɑːtʃ] *n.* [化]淀粉；刻板，生硬【17】

start-up ['stɑːtʌp] *n.* 启动
　　　　a. 启动阶段的；开始阶段的（异体字 startup）【3】

steadily ['stedili] *adv.* 稳定地；稳固地；有规则地【3】

steam stripping 汽提；蒸汽脱附【8】

stereospecific [,steriəuspi'sifik,,stiə-] *a.* [化]立体有择的，立体定向的[亦作 stereoregular]【14】

stirrer ['stəːrə] *n.* 搅拌器【7】

stoichiometric [,stɔikiə'metrik] *a.* 化学计量的；化学计算的【2】

stoichiometry [,stɔiki'ɔmitri] *n.* 化学计量学【2】

stripper ['stripə] [化] 汽提塔；剥离器【12】

stripping ['stripiŋ] *n.* 剥离；剥脱；拆封
　　　　v. 剥去；脱掉；拆除【8】

styrene ['stairiːn, 'sti-] *n.* [有化] 苯乙烯【14】

subdivided [,sʌbdi'vaid, 'sʌbdivaid] *vi.* 细分，再分 *vt.* 把…再分，把…细分【5】

subsequently ['sʌbsikwəntli] *adv.* 随后，其后；后来【4】

substance ['sʌbstəns] *n.*（化学成分明确的）物质；实质【1】

substantial [səb'stænʃəl] *a.* 1. 坚固的；结实的 2. 大量的，可观的【5】

substantially [səb'stænʃəli] *adv.* 实质上；大体上；充分地【15】

substitute ['sʌbstitjuːt, -tuːt] *n.* 代用品；代替者 *vi.* 替代 *vt.* 代替【21】

sufficient [sə'fiʃənt] *a.* 足够的；充分的【8】

sulfa ['sʌlfə] *a.* 磺胺的；磺胺药剂的【19】

sulfate ['sʌlfeit] *n.* 硫酸盐 *vt.* 使成硫酸盐；用硫酸处理；【17】

sulfide ['sʌlfaid] *n.* [化]硫化物【8】

sulfonation [,sʌlfə'neiʃən] *n.* [有化] 磺化【11】

sulfur ['sʌlfə] *vt.* 用硫黄处理 *n.* 硫黄；硫黄色【13】

sulfuric [sʌl'fjuərik] *adj.* 硫黄的；含多量硫黄的；含（六价）硫的【9】

surfactant [sə:'fæktənt] *n.* [化]表面活性剂 *a.* [化]表面活性剂的【16】

surroundings [sə'raundiŋz] *n.* (周围的)环境[事物]【4】

susceptible [sə'septəbl] *a.* 易受影响的；易感动的；容许…的 *n.* 易得病的人【13】

suspension [sə'spenʃən] *n.* 暂停；悬浮；停职【4】

syngas ['singæs] *n.* 合成气（指一氧化碳和氢的混合物，尤指由低级煤生产的可燃性气体，主要用于化学和生物加工以及甲醇的生产）【10】

synonymous [si'nɔniməs] *a.* 同义的；同义词的；同义突变的【16】

synthetic [sin'θetik] *a.* 综合的；合成的，人造的【8】

T

tabular ['tæbjulə] *a.* 列成表格的；扁平的【1】

take into account 考虑；重视；体谅【3】

taper ['teipə] *vt. & vi.*(使)一端逐渐变细；(使)成锥形；逐渐变小【6】

technique [tek'niːk] *n.* (工艺或技术)技巧；技术【19】

temptation [temp'teiʃən] *n.* 引诱；诱惑物【20】

tendency ['tendənsi] *n.* 倾向，趋势；癖好【16】

tensile ['tensail, -səl] *a.* [物] 张力的；拉力的；抗张力的【15】

termination [ˌtə:mi'neiʃən] *n.* 结束，终止【14】

terminology [ˌtə:mi'nɔlədʒi] *n.* 术语，术语学；用词【2】

tert-butyl [tə:t-'bju:til] *n.*[化] 叔丁基【10】

the aged catalyst 老化的催化剂【13】

the critical micelle concentration 临界胶束浓度【16】

the ebullated bed reactor 沸腾床反应器【18】

the lyophilic part 亲水部分【16】

the underlying surface 基质表面【17】

the wider community 广大市民【20】

thermal ['θə:məl] *a.* 热的，热量的【12】

thermal cracking [油气] 热裂解【12】

thermodynamic [ˌθə:məudai'næmik, -di-] *a.* 热力学的；使用热动力的【2】

thermoplast ['θə:məuplæst] *n.* 【化学】热塑性塑料【15】

thermoplastic [ˌθə:məu'plæstik] *a.* 热塑性的 *n.*[塑料] 热塑性塑料【15】

thickness ['θiknis] *n.* 厚度；层；含混不清；浓度【6】

to some extent 在一定程度上；在某种程度上【10】

toluene ['tɔljui:n] *n.* [有化] 甲苯【11】

toughness ['tʌfnis] *n.*[力] 韧性；有黏性【15】

toxicity [tɔk'sisəti] *n.* [毒理学] 毒性，毒力【20】

transfer [træns'fə:] *vt. & vi.* 转移；迁移【4】

transient ['trænziənt, -si-, -ʃənt, 'trɑ:n-] *a.* 短暂的；路过的
　　　　　　　　　　　　　　　n. 瞬变现象【3】

transparency [træns'pærənsi, -'pɛə-, trænz-, trɑ:n-] *n.* 透明，透明度【15】

triangular [trai'æŋgjulə] *a.*三角(形)的【6】

triglycerides [trai'glisəraid, -rid] *n.* 甘油三酸酯【17】

trioxide [trai'ɔksaid] *n.* 三氧化物【9】

truncated [trʌn'keitid, 'trʌŋk-] *a.* 缩短了的；被删节的；切去顶端的【9】

tub [tʌb] *n.* 浴盆，桶【15】

tube sheet 管板【6】

tube [tju:b] *n.*管，软管【6】

turbine ['tə:bain, -bin] *n.* [动力] 涡轮；[动力] 涡轮机【22】

turbulence ['tə:bjuləns] *n.*气体或水的涡流，波动【6】

U

ubiquitous [ju:'bikwitəs] *a.* 普遍存在的；无所不在的【10】

ultimately ['ʌltimətli] *adv.* 最后；根本；基本上【18】

unconsumed [ʌnkən'sju:md] *a.* 未遭毁灭的；未耗尽的；未吃光的【3】

undergo [ʌndə'gəu] *vt.* 经历，经受；忍受【2】

unimers ['ju:nimə(r)] *n.* [化]单聚体【16】

UOP abbr. 万国油品公司（Universal Oil Products Company）【13】

V

vacuum ['vækjuəm] *n.* 真空
　　　　　　　　　　　a. 真空的【11】

valid ['vælid] *a.* 有效的，有根据的；正当的【2】

vanadium [və'neidiəm] *n.*[化]钒【9】

vapor ['veipə] *n.* 蒸汽；烟雾
　　　　　　　　vt. 使…蒸发；使…汽化
　　　　　　　　vi. 蒸发；吹牛；沮丧【4】

vaporization [ˌveipərai'zeiʃən, -ri'z-] *n.* 蒸发；喷雾器；蒸馏器【4】

variable ['vɛəriəbl] *n.* [数]变量；可变物，可变因素【3】

variation [ˌvɛəri'eiʃən] *n.* 变化，变动(的程度)【7】

various ['vɛərəs] *a.* 各种各样的；多方面的【1】

vary ['vɛəri] *vi.* 变化；[生]变异【8】

vary in 在…方面变化；在…方面有差异【19】

velocity [vi'lɔseti] *n.* 速率；迅速；周转率【5】

velocity [vi'lɔsiti] *n.* 速度【6】

vent [vent] *vi.* 放出
　　　　　　n. 出口；通风孔【8】

version ['və:ʃən] *n.* 版本；译文；倒转术【13】

vertical ['və:tikəl] *a.* 垂直的，竖的【4】

vessel ['vesəl] *n.* 容器，器皿；脉管，血管；船，舰【3】

via ['vaiə] *prep.* 取道，通过；经由【10】

viable ['vaiəbl] *a.* 可行的【18】

vinegar ['vinigə] *n.* 醋【9】

visbreaking ['vis,breikiŋ] *n.* [油气] 减黏裂化，减黏轻度裂化；减低黏度【12】

viscosity [vi'skɔsəti] *n.* [物] 黏性，[物] 黏度【14】

vitriol ['vitriəl] *n.* 硫酸，硫酸盐【9】

volatile component　易挥发组分；轻组分【4】

volatile ['vɔlətail] *a.* 易变的，反复无常的，易激动的，(液体或油)易挥发的【4】

volume ['vɔljuːm] *n.* 体积；容积，容量【7】

W

wastage ['weistidʒ] *n.* 损耗；消瘦；衰老【22】

water-tight connection.　防水连接【15】

weeping ['wiːpiŋ] *a.* 哭泣的，滴水的；垂枝的【5】

weir [wiə] *n.* 溢流堰【5】

weld [weld] *vt. & vi.* 焊接；熔接【6】

wetting ['wetiŋ] *n.* 润湿【17】

whereas [hwɛə'æz] *conj.* 然而；鉴于；反之【17】

windmill ['windmil] *n.* 风车；风车房；旋转玩具；[口]直升机

vt. 使旋转

vi. 作风车般旋转【22】

withdraw [wið'drɔː, wiθ-] *vt.* 撤退；收回；撤销；拉开

vi. 撤退；离开【3】

woody ['wudi] *a.* 木质的；多树木的；木头似的【10】

worn-out ['wɔːn'aut] *a.* 磨破的；穿旧的；不能再用的【12】

Z

zeolite ['ziːəlait] *n.* 沸石【11】

Ziegler-Natta　齐格勒催化剂【15】

zinc [ziŋk] *n.* 锌【8】

zwitterionics [,zwitərai'ɔnik] *n.* 两性离子

a. 两性离子的【16】

参 考 文 献

[1] 赵宣，郑仰成.科技英语翻译. 北京：外语教学与研究出版社，2006.

[2] 保清，苻之.科技英语翻译理论与技巧. 北京：中国农业机械出版社，1983.

[3] 张道真.实用英语语法. 北京：外语教学与研究出版社，1995.

[4] Richard M.Felder, Ronald W.Rousseau. Elementary Principles of Chemical Processes(3rd Edition).The United States of America: John Wiley & Sons, Inc. 2005.

[5] Warren L.McCabe, Julian C.Smith, Peter Harriott. Unit Operations Of Chemical Engineering (5th Edition) . Singapore: McGraw-Hill,Inc. 1993.

[6] E.Bruce Nauman. Chemical Reactor Design Optimization and Scale up. The United States of America: The McGraw-Hill Companies.2002.

[7] Peter J. Dunn, Andrew S. Wells, and Michael T. Williams. Green Chemistry in the Pharmaceutical Industry. The Federal Republic of Germany: WILEY-VCH Verlag GmbH & Co. KGaA. 2010.

[8] Jacques des Cloizeaux. Polymers in Solution. The United States of America: Oxford University Press. 1989.

[9] Krister Holmberg, Bo Jonsson, Bengt Kronberg and Bjorn Lindman. Surfactants and Polymers in Aqueous Solution. Great Britain: John Wiley & Sons, Ltd. 2002.

[10] Martyn Poliakoff and Pete Licence. Green chemistry. Nature, 2007, (6)450:810-812.

[11] Sami Matar. Chemistry of Petrochemical Process. The United States of America: Gulf Publishing Company. 2000.

[12] http://www.eoearth.org/article.

[13] http://en.wikipedia.org/wiki.